ADOLF CLUSS ARCHITECT

GHI STUDIES IN GERMAN HISTORY

German Historical Institute, Washington, D.C.

in association with

Berghahn Books, New York *and* Oxford

ARCHITECT

Adolf Cluss

FROM GERMANY TO AMERICA

Edited by Alan Lessoff *and* Christof Mauch

The Historical Society of Washington, D.C., *and* Stadtarchiv Heilbronn
in association with Berghahn Books, New York *and* Oxford

A Bergamot Book

A Bergamot Book
www.bergamotbooks.com
Edited by Gail D. Spilsbury
Designed by Carol Beehler

The publication of this book has been made possible through a
generous grant from the Transatlantic Program of the Federal
Republic of Germany, with funds from the European Recovery
Program (ERP) of the Federal Ministry of Economics and Labor
(BMWA). It was printed with the support of the German
Historical Institute, Washington, D.C., and Georg Kohl GmbH,
Brackenheim, Germany.

Adolf Cluss, Architect: From Germany to America accompanies the
Adolf Cluss exhibitions at both the Charles Sumner School
Museum in Washington, D.C., and the Stadtarchiv Heilbronn,
Germany, September 2005 to February 2006.
www.adolf-cluss.org

The Stadtarchiv Heilbronn publishes a German version of this
book under the title *Adolf Cluss, Revolutionär und Architekt: Von
Heilbronn nach Washington;* ISBN 3-928990-92-6.

Library of Congress Cataloging-in-Publication Data

Adolf Cluss, architect: from Germany to America / edited by
Alan Lessoff and Christof Mauch.
p. cm.
Includes bibliographical references and index.
ISBN 1-84545-052-3 (pbk.)
1. Cluss, Adolf, 1825-1905—Criticism and interpretation.
2. Architecture—Washington (D.C.)—19th century. I. Lessoff,
Alan. II. Mauch, Christof. III. Cluss, Adolf, 1825–1905.

NA737.C5A83 2005
720.92—dc22

Cover: Cluss and Schulze, National Museum building,
ca. 1885–90, Smithsonian Institution. See page 130.
Inside back cover: Washington, 1892, at the end of Adolf
Cluss's architectural career. Courtesy Albert Small Washington
Collection.
Title page: Adolf Cluss, Washington, 1900. See page 100.
Map page 70: Gene Thorp, Cartographic Concepts, Inc., 2005.

ISBN 1-84545-052-3

CONTENTS

*T*HE ADOLF CLUSS PROJECT, with its many compo-
nents on both sides of the Atlantic, has a long history of
bringing individuals and organizations together in search of
common themes. In 1996, the Goethe-Institut Washington/
German Cultural Center moved to its current home on
Seventh Street NW, in the heart of Washington's "Old
Downtown." At the time, this neighborhood looked a bit
shabby, but with its attractive mixture of nineteenth-century
and more modern buildings, the Seventh Street corridor has
become once again a vibrant part of the city. Like all newcomers, we became curious about our new surroundings.
We soon found out from friends at the Historical Society of
Washington, D.C., that this part of Washington had a rich
ethnic heritage, profoundly marked by German-speaking
immigrants in the nineteenth century. And that among this
community was a German-born architect named Adolf Cluss,
who had been remarkably influential in making Washington
into a city worthy of being the capital of a great and unified
republic after the American Civil War.

   In the course of research for walking tours of the neighborhood and for our Web site on German American sites in
downtown Washington, we discovered more and more about
this intriguing man, whose work as an architect and social
thinker survives today in only a few beloved buildings; the
rest having been swept away by successive tides of marble

and white limestone. After meeting Joseph L. Browne, who
had been doing independent research on Cluss in Germany,
we decided to explore additional ways to understand Cluss
in the context of nineteenth-century, German American life
in Washington. We approached friends at the Historical
Society of Washington, D.C., the Charles Sumner School
Museum and Archives, and the Smithsonian's Office of
Architectural History and Preservation and discovered that
people in each organization had been researching Adolf Cluss
independently of one another. When we contacted the
German side, we discovered that the City of Heilbronn, and
the meticulous historians at its City Archives (Stadtarchiv
Heilbronn), knew about Adolf Cluss and found the man's
life and work most intriguing. As the German historians took
a closer look at Adolf Cluss, they realized that the history of
this emigrant radical and architect and his family were good
means to illustrate Heilbronn's place in the nineteenth
century and its connections to the 1848 revolution as well as
to emigration. Soon, the German Historical Institute in
Washington expressed a strong interest in a general effort
to rediscover German aspects of Washington history.
Thus the Adolf Cluss Project is the result of a consortium's
efforts in pursuit of knowledge and understanding of
history on both sides of the Atlantic. This book, which brings
to light so many fascinating issues about European-American
relationships and the reinvention of the capital of the
American republic in the second half of the nineteenth

century, is one of the concrete results of so many peoples' efforts to reclaim part of a previously neglected past.

It is hard in the year 2005 to imagine what Washington was like when Adolf Cluss arrived in it in 1849, or even what it was like when Cluss died in 1905; except for its street plan and a few notable buildings, Washington has been completely transformed from its muddy provincial conditions of the mid-nineteenth century. It has also changed from the handsome red-brick city it had become by 1900. In the second volume of *The Reminiscences of Carl Schurz*, published in 1907 by a well-known German political émigré of 1848, the journalist, former United States Senator, and Secretary of the Interior recalled the Washington of 1854 and compared it to the city he knew at the beginning of the twentieth century—in other words, before and after Adolf Cluss's architectural career:

> My first impressions of the political capital of the great American Republic were rather dismal. Washington looked at that period like a big, sprawling village, consisting of scattered groups of houses which were overtopped by a few public buildings. . . . The departments of State, of War, and of the Navy were quartered in small, very insignificant-looking houses which might have been the dwellings of some well-to-do shopkeepers who did not care for show. There was not one solidly built-up street in the whole city—scarcely a block without gaps of dreary emptiness.
>
> . . . The streets, ill-paved, if paved at all, were constantly covered with mud or dust. . . . Washington was called "the city of magnificent distances." But there was nothing at the ends of those distances, and, excepting the few public buildings, very little that was in any way interesting or pleasing. In many of the streets, geese, chickens, pigs, and cows had still a scarcely disputed right of way. The city had throughout a slouchy, unenterprising, unprogressive appearance, giving extremely little promise of becoming the beautiful capital it now is.

If Carl Schurz, writing in 1907, could refer to the city as having become a "beautiful capital," it was thanks in large part to the vision, expertise, professional competence, and persistent efforts of Adolf Cluss and his colleagues. As we look at the few remaining Cluss buildings, we must reflect on what has been lost, but also at what has been preserved—and what cries out for preservation now.

Our deepest thanks go to all the institutions in Germany and the United States who have made this book and project possible, particularly to the Transatlantic Program of the Federal Republic of Germany, with funds from the European Recovery Program (ERP) of the Federal Ministry of Economics and Labor (BMWA), which provided the critical financial support for this publication. Special thanks also to the coeditors, Alan Lessoff and Christof Mauch, for their patient work with all the contributors to the volume. Thanks as well to David Lazar for his careful work as an editor and translator, to Helena Johnson for her excellent proofreading job, and to Alexander O. Trotter for indexing the book. We also thank Gail Spilsbury, whose eye for detail and fine esthetic sense have proved invaluable to the book's success. Finally, we wish to express our gratitude to Carol Beehler for the elegance of the book's design.

We all hope that this book will enable Washingtonians and visitors alike to open their eyes anew and appreciate the history, ideas, and human efforts that lie hidden behind the facades and underneath the streets of this international capital.

William Gilcher
Goethe-Institut Washington, D.C.

JOSEPH L. BROWNE *and* ALAN LESSOFF

AMONG THE CROWD at the inauguration of President Zachary Taylor in March 1849 stood a sandy-haired, twenty-four-year-old man, over six feet in height. He was Adolf Cluss, a veteran of the failed German Revolution of 1848, who had arrived in New York only five months earlier. Intrigued by the 1848 presidential campaign, Cluss traveled to Washington, D.C., to observe the finale of the rituals by which the American republic chose its leader, a dramatic contrast to the oligarchic and autocratic methods he had opposed in his home country.[1] Cluss decided to stay in the American capital to witness republican government firsthand. After settling in Washington and devoting time to working, studying, and learning about his new country, Cluss gradually resumed political activity within the network of émigré German activists spread throughout the cities of the Northeast and Midwest. He also resumed correspondence with his mentor and friend, Karl Marx, then operating from his own exile in London. "He is one of our best and most talented men," the communist leader wrote of Cluss's activities in America.[2]

In his early years in America, Cluss anticipated returning home to participate again in Germany's movement for political and social reform. But his life took an unanticipated turn that mirrored the experiences of numerous veterans of Germany's failed revolution who found professional success

in the United States. Cluss's experience as a draftsman and surveyor enabled him to find work in a variety of federal agencies. In 1862, after more than a decade of honing his skills and developing his knowledge of Washington, he went into private practice as an architect and civil engineer. Over the next thirty years, Cluss exerted considerable influence on Washington's appearance and infrastructure. The former German revolutionary became the American capital's leading architect during the decades when Washington developed from a "struggling, shabby, dirty little third-rate Southern town" into an elegant, pleasant capital city that residents proudly, if prematurely, declared worthy of comparison to Paris or Berlin.[3] By 1890, he had designed four buildings on the National Mall. His innovative school buildings had brought Washington's public school system international acclaim. His mansions were fixtures of fashionable new neighborhoods such as Farragut Square and Dupont Circle. Remarkably versatile, he designed the capital city's first modern markets and its first apartment building, while also participating in the creation of Washington's sewage system and the grading and paving of its streets.

This book explores Cluss's journey from youthful revolutionary in Mainz to innovative Washington architect. The first four essays follow Cluss from Germany to America. Christhard Schrenk and Peter Wanner begin with a review of Cluss's childhood in Heilbronn, a town in Württemberg in southwestern Germany. The political activities that culminated in Cluss's playing a noteworthy role in the Revolution of 1848, despite being only twenty-three years old, are discussed by Sabine Freitag in the second essay. Sabina Dugan's study is next; she traces Cluss's journey to America and his gradual transformation from German émigré to German American professional. Kathleen Neils Conzen's essay profiles the distinctive German community in Washington of which Cluss became a distinguished member.

A photo essay on page 68 depicts the ways that Cluss shaped Washington during his long career and also traces the fate of his buildings and his city amid sweeping changes in architectural style and urban life that marked the twentieth century. The final five essays consider Cluss as architect and engineer. Richard Longstreth relates Cluss's work to international trends in architecture and urban design, while Alan Lessoff recounts Cluss's ill-fated venture into municipal engineering and urban planning in the 1870s as a member of Washington's legendary territorial government. Next, architectural historian Cynthia Field explicates Cluss's best-known surviving building, the Smithsonian's National Museum, now known as the Arts and Industries building. Tanya Edwards Beauchamp reviews Cluss's public school design, an architectural form for which he won renown in his lifetime. In the book's final essay, Helen Tangires considers Cluss's contribution to the design of public markets, another form of architecture that flourished in his lifetime in Europe and North America.

Born in 1825 into a family of builders and architects in the manufacturing city of Heilbronn, young Cluss had admired the drawings of his architect uncle and witnessed his father's building and quarrying businesses. When he was nineteen, Cluss became an journeyman carpenter, the typical career path for a future architect. By 1846, he worked in Mainz as a draftsman for a new railroad along the Rhine.[4]

Cluss had grown up in a revolutionary age. Following the invasion of French ideas under Napoleon, many middle-class Germans had hoped to unite the hodgepodge of German monarchies into a republic like the widely admired American example. Cluss was among the many young German men who joined gymnastic clubs—in German, *Turnvereine*—which provided cover for illegal political discussions. In his travels, Cluss had witnessed the hardships of itinerant workers and the rural poor. He boasted that from 1846 on, he was "always with the workers." Attracted by the German political refugee community in liberal Belgium, Cluss even moved for a brief period to Brussels. Befriended there by Karl Marx, the leader of the new Communist League, Cluss publicly defended Marx's ideas. When revolution swept away the monarchy in France in February 1848, igniting rebellions in German states like Hesse, Cluss hurried back to Mainz.[5]

Party leaders then elected the twenty-three-year-old Cluss vice president of the city's Communist League as well as secretary of a workers' educational association. In March 1848, a reading of a new pamphlet cowritten by Marx and Friedrich Engels, the *Communist Manifesto*, further stirred Cluss's already vibrant enthusiasm. "Full of the fire of youth," a colleague recalled, Cluss lectured to the workers and wrote newspaper articles about education, public opinion, and the proletariat. He also established party branches in nearby towns. Like Marx, Cluss argued in his speeches and articles that class conflict was inevitable. "We are momentarily confronting the battle of labor against capital, brought about by the domination of the non-propertied by the propertied," Cluss wrote. He stopped short of calling for revolution, but argued that the proletarian "can work, wants to work, and will do so contentedly, plentifully, and well," but the worker also demands "an appropriate pay for his labor." Cluss disagreed with socialists who called for equal wages, demanding instead that "the rarer talent must be paid better than the more common; the engraver and the draftsman must be paid better than the helper."[6]

The German revolutions in Hesse soon collapsed, and in May Prussian troops reasserted control in Mainz. At the Frankfurt Democratic Congress in June, Cluss and other workers' representatives disagreed with middle-class democrats. In the meeting hall, the American flag—a symbol of constitutional republicanism—hung next to the black, red, and gold flag of the German revolution. Still, the congress took only tentative steps toward the republic that Cluss favored. Cluss decided to observe personally the world's only major republic. He sailed to New York one month later.[7]

While in Washington in March 1849, Cluss found a job

as a surveyor for the United States Coast Survey, working for six months mapping the Chesapeake Bay and the Atlantic coasts of Maryland and Virginia. By mid-1850, he embarked on a new job as a draftsman at the Washington Navy Yard.[8] Though Cluss initiated correspondence with Communist League member Wilhelm Wolff in London in March 1850, Karl Marx took little interest in Cluss until November 1851, when Marx felt threatened by political rivals who had traveled to the United States. Marx then began an animated, four-year exchange of letters with Cluss. This correspondence and Cluss's exchanges with other figures in the German radical network on both sides of the Atlantic shaped Cluss's first years in America. "Few mortals other than yourself can boast of having received letters from me on four successive days," Marx admitted. Cluss's letters sparked the communist leader's interest: "I have just had a most thrilling letter from Cluss," he once remarked to Engels.[9]

In Washington, Cluss again assumed a leadership role in the communist movement. Joseph Weydemeyer, a follower of Marx who settled in New York in 1851, reported to Engels: "The only way for us to get influence here and control the unions is to transplant the [Communist] League on American soil, on which Cluss and I have also agreed on the essentials." Marx hoped that Cluss would combat his enemies in America such as Gottfried Kinkel and Wilhelm Weitling. Cluss also aided Marx as a propagandist and financier. He invested money in Weydemeyer's *Die Revolution* that survived for only two issues, and he helped Marx publish *The Eighteenth Brumaire of Louis Bonaparte* in New York, an analysis of events in France that was not published in Europe until 1869. Cluss wrote and suggested weekly articles for *Die Reform*, a communist newspaper in New York nurtured by Marx and edited by Weydemeyer. Cluss also helped to finance the newspaper, investing money he obtained through inheritance or subterfuge from his bourgeois family. Cluss lost most of his investment when the newspaper failed in 1854.[10] As early as 1852, however, he questioned the movement's future. The politics of class warfare appealed to few workers in the United States; Cluss "doubted that the Communist League would gain much in coming years." Political apathy reigned. "During public meetings," he com-

plained, "half [of the audience] sleep during a debate and the other half play cards. It is enough to make one insane."[11]

Cluss mostly filled his letters to Marx and other party leaders with political news, gossip, and publishing hopes. In 1852, however, he made mention of a spirited, beautiful sixteen-year-old girl from Baltimore. Cluss met Rosa Schmidt and her parents at a political meeting. Jacob Schmidt, a teacher at Baltimore's free-thinking Zion Church school, and his wife, had immigrated from the Palatinate in the 1830s. While they held liberal views about religion and Germany's future government, they disagreed with communist ideology. Thus Adolf and Rosa did not get off to a good start. Cluss joked, "The young girl . . . has been rude to me wherever she could, and the old man wants me beaten up in case I enter their house. Of course, I used this for bad jokes, which intensified their anger." As his attachment to communism waned in the following years, a friendship with Rosa deepened. Marx speculated that Rosa and her family had undermined Cluss's loyalty to the communist movement.[12]

In his first years in America, Cluss expected the outbreak of a new revolution in Germany and vowed to return "as soon as the Fatherland calls." At times, life in Washington depressed him. "I would not mind leaving Washington, this rotten nest. . .," he remarked in 1852, adding, "only animalized people live here." He described the capital city as "a village," its people so spread out that one "had to take a trip" to go from one house to another. One year later he confessed, "I hope . . . to soon be able to shake Washington's dust forever from my feet." Cluss traveled through New England, New York, Canada, and parts of the Midwest and the South. Cincinnati headed his list of possible places to move.[13]

Like other German Forty-eighters, Cluss searched for new ways to express his social conscience. In 1855, he became a United States citizen and secured a promising job in the Treasury Department drawing plans for federal buildings. Cluss became a familiar figure in Washington's distinctive German community. He was active in the Washington *Turnverein* and in the late 1850s, joined Washington's small but vocal antislavery Republican Party. By 1860, Cluss was well acquainted with Washington abolitionist and Republican leader Lewis Clephane and Baltimore party leader Georg Wiss, both Lincoln supporters at the party's Chicago convention.[14]

Though he sent fewer letters and newspapers to Marx, Cluss felt a lingering loyalty. After a reunion with his family in Württemberg in 1858, Cluss journeyed to London to talk to the communist leader, but found he was away. Jenny Marx wrote to her husband, then visiting Engels in Manchester, that Cluss, "heart brimful," had promised to return. Still uncertain about whether he wanted to maintain his old radical connections, Cluss instead sent Marx a letter of apology for not returning. The two never contacted each other again. Cluss had many good reasons to abandon Marx. His letters never revealed much interest with theoretical matters, a trait that Jenny Marx noted when she told him that some of his friends preferred him "in a less theoretical vein and would like you always to remain the same old humorous, light-hearted Cluss." He did not want to subject his future family to the kind of poverty Jenny Marx and her children endured. (Marx's wife had once written to Cluss asking for money so she could feed her children.) In a country with so much land and so many opportunities, Cluss knew that communism would have little appeal for American workers. For the rest of his life, though, Cluss saved letters written to him by Jenny and Karl Marx. Later in his life, he saved an obituary of Marx and in the 1890s acquired a new copy of the *Communist Manifesto*.[15]

Cluss returned to America in 1858 and married Rosa Schmidt. They lived for the next thirty-five years in a modest row house on Second Street in northwest Washington, where they raised seven children. Cluss again worked at the Navy Yard under Captain John Dahlgren, then modernizing the Navy's weaponry. While researching new weapons during the Civil War, Cluss launched his architectural career by designing a foundry for the Navy.[16] With his first partner, Joseph W. von Kammerhueber, also a Navy Yard employee, he launched a private architectural practice in 1862. The new partners won a competition to design a multiclassroom school to supersede Washington's one-room buildings, the first of eight innovative, award-winning public schools Cluss planned. Over the following decades, Cluss, usually working with a partner who was a German or Austrian immigrant, designed or renovated more than sixty Washington buildings.[17]

Cluss's desire to build model schools grew out of his commitment to republican government. In the schools Cluss designed for Washington, he employed the latest pedagogic theories and the newest construction, ventilation, and heating technologies. His two surviving schools attest to the importance that he and other reformers attributed to public education. "These were model schools . . . they towered over the skyline, which was then less imposing . . . they were supposed to inspire, uplift, and educate." Cluss intended nothing less for Franklin School. "The pervading spirit of its design was the Renaissance," he proclaimed at its dedication in 1869. Its prominent location on Franklin Square near the White House made it a natural destination for tourists as well as visiting educators. His handsome Charles Sumner School, built for African American children, was also a model school—a dramatic symbol of opportunity for its first students, former slaves and the children of former slaves.[18]

Cluss also wanted to dignify public spaces like the Center Market. He counted among the numerous architects on both sides of the Atlantic who were attracted to public market halls, because such halls offered an essential service while serving as a community meeting place and a city landmark. With its high towers and two-story, interior hall, Cluss's market ennobled the hub of the business district at Seventh Street and Pennsylvania Avenue, halfway between the White House and the Capitol. Though the federal government demolished the Center Market in 1931, the Eastern Market, also designed by Cluss, still invigorates and unites its Capitol Hill neighborhood.[19]

Other Cluss public buildings included six churches, a Masonic hall, a department store, Baltimore's Concordia Hall, buildings for the departments of Agriculture and Interior, and two museums. As the Smithsonian's architect for a quarter of a century, Cluss renovated the Smithsonian Institution building—the Castle—following a fire in 1864 and executed improvements in the building in later years. He and his partner Paul Schulze also designed the festive National Museum (today's Arts and Industries building). The National Museum vividly illustrates the architectural principles and ideas that engaged Cluss's lively imagination. Opened in 1881, its first event was the Inaugural Ball for President James Garfield, for which Cluss chaired the reception and promenade committee. Cluss and Schulze also designed the Army Medical Museum located on the Mall, though Cluss complained to the Army Corps of Engineers that congressional cost cutting would jeopardize the "dignity of a public building" and feared "fastening a nightmare upon a beautiful landscape." By 1890, Cluss had designed four of the five buildings on the Mall: the two museums, Center Market, and the Department of Agriculture.[20]

Concerned with the appearance of the city's residential streets and squares, Cluss competed in Washington's booming housing market. He criticized the economic forces that had previously produced houses "from Maine to Texas . . . in the same strictly utilitarian haphazard character." For the capital city, he fashioned row houses, shop-front houses, and the city's first apartment building in the same style as most of his public buildings—the red-brick, *Rundbogenstil* or Second Empire appearance considered progressive in the post—Civil War years. By working with wealthy clients at prominent residential locations such as Farragut Square, Franklin Square, Thomas Circle, Dupont Circle, and Massachusetts and Connecticut avenues, Cluss "had done more than anyone else," the *New York Tribune* editorialized, "to foster an improved style of private architecture in the Nation's Capital." All his residential buildings were razed in the twentieth century, victims of commercial and government expansion in the heart of the city.[21] Still, as Richard Longstreth argues, Cluss's status as Washington's "pioneer" professional architect allowed him to exert an influence on the capital city's appearance that outlasted the effort during the twentieth century by Beaux Arts and modernist architects to purge the red-brick, "Victorian" city he helped to create.

Despite Cluss's busy private practice, public service always beckoned him. He held long-term consulting positions with the District of Columbia and the Smithsonian Institution. Working as a consulting engineer for the city government in 1864, he and Kammerhueber prepared a plan to build a citywide sewage system and rebuild the moribund Washington City Canal. While not implemented, their report stimulated a six-year debate that helped unite Republican reformers like Cluss behind a plan for a district-wide, territorial government, a Board of Public Works, and a program to modernize the city.[22] As Henry Cooke, the first territorial governor, explained to a meeting of German Republicans, the reformers hoped "the capital of the nation might be made worthy of its position as the political metropolis of the country, and the metropolitan representative of the grandeur, the culture, and the energy of the republic." Cluss supported Republican goals and party leaders. He led a successful fight to keep Germans in the party organization in 1861. He served on inaugural committees in 1865 and 1869, and he was elected president of the German Republicans of Washington on the eve of congressional approval of the territorial system.[23] Appointed building inspector under the new territorial government in 1871, Cluss rewrote the city's building regulations and included new provisions for fireproofed and ventilated buildings as well as new codes for Washington's distinctive bays, porticos, and towers. Using permits, inspections, warnings, and court actions, Cluss initiated enforcement of these improved regulations.[24]

A year later, President Ulysses S. Grant, a proponent of modernizing Washington, appointed Cluss to the post of city engineer and member of the Board of Public Works. Cluss oversaw the ambitious, costly plan to modernize the city developed by the board's head, Alexander Shepherd. Cluss and Shepherd had known one another since the 1850s when both had joined the new Republican Party. Cluss's involvement with Shepherd's Comprehensive Plan of Improvements led to the most dramatic, wrenching episode in Cluss's American career.

As city engineer, Cluss superintended extensive street grading and paving, as well as the design and building of the city's sewage system. For the first time, Washington could boast drained, well-paved streets, although technical flaws in this work would soon necessitate its costly replacement. More successful was Cluss's supervision of efforts to narrow Washington's wide streets and to encourage property owners to plant gardens on the leftover right-of-way in front of their houses. Supervising a tree-planting commission, he labored to turn Washington's streets into "one vast garden . . . its squares and circles clad with green grass, left free for repose between trees and hardy shrubs." The capital won recognition for these improvements in both the national media and tourist publications and promotions.[25] The city's progress, however, imposed a cost that Cluss refused to pay. In 1874, he testified before a congressional committee and disclosed mismanagement in the Board of Public Works and influence peddling in Shepherd's relations with contractors. He criticized Shepherd's dictatorial methods. Shepherd retaliated by requesting that President Grant fire Cluss from the Board of Public Works, ending his career as a municipal engineer and city planner. In the following years, Cluss remained active as an adviser and consultant to the District of Columbia Board of Commissioners, which replaced the territorial system as Washington's local government, and to the Army Corps of Engineers, which took over management of the city's public works.[26]

Optimistic about "the progressive spirit of the age," the architect-engineer spoke out in national media about urban problems. He called for a federal board of public works to oversee building standards and promote new technology.[27] At a time when experts still debated the best street paving material, he argued—based in part on his misadventures with other materials—that a newly developed substance called asphalt was superior to wood, stone, or concrete. Citing Germany's experience, he also proposed underground pipes built by the Post Office Department to house telegraph wires for the safety of pedestrians and the protection of shade trees. In an age of unregulated capitalism, Cluss argued that private business should not have the right "to interfere with the safety of the community or of neighbors or to disfigure a city or public place." The urban reforms he favored all underscored concern with public health, especially for the poor: "Justice should be done . . . to the demands of health for the poorer classes . . . frequently doomed to live in alleys and lanes."[28]

Though Cluss believed in the use of government power to shape the capital city and tackle urban problems, he argued against some projects promoted by Congress. He criticized the use of the ancient form of the obelisk for the Washington Monument. As a symbol of military and imperial glories in Egypt, Babylon, and Rome, the obelisk, he said, dishonored "such a humane man" as Washington as well as the ideals of the American republic. Cluss arranged for publication of his views in the *New York Tribune* and in Washington's *Sunday Chronicle*.[29]

Throughout his professional career, Cluss played a role in the American Institute of Architects (AIA). He joined the national organization in 1867, attended many national conventions, and often presented technical and historical papers. He lectured about chimneys and mortars, the problems of dampness and acoustics in buildings, and the history of public architecture in Washington and Mexico City. On behalf of the AIA, he wrote a plea for reform of the federal Supervising Architect's office. Cluss joined other Washington architects to form the local branch of the AIA in 1887, served as the second president, and remained an active member to the end of his life.[30]

Complaining of competition among fellow architects— "the undignified scramble and intrigues of men to cut each other's throats"—Cluss retired from private practice in 1889. Upon the recommendation of Colonel John Wilson of the Army Corps of Engineers, the Secretary of the Treasury appointed Cluss as inspector of public buildings for the federal government. He traveled throughout the country inspecting new government buildings, including the Ellis Island facility for immigrants. He analyzed problems in old buildings such as the United States Capitol. *The Brooklyn Eagle* reported that on Cluss's visit to an unfinished post office, the sixty-five-year-old "climbed up ladders and across narrow planks on the unfinished floor a hundred feet in the air with an agility that stumped an *Eagle* reporter who was with him." Despite recommendations from former Senators Justin Morrill and Carl Schurz, as well as from William Steinway and General John Wilson among others, in August 1894, President Grover Cleveland's administration removed him because he was not a Democrat.[31]

Cluss's long devotion to the community's health and safety did not spare him from the scourges of nineteenth-century city life. In 1886, his son Adolph, age twenty-three, a clerk working for Cluss, died of typhoid fever. Between

1893 and 1894, two other sons and his wife died. Seventeen-year-old Richard died of tuberculosis in April 1893, and a year later Cluss's wife, Rosa, succumbed to a lengthy respiratory illness. Six months later, his twenty-nine-year-old son, Carl, a pharmacist, died of typhoid fever. Following those tragedies, Cluss and two daughters, Flora and Anita, moved to the home of his oldest daughter and her husband, Lillian and William Daw, above Daw's pharmacy at Twenty-third and H streets, NW. An inveterate traveler, Cluss joined his daughters on trips to Niagara Falls and Harpers Ferry and attended many performances by his daughter Anita, a professional harpist. Anita Cluss performed in Washington, New York, and Europe and on the summer circuit in Asbury Park, Saratoga Springs, and Chautauqua.[32]

Cluss continued to work as a builder into his seventies. He superintended construction of an addition to the Government Printing Office and renovation work at the White House. He also designed, at no charge, a summer home for the Washington Hospital for Foundlings.[33]

Following the deaths of his sons and wife, Cluss twice returned to his homeland. He renewed family ties in a now-united German empire, meeting for the first time many of his nieces and nephews. On a long pilgrimage in 1898, the fiftieth anniversary of his emigration to America, the seventy-three-year-old Cluss revisited the sites of his youthful revolutionary activities, where he had once hoped to build a new society and design a German republic, still elusive goals in Wilhelmine Germany. Before his return to America, Cluss's family presented him with a silver cup, on which they had engraved a German and an American coat of arms, an expression of their friendship and loyalty to each other and their two countries. In the last years of his life—the first five years of the new century—he wrote letters to his brother, sisters, and many nieces and nephews and their children in Germany. Cluss reported on his new drawings and his gymnastic exercises. He sent postcards illustrating the frescoes that he admired in the Library of Congress building. He retold the story of an 1846 *Turnfest* in Heilbronn, to which he had led a delegation of Mainz *Turner*.[34]

He also mulled over a copy of the 1902 McMillan plan that would redesign Washington's National Mall and downtown, dooming many of his buildings. In 1902, at one of the last meetings of the Washington branch of the AIA that Cluss attended, the members examined the drawings for a new Agriculture Department headquarters that would replace Cluss's 1867 building. Guided by the McMillan Plan, Cluss's successors, including the architect-pallbearers at his 1905 funeral, planned a new Washington of grand vistas and white, neoclassical Greco-Roman buildings.[35] In its obituary for Cluss, the *American Architect and Building News* forecast the future of the architect's buildings in the twentieth century. Though his work included "very carefully constructed buildings believed to be practically imperishable, the work accomplished by Adolf Cluss . . . is doomed to disappear before long, all the more because it is mainly to be found in Washington, and for the most part, ill accords with the monumentally architectural character that the city is so rapidly acquiring."[36]

This pronouncement proved prescient. Of the dozens of buildings on which Cluss worked, only eight remain. Yet the monumental, neoclassical Washington that took shape in the early twentieth century existed on an imperial scale seemingly inappropriate for a democratic republic. The post–World War II Washington of nondescript, modernist glass office buildings, urban renewal zones, and automobiles seemed to lack personality altogether. By the start of the twenty-first century, Washingtonians, like urban dwellers elsewhere, evinced a nostalgia, perhaps well-founded, for the city that Cluss left behind, with its eclectic, red-brick buildings and its pedestrian-friendly, tree-lined boulevards. Throughout Europe and North America, urban preservationists now fight to preserve their remaining Second Empire and Victorian buildings, the sorts that Cluss created. Renewed appreciation for architects such as Cluss perhaps signals a longing for a form of city and a way of urban life that Western societies left to decay and then threw away. As Cluss, the person and the buildings he designed, were indicative of the nineteenth century, so the renewed interest manifested by this book is a symptom of a widespread dissatisfaction with both the scale and appearance of cities in the present. 🏵

NOTES

Abbreviations

MECW   Karl Marx and Friedrich Engels: Collected Works
MEGA   Karl Marx—Friedrich Engels Gesamtausgabe
MELA   Karl Marx and Friedrich Engels: Letters to America
NARA1   National Archives and Records Administration, Washington, D.C.
NARA2   National Archives and Records Administration, College Park, MD
RCHS   Records of the Columbia Historical Society, Washington, D.C.

1. Adolf Cluss to Ferdinand Wolff, 3 March 1850, *Der Bund Der Kommunisten: Dokumente und Materialien*, 3 vols. (Berlin, 1982), 2:151.

2. Karl Marx to Joseph Weydemeyer, 19 December 1851, in Richard Dixon, ed. and trans., *MECW*, 50 vols. (New York, 1975), 38:519.

3. *The Nation*, 30 March 1871.

4. Werner A. Cluss, "Die Geschichte der Familie Cluss" (unpublished typescript, 1932, copy on deposit in the City Archives of Heilbronn), 1; Wanderbuch, 27 June 1844, Staatsarchiv Ludwigsburg F 173, Bü. 47, 97—98, no. 90. *Affairs of the District of Columbia*, 43d Cong., 1st sess. (June 16, 1874), S. Rept. 473, Testimony, 2049.

5. Theodore S. Hamerow, *Restoration, Revolution, Reaction: Economics and Politics in Germany, 1815—1871* (Princeton, 1958), 58—59; Cluss's activities in 1846—48 are detailed in Welta Pospelowa, "Adolf Cluss—ein Mitglied des Bundes der Kommunisten und Kampfgefährte von Marx und Engels," *Marx-Engels Jahrbuch* (Berlin, 1980), 87—91.

6. Pospelowa, "Adolf Cluss," 92; Paul Stumpf to August Bebel, 24 September 1895, in Heinz Monz, ed., *Die Verbindung des Mainzer Paul Stumpf zu Karl Marx und Friedrich Engels* (Darmstadt, 1986), 306—8; Michael Wettengel, *Die Revolution von 1848/49 im Rhein-Main-Raum* (Wiesbaden, 1989), 138, 143; Adolf Cluss, "Über die Ursachen und das Wesen des Proletariats," *Der Demokrat*, 21 May 1848, 41—42; Adolf Cluss, "Louis Blanc und die neueste Phase seines Strebens," *Der Demokrat*, 7 May 1848, 29—30.

7. Wettengel, *Die Revolution von 1848/49*, 180; Gerhard Beier, *Arbeiterbewegung in Hessen* (Frankfurt am Main, 1984), 92—93; Karl Obermann, *Joseph Weydemeyer: Pioneer of American Socialism* (New York, 1947), 33; Passenger Ship List, SS *Zurich*, 15 September 1848, Microfilm 1062, 4, NARA.

8. Cluss to Wolff, 3 March 1850, *Der Bund der Kommunisten*, 2:151; Cluss to Joseph Weydemeyer, *MEGA* 1987, Part 3, 20 December 1851, 5:487.

9. Cluss to Wolff, 3 March 1850, *Der Bund der Kommunisten*, 2:151; The first known letter from Marx to Cluss was 28 November 1851, and the first letter from Cluss to Marx is dated December 1851. See *MEGA* 1987, Part 2, 4:252 and *MECW* 1975, 38:496. For Marx's comments on Cluss letters, see *MECW* 1975, 15 May 1852, 39:105, 26 April 1853, 39:315.

10. Karl Obermann, "The Communist League: A Forerunner of the American Labor Movement," *Science and Society* 30 (Fall 1966): 434; Pospelowa "Adolf Cluss," 107. For an overview of publication efforts in which Cluss was involved, see Karl Obermann, *Joseph Weydemeyer: Ein Lebensbild/1818—1866* (Berlin, 1968), 260—327. Cluss detailed his financial contributions and losses in letters to Marx: *MECW* 1975, 5 August 1852, 38:162—63; *MEGA* 1989, Part 3, 25 May 1854, 7:380. For Cluss's 1850 inheritance see Peter Wanner, "Kommunist der ersten Stunde und Baumeister Washingtons—Adolf Cluss (1825—1905)," in Christhard Schrenk, ed., *Heilbronner Köpfe* II (Heilbronn, 1999), 27.

11. Cluss to Weydemeyer, 12 November 1852 and 26 March 1853, quoted in Obermann, *Joseph Weydemeyer*, 439, 446; Cluss to Weydemeyer, 27 December 1851, *Zeitgenossen von Marx und Engels: Ausgewählte Briefe aus den Jahren 1844 bis 1852* (Amsterdam, 1975), 432.

12. Cluss to Weydemeyer, 2 January 1852, and 25 May 1852, *MEGA* 1987, Part 3, 5:487. On Jacob Schmidt and the Zion School, see Gustav Körner, *Das Deutsche Element in den Vereinigten Staaten von Nordamerika, 1818—1848* (New York, 1884), 400—402; and Klaus Wust, *Zion in Baltimore, 1755—1955* (Baltimore, 1955), 76—78. Marx noted that Cluss had married someone he met at the house of Dr. Georg Wiss, a Baltimore supporter of Kinkel, Weitling, and Willich, his political enemies. See *MECW* 1975, 17 December 1858, 40:363; Alexander Trachtenberg, ed., *MELA*, 1 February 1859 (New York, 1953), 60.

13. Cluss to Wolff, 3 March 1850, *Der Bund Der Kommunisten*, 2:151; Cluss to Weydemeyer, *MEGA* 1987, Part 3, 30 May 1852, 5:527; 16 August 1852, 5:558; 4—5 April 1852, 5:148.

14. Bruce Levine, "In the Heat of Two Revolutions: The Forging of German-American Radicalism," in *Struggle the Hard Battle*, Dirk Hoerder, ed. (DeKalb, 1986), 39; Antoinette J. Lee, *Architects to the Nation: The Rise and Decline of the Supervising Architect's Office* (New York, 2000), 48; Cluss to Karl Marx, 22 July 1852, *MEGA* 1987, Part 3, 5:444; Lewis Clephane, *Birth of the Republican Party* (Washington, 1889), 5; Dieter Cunz, *The Maryland Germans: A History* (Princeton, 1948), 274, 299—301.

15. Engels to Jenny Marx, 11 May 1858, *MECW* 1975, 40:313; Jenny Marx to Cluss, 30 October 1852, *MECW* 1975, 39:579; Jenny Marx to Engels, 27 April 1853, *MECW* 1975, 39:581.

16. Edward Marolda, *Washington Navy Yard* (Washington, 1999), 17—20; *National Cyclopedia of American Biography*, s.v. "Cluss, Adolf," 4:507; Adolf Cluss Buildings, Office of Architectural History and Historic Preservation, Smithsonian Institution, 2004 (page 174, this volume).

17. J. Ormond Wilson, "Eighty Years of the Public Schools of Washington—1805 to 1885," *RCHS* 1 (October 1897): 141—43, 159—60; Adolf Cluss Buildings.

18. William J. Reese to Cluss Exhibition Project, 21 January 2003, 4; *The Franklin School Building* (Washington, n.d.), 9—10. An early example of the Franklin School as a tourist attraction is in *The National Capital Explained and Illustrated* (Washington, 1872), 48. See expectations expressed at the dedication of the Charles Sumner School, 2 September 1872, *The Charles Sumner School* (Washington, 1986), 13—25.

19. Helen Tangires, "Contested Space: The Life and Death of Center Market," *Washington History* 7 (Spring—Summer 1995): 56—57, 59—60; Christopher Weeks, *Guide to the Architecture of Washington, D.C.* (Baltimore, 1994), 47.

20. Adolf Cluss Buildings; Tanya Edwards Beauchamp, "Adolf Cluss: An Architect in Washington during Civil War and Reconstruction," *RCHS* 48 (1971—1972), 345—47; *Inaugural Program* (Washington, 1881), 2; Cluss to Colonel Thomas L. Casey, Records of the Office of Public Buildings and Grounds, Letters Received Pertaining to the Construction of the Army Medical Museum, Entry 187, Box 1, RG 42, NARA.

21. Adolf Cluss, "Architecture and Architects at the Capital of the United States from Its Foundation until 1875," *Proceedings of the Tenth Annual Convention of the American Institute of Architects* (Washington, 1877), 44; Adolf Cluss Buildings; *New York Daily Tribune*, 26 October 1876.

22. *Report and Documents on the Present State, and the Improvement of the Washington City Canal* (Washington, 1865); Alan Lessoff, *The Nation and the City: Politics, "Corruption," and Progress in Washington, D.C., 1861—1902* (Baltimore, 1994), 53, 89—90; "German Republicans," *Evening Star*, 17 November 1871.

23. "Breakers Ahead! Fatherlands and Other Lands on the 'Qui Vive,'" *Evening Star*, 10 January 1861; "Great Times at the Wigwam," *Evening Star*, 11 January 1861; *National Daily Intelligencer*, 1 March 1865; "German Republicans: Ratification Meeting," *Evening Star*, 14 April 1871.

24. "Report of the Inspector of Buildings," in Board of Public Works, *Annual Report*, 1872, 91–92; For Cluss's approach to enforcement, see "Francis Dainese v. Henry Cooke, et al. Defendants," Supreme Court of the District of Columbia, Equity Docket 12, Number 2993, RG 21, NARA.

25. Beauchamp, "Adolf Cluss," 348–49; "Report of the Chief Engineer," Board of Public Works, *Annual Report*, 1873, 13–14. For Grant's attitude towards the capital, see Kenneth R. Bowling, "From 'Federal Town' to 'National Capital': Ulysses S. Grant and the Reconstruction of Washington, D.C.," *Washington History* 14 (Spring–Summer 2002): 14. The following reveal some of the praise for the changes made in the city: "Life at the Capital," *Lippincott's Magazine* 12 (December 1873): 651–53; George Alfred Townsend, "New Washington," *Harper's New Monthly Magazine* 90 (April 1875): 657–74; E. V. Smalley, "The New Washington," *The Century Magazine* 27 (March 1884): 117–23; F. W. Fitzpatrick, "Centennial of the Nation's Capital," *The Cosmopolitan* 14 (December 1900): 309–11. For the promotion of tourism in Washington, see Catherine Cocks, *Doing the Town: The Rise of Urban Tourism in the United States, 1850–1915* (Berkeley, 2001), 36–40, 123.

26. For Cluss's testimony, see *New York Times*, 21–23, 25–26 May 1874; James H. Whyte, *The Uncivil War: Washington During Reconstruction, 1865–1878* (New York, 1958), 272. Examples of Cluss's advisory roles are found in "The City Sewage," *Washington Post*, 21 May 1878; "The Jefferson School Building Loss," *Washington Post*, 17 February 1882; Adolf Cluss to Colonel John M. Wilson, 1 October 1888, Records of the Office of Public Buildings and Public Parks of the National Capital, Letters Received, Entry 87, Box 26, Number 786, RG 42, NARA; "Looking after Our Health," *Washington Post*, 25 May 1878.

27. *The Office of the Supervising Architect: What It Was, What It Is, and What It Ought to Be* (New York, 1869), 8. Though published under the pseudonym Civitas, Cluss signed his name on a copy deposited in the AIA archives and is the presumed author.

28. Adolf Cluss, "Modern Street-Pavements," *Popular Science Monthly* 7 (May–October 1875): 80–89.

29. Cluss, "Architecture and Architects at the Capital," 39, 44. The views of other architects about the Washington Monument are related in "The American Institute of Architects and the Washington Monument," *Sunday Chronicle*, 11 October 1876. Cluss's lengthy attack is found in "A Letter from Adolf Cluss," *New York Daily Tribune*, 18 February 1875; and "The Washington National Monument," *Sunday Chronicle*, 10 December 1876 and 17 December 1876.

30. Cluss's AIA meeting papers are reproduced in the following: "American Institute of Architects," *New York World*, 18 November 1869; *Baltimore American*, 20 November 1875; Cluss, "Architecture and Architects at the Capital"; "On Science of Sound," *Washington Post*, 3 November 1898.

31. Cluss to "Dear Sir," an unknown recipient at the Washington chapter of the American Institute of Architects, 2 March 1889, AIA Archives, RG 801, SR 1, Box 3, folder 1889 AC, Incoming Correspondence; James H. Windrim, to Colonel J. M. Wilson, 25 June 1889, Records of the Office of Public Buildings and Public Parks of the National Capital, Entry 87, Letters Received, 1889, Box 29, 651, RG 42, NARA; "Looking at the Building," *Brooklyn Eagle*, 11 November 1889, 6; Proceedings of the Senate Committee of Immigration and the House Committee on Immigration and Naturalization, Acting Jointly at Ellis Island, New York Harbor, 5 March 1892, 52d Cong. 1st sess., CIS Microfiche Group 2, SuDoc Y.4Im6/1:Im6/1, 581, NARA; W. G. Emery to William Windom, 13 June 1889; Justin S. Morrill to William Windom, 18 June 1889; William Steinway to Daniel S. Lamont, 24 August 1894, Records of the Department of the Treasury, Letters Received, Entry 27, RG 56, NARA; "Inspector Cluss Removed," *Washington Post*, 1 September 1894.

32. "Adolph S. Cluss," *Evening Star*, 8 September 1886; Certificates of Death, Department of Health, District of Columbia, 3 April 1893, 10 April 1894, and 12 October 1894; "The Clarendon, The Most Popular Hotel in Saratoga Springs" (advertisement), *Brooklyn Eagle*, 2 July 1898; "City Personals," *Washington Post*, 24 July 1888; R. Metzentien to Cluss, 12 January 1903, Cluss Papers, Smithsonian Institution Castle Collection, Gift of William S. Shacklette.

33. Cluss to Office of Public Buildings and Grounds, 1895, Office of Public Buildings and Grounds, Entry 90, Index to Letters Received, Vol. 7, Nr. 349, RG 42, NARA; Cluss to Office of Public Buildings and Grounds, 1896, Entry 90, Nr. 936, RG 42; Robert W. Gibson to Cluss, 10 May 1900, Cluss Papers; Louise W. Smith to Cluss, 12 December 1889, Cluss Papers.

34. "Die Geschichte der Familie Cluss," 7. The silver cup and letters are found in the Cluss Papers. Anna de Millas to Cluss, 11 May 1903; Cluss to Sophia de Millas, 14 September 1904, in private collection (copy on deposit in the City Archives of Heilbronn).

35. "Washington, D.C.—Diagram of a Portion of City Showing Proposed Sites for Future Public Buildings," Cluss Papers; "Minutes," 1 November 1901, AIA Archives.

36. *American Architect and Building News* 88 (5 August 1905): 41.

PART 1 Heilbronn, Revolution, Exile, and a New Home

Adolf Cluss in Heilbronn—His Formative Years

CHRISTHARD SCHRENK *and* PETER WANNER

ADOLF CLUSS was born on July 14, 1825, "noon time, 11:00 to 12,"[1] in the former imperial city of Heilbronn on the Neckar River in the Kingdom of Württemberg in southwestern Germany. He was born on the Klostergasse in the medieval heart of the city (fig. 1).[2] The later revolutionary considered it a good omen that his birthday coincided with the anniversary of the French Revolution. "Your baby can only be envious of me. Since I, as it just occurs to me, was born on the anniversary of the storming of the Bastille," he was to write to a friend in New York.[3]

Adolf Cluss was the fifth child of Johann Heinrich Abraham Cluss (1792–1857), citizen and master workman in Heilbronn, and Anna Christine Neuz (1796–1827). His father descended from a wealthy family of master craftsmen in the building trades. His mother, the daughter of an innkeeper, came from a village near Heilbronn. Heinrich Cluss, as Adolf's father was known, owned a large wine press, which was located next to the family's house. He used it to produce wine from grapes grown in his vineyards.

"I was called Cluss when I was born, and an 'Adolf' was added a few weeks later with the blessing of the Schwabian state church," Cluss later wrote.[4] On July 31, 1825, Adolf

Cluss was baptized in Heilbronn in the Lutheran Kilian's Church (fig. 2). The social standing of those attending the baptismal ceremony helps to define the social position of the Cluss family, which was between the craftsmen and the new upper class. Cluss's godparents were his aunt and uncle, Caroline and Johann Ludwig Reiner. Caroline Reiner, Heinrich Cluss's sister, had founded a coffee, tobacco, and grocery business with her husband. This successful firm was converted into a tobacco factory in 1820. After Johann Ludwig Reiner's death, his widow managed the factory. Heinrich Cluss was a partner in his sister's business.

Jakobine Roth, also named in the records of Cluss's baptism, was an unmarried relative of Adolf's mother. Her father was the mayor of the village of Neckargartach. She helped to run the Cluss family household, and in 1827, following the death of Adolf's mother, she became the second wife of Heinrich Cluss.

The Lutheran Cluss family had its roots in Silesia. It migrated to Württemberg after 1648. In 1782, Adolf's grandfather, Georg Andreas Cluss (1750–1822), settled in Heilbronn and became a citizen of the city. A mason and construction foreman, he was the fourth generation of the Cluss family to work in the building trades. Georg Andreas Cluss had seven children. Adolf Cluss's father Heinrich was the youngest son. His brother Carl Cluss (1784–1831) became an architect, and his skill as a draftsman caught the admiring eye of Adolf Cluss. Carl apparently died in a

Fig. 2. Kilian's Church, Heilbronn, in 1865. Cluss grew up in the immediate vicinity of the church. Stadtarchiv Heilbronn.

psychiatric institution. "It seems to have been a prejudice of the time that insane people, even those with very agreeable temperaments, were seldom spoken of and then only in very hushed voices," Adolf later wrote, "For this reason, I know very little about this man, whose posthumous papers and drawings inspired tremendous respect in me as a young man. It always saddened me that we heard so little about him."[5]

The Cluss family exemplifies the changes in the social structure of Heilbronn. Georg Andreas accumulated wealth as a skilled construction worker and invested in his children's businesses. From the period of Germany's rapid industrial expansion in the early 1870s, Georg Andreas's descendants belonged to Heilbronn's *Hautevolee*, the upper class comprised of families linked by ties of blood and marriage.

Heilbronn in the First Half of the Nineteenth Century

At the end of the eighteenth century, Heilbronn was a flourishing imperial city, and as such, enjoyed a high degree of political independence.[6] In governing, its political elite was strongly influenced by Enlightenment ideas. Heilbronn's population at century's end stood at approximately 7,000 inhabitants; another 3,000 resided in four villages located within the city limits. Almost all of the city's residents were Protestants.

Through the late eighteenth century, Heilbronn's residents had earned their livings from growing fruit and vegetables and producing wine. International trade had become steadily more important over the course of the century. Merchants in Heilbronn, particularly those engaged in international wholesale trade, increasingly invested in mills to process commodities such as oilseeds, tobacco, and wood. This development can be seen as an early stage in Heilbronn's industrialization.

Heilbronn covered a comparatively small area, some 25 square miles. Despite its size—or perhaps because of it—the city enjoyed an exceptionally favorable financial situation. All classes dwelling in the city enjoyed favorable economic circumstances, which contributed to a basic consensus within the community. For most imperial cities, the second half of the eighteenth century was a time of economic stagnation and indebtedness. In Heilbronn, by contrast, it was an era of growth and prosperity (fig. 3).

It thus came as a shock to Heilbronn when this period of imperial freedom came to an end suddenly in the aftermath of the Napoleonic Wars. The city did all it could to resist curtailment of its political prerogatives, but it could not hold back the historic movements that were reshaping the entire continent. In September 1802, the Duchy of Württemberg, against which Heilbronn had for centuries maintained its independence, took de facto possession of the wealthy imperial city on the Neckar, an action that received legal sanction in February 1803.

In due course, the Duchy of Württemberg established administrative and governmental structures in Heilbronn, and the city received a new constitution. There was, however, clear continuity in the leadership of local offices after

Fig. 3. The Heilbronn Market Square in 1820. Aquatint by Carl Doerr. The Market Square was the center of commercial activity in the city. Goods were stored in the Rathaus (city hall, left) until the end of the nineteenth century. Stadtarchiv Heilbronn.

1802 to 1803. Unlike their counterparts in other cities, the citizens of Heilbronn did not turn away from politics to seek refuge in the private sphere during the so-called Biedermeier era. Rather, they channeled their energy into commerce and industry.

A number of wholesalers in Heilbronn who were not averse to taking risks recognized the opportunity that came with the city's unavoidable integration into what in 1805 became known as the Kingdom of Württemberg. They decided to take a radical step towards diversification and invested their capital in the creation of completely new economic sectors. By 1830, a dozen large-scale industrial enterprises existed in Heilbronn that, together, employed about 450 people (fig. 4).

Fig. 4. View of Heilbronn in 1830. Colored lithograph by the Brothers Wolff. The smokestacks are one indication of the early stage of the city's industrialization. Note, though, that the boat in the foreground is still horse-drawn. Private collection.

Fig. 5. The Heilbronn Hospital in 1857. Watercolor by Gustav Schmoller. When Adolf Cluss was young, Heilbronn was a living museum of architectural history. This view shows the hospital's baroque facade and, in the background, the Renaissance tower of Kilian's Church. Stadtarchiv Heilbronn.

The cooking oil and tobacco industries were prominent areas of specialization from the beginning of Heilbronn's industrialization in the late eighteenth century. The production of cooking oil became increasingly important over the course of the nineteenth century; by 1914, Heilbronn accounted for one third of the oil produced in the German Empire. Heilbronn's food products and tobacco industries diversified considerably during the nineteenth century. The firm Knorr, which earned an international reputation with its line of soups, is a notable example.

The paper industry provides an ideal illustration of the process of industrialization in Heilbronn. At the beginning we find the wealthy, venerable firm of the Rauch Brothers. In 1822, due to poor business prospects, the firm withdrew from trade. It retooled its oil and tobacco mills and began producing paper. The Rauch Brothers were the first in southern Germany to attempt the mechanical production of paper in uncut rolls. And this experiment proved to be extremely successful economically. With their new method of producing paper the Rauch Brothers introduced a rapid and radical restructuring of the paper industry.

While the textile industry assumed a key position in the Kingdom of Württemberg during the nineteenth century, it

was the paper industry that drove industrialization in Heilbronn. The city quickly also became a center for the production of paper-making machines and a leading market in the paper trade.

The pace of industrialization in Heilbronn accelerated from the middle of the nineteenth century on. A number of sectors blossomed (chemicals, foodstuffs), and others died out. By the end of the century, Heilbronn was one of southwestern Germany's major industrial centers. According to the 1895 industrial statistics gathered in Württemberg, 10,099 people were employed in Heilbronn, of whom 8,965 worked in 361 commercial and industrial enterprises. Only the capital city of Stuttgart had more workers in industry.

The city's rapid industrialization was accompanied by an enormous increase in population. Heilbronn had one of the highest growth rates among cities in the Kingdom of Württemberg. As a result of both a rising birth rate and migration, its population grew more than five-fold over the course of the nineteenth century—to 37,900 by 1900. That unprecedented rate of growth was not to be equaled in any later period of the city's history.

Not only the population, but also the physical limits of Heilbronn grew. In 1830, there were no residential buildings and only a handful of commercial and industrial structures outside the limits of the old core of the imperial city, an area of approximately 65 acres. From 1836 on, responsibility for planning the systematic expansion of the city fell to the city architect. This position was filled in 1838 by Ludwig de Millas, Adolf Cluss's brother-in-law. By the end of the nineteenth century, the development of new suburbs had increased the settled area of Heilbronn to about 1,100 acres.

All this growth naturally had an effect on the appearance of the city. For centuries, the area of the old city, surrounded by a wall, remained practically unchanged (fig. 5). Within this area, however, there was constant reconstruction and alteration of existing structures according to prevailing tastes. The result over time was a mix of architectural styles dominated by *Fachwerk* (half-timbered) houses and large stone buildings. By contrast, the buildings constructed during the nineteenth century in the areas beyond where the old city

Fig. 6. The Heilbronn train station in 1848. Lithograph by the Brothers Wolff. Stadtarchiv Heilbronn.

Fig. 7. The Wilhelmsbau (right) in 1910. This prominent building was built by Heinrich Cluss in 1843 to 1845 and was known as the Clussbau for several decades. Stadtarchiv Heilbronn.

walls had stood were characterized above all by facades of local sandstone. Master workmen in Heilbronn, such as Heinrich Cluss, quarried the stone in their individual allotments in the massive stone quarries in the mountains east of the city and marketed this valuable building material throughout the region and beyond. Heinrich Cluss had his own warehouse on the Heilbronn waterfront and sent numerous shiploads of sandstone down the river. Stone quarried and sold by Cluss ended up, for instance, in the Cologne Cathedral.[7]

Urban development in Heilbronn centered on the railroad in the west (fig. 6) and the still standing Wilhelmsbau (Wilhelm's building) in the south (fig. 7). No sooner had the first train rolled down the track in Germany in 1835 than this new means of transportation became the subject of discussion in Heilbronn. Concrete plans for the first rail line in the Kingdom of Württemberg—a link connecting Stuttgart, the capital, with Heilbronn—did not, however, take shape until 1845. After a number of options were considered, it was decided to locate Heilbronn's train station on the west bank of the Neckar in front of the bridge over the river. This location provided a direct connection to the steamboats that traveled daily down river to Mannheim.[8]

In histories of Heilbronn, the plans for the train station are discussed in connection with Heinrich Cluss's construction of what is now known as the Wilhelmsbau south of the old city center (fig. 7). It is assumed this building was envisioned as a railroad hotel for the eventuality that the train station would be located in the southern part of the city. There is, however, no mention of the building serving as a hotel in the proposal to construct a "substantial building . . . in [Byzantine] rounded arch style" that Heinrich Cluss presented to the city council on August 10, 1843.[9] And by the time the first plans for a rail link to Heilbronn were being drafted in 1845, the apartments in the "Cluss Building" had already been rented.[10]

Heinrich Cluss's Businesses

Along with his construction businesses, Heinrich Cluss also owned vineyards and a winery. He invested in real estate ventures and sold sandstone from his allotment in the Heilbronn quarries. All of this commercial activity occupied him to such a degree that he declined election to the City Council in 1835—"as much as the undersigned thankfully acknowledges the trust placed in him by a respectable number of his fellow citizens who suggested that he be elected into the City Council."[11]

Heinrich Cluss's larger construction projects included two bridge contracts in the region. In 1824, he took over the construction of a stone bridge over the Kocher River north of Heilbronn. Adolf Cluss might have experienced something of another of his father's bridge projects as a child. Between 1832 and 1835, Heinrich Cluss was engaged in the construction of a bridge over the Enz River at Besigheim, over which the main road connecting Heilbronn and Stuttgart would run. As with other large projects, Cluss hired several construction workers (stonecutters and masons), and, as the "entrepreneur" in charge of the project, he had to make a security deposit of 10,000 gulden before construction could begin.[12]

For this extensive construction activity it was certainly not a drawback that Caroline Cluss, Heinrich's oldest daughter, married the city's chief architect (*Stadtbaumeister*), Ludwig de Millas (1808–1890). In September 1838, de Millas took over responsibility for planning the extension of the city beyond its medieval core. Heinrich Cluss was interested above all in the city's growth to the south, where he had begun to buy property in 1830 to 1831 and was to erect the Cluss Building mentioned above.

In 1847, Heinrich Cluss, although only fifty-five years old, turned his firm over to his eldest son, Carl. On the occasion of this transfer, the "entire team of workers who had been employed by Mr. Cluss [expressed] publicly their gratitude" to him and wished him "God's rich reward."[13] Heinrich Cluss did not, however, simply go into retirement. He had become a member of the City Council, and the newly established fire department chose him as commandant.[14]

It was no accident that Heinrich Cluss was active in wine

Fig. 8. Kilian's Square, Heilbronn, 1837. Lithograph by the Brothers Wolff. Adolf Cluss grew up in the vicinity, and he was certainly influenced by memories of markets such as this. Städtische Museen Heilbronn.

production as well as construction. Heilbronn had been a center of viticulture from its earliest days and remains one today. Like his father, Heinrich Cluss systematically acquired vineyards and produced wine. In June 1827, he bought the building neighboring the family's house in the Klostergasse, "a cellar . . . with a large barn on top of it containing a sizeable wine press."[15] Heinrich Cluss also experimented with varieties of grapes that were unknown in the Heilbronn region. Two of his wines—including "a very fine wine with delicate bouquet and beautiful astringency that can be placed alongside famed red wines"—won prizes at the 1846 Convention of German Wine and Fruit Producers in Heilbronn.[16]

Adolf Cluss appreciated his father's wines. In 1854, he wrote to Joseph Weydemeyer, "My old man (jack ass) never wrote me how much the little cask would hold. I only know that it is an excellent 1846 red wine from the Neckar Valley (the old man's own)."[17]

Family Stories

We hear nothing about Adolf Cluss between his baptism in 1825 and his being issued a journeyman's book (*Wanderbuch*) in June 1844.[18] For this period, we have only indirect sources that throw light on Cluss's family, his immediate environment, the schools he attended, his teachers and his classmates (fig. 8).

Adolf Cluss was not yet two years old when his mother died in 1827. To honor his deceased wife, Heinrich Cluss had a memorial erected in the cemetery.[19] For Adolf Cluss, the youngest child in the family, Anna Cluss's death must have been an event of far-reaching consequences, although he never mentioned it later. Barely six months after the funeral, Heinrich Cluss married Jakobine Roth, a niece of his deceased wife who had lived in the household for several years.

The life of the Cluss family was shaped by the father's many business activities. We can only assume that Adolf was introduced at an early age to the building trade by his father, his brother-in-law, and his older brother. In the history of the family, Heinrich Cluss is portrayed as severe, "almost a tyrant." That perhaps helps to explain Adolf's personality. He rebelled early on, and he never had anything good to say about his father in his correspondence.

Heinrich Cluss apparently did not appreciate music. When his daughter Pauline wanted to attend a concert by Franz Liszt in November 1843, he said no: the admission price of two gulden was too much for a single musician.[20] His children were not, however, deterred from their interest in music. Adolf was eventually to become a member of the Washington *Sängerbund*, for example, and his sister Henriette, together with her son Hugo Faisst, backed the composer Hugo Wolf.

One of Heinrich Cluss's character traits did, however, appear in Adolf. Heinrich repeatedly took active part in social causes. In February 1844, for example, he took the initiative in collecting donations for victims of a mining accident.[21] His will made several "bequests for benevolent purposes"—to a hospital, an elementary school, and charities for the local poor.[22]

Cluss's father seems to have been a model for his son in another respect. Heinrich Cluss was extremely fond of traveling, and his travels took him to London, Rotterdam, Antwerp, and Strasbourg, among other places.

At School

Like all the children his age, young Adolf attended a *Volksschule* (public primary school); he probably entered school in 1831, most likely the boys' school located in the Klostergasse in Heilbronn. Religion and ethics were the main subjects, followed by reading, writing, and arithmetic.

Fig. 9. The Heilbronn Gymnasium in 1830. Lithograph by the Brothers Wolff. Adolf Cluss attended school in this building; he was probably enrolled in the school's *Realklasse* from 1833 to 1841. Städtische Museen Heilbronn.

Music classes were primarily devoted to practicing Protestant hymns.

After two years of *Volksschule*, boys had the opportunity to transfer to the *Gymnasium* (high school); beginning in 1827, it was possible for students in Heilbronn to switch to a *Realklasse* (vocational track), after three years of *Gymnasium*. The *Realklasse* emphasized new educational subjects so that students could "receive a higher education as future businessmen, professionals, artists, etc., without having to devote themselves to university studies."[23] The *Realklasse* was eventually turned into a school of its own, but in Cluss's youth the *Gymnasium* and the *Realklasse* were housed in the same building in the Karlsstrasse, and they shared a principal and some faculty (fig. 9).

Adolf Cluss probably began at *Gymnasium* in 1833. The later course of his life suggests he opted for the *Realklasse*; if indeed he did, his school years would have come to an end in 1841. Several of the teachers who might have taught him were to become politically prominent in years leading up to the 1848 revolution and may thus have laid the foundation for Cluss's participation in the communist movement. Among these teachers were Christian Märklin, who had started teaching at the Heilbronn *Gymnasium* in August 1840, and Carl Friedrich Schnitzer, who joined the school faculty in March 1837.

Johann Franz Arnold may also have belonged to the circle of teachers who had instructed Adolf Cluss. He began teaching English in the *Realklasse* in 1831. His son Franz, born 1829 in Heilbronn, emigrated like Adolf Cluss to the United States. He could well be the Franz Arnold whom Cluss describes in a letter to Weydemeyer from 1852 as a "Fresco painter from Heilbronn,"[24] and in another as "a young man not without talents, although only one to one-and-one-half years ago he was still an immature twit *[ein grosser Laffe]*." In that second letter, Cluss goes on to report, "because of a cute, silly little girl, Rosa Schmidt in Baltimore, he nearly turned his back on his whole political engagement; it was only the old man Schmidt's refusal to give his blessing to this marriage that in part saved him from this fiasco."[25] As he wrote that letter, Adolf Cluss most certainly could not have imagined that he himself would marry this very same Rosa Schmidt in 1859.

Among Cluss's friends in Heilbronn were the brothers Wilhelm and Carl Pfänder. Wilhelm Pfänder (1826–1905) was Cluss's schoolmate; like Cluss, he was an enthusiastic member of a sports club *(Turnverein)* and was also to emigrate to the United States. Wilhelm Pfänder participated in the founding of the town of New Ulm, Minnesota. Carl Pfänder (1819–1876) belonged, like Adolf Cluss, to the inner circle around Karl Marx and lived in London from 1845 on.

In his youth, Cluss was also "close friends"[26] with August Bruckmann (1824–1864). Son of a silverware manufacturer, Bruckmann was a member of the Heilbronn *Turnverein*, which he headed in 1848 to 1849. He played an active part in the revolution of 1848; after a brief imprisonment, he emigrated to France in 1849 and later relocated to Russia.[27]

We know for certain that Adolf Cluss knew Wilhelm Doderer (1825–1900), a classmate of the same age who also attended the *Realklasse* of the Heilbronn *Gymnasium*. After 1840, Doderer worked "with an industrious construction foreman"[28] as a mason and stone cutter on Kilian's Church before he passed the Württemberg state exam in the building trades and attended the Berlin Academy of Architecture. This career path was typical of architects in the nineteenth century.

Carl Cluss (1819–1870), Adolf's older brother, also became an architect. After finishing school, he became an apprentice mason and stonecutter in his father's firm. He passed his master's exam in 1844,[29] and then, like Doderer, went on to study architecture in Berlin.

Adolf Cluss started off in one of the building trades as well. He was a journeyman carpenter when he applied for his journeyman's book *(Wanderbuch)* on June 27, 1844, at the registry office in Heilbronn. Traveling journeymen were required to carry a *Wanderbuch*, in which masters would record how long they were employed at each work site.

Heilbronn, City of Innovation

Nineteenth-century Heilbronn was marked not only by enormous growth in population and area but also by an unusual openness to technological and intellectual innovation. The city's Protestant, politically liberal middle class believed strongly in the idea of progress.

In 1848, Heilbronn became the final stop on Württemberg's first—and for a time only—rail line. Through its own initiative, the city developed into a hub for what were then the two most modern forms of transportation: the locomotive and the steamship. As the railroad began to surpass steamships, Heilbronn answered the challenge by using a new technology: chain-driven freighters that could carry large cargoes along the Neckar at rates competitive with rail.

A modern, middle-class society took shape in Heilbronn in the *Vormärz* era between the Napoleonic Wars and the 1848 revolution. A nationalist outlook began to spread throughout the land; one manifestation of this trend was the proliferation of societies and associations. Social clubs, choral societies, gymnastic clubs, and associations of prominent citizens were established across Germany. The first choral society in Heilbronn, the *Singkranz*, was formed in 1818. The city's first gymnastics club, the *Turngemeinde*, was established in 1845, the same year as the first club of local notables, the *Grässle-Gesellschaft.*

Heilbronn hosted a number of large gymnastic and choral festivals during the 1840s that had resonance far beyond the city and its environs. These festivals combined sports and music with political and social ideas and attracted many enthusiastic young participants such as Adolf Cluss. The 1840 Pentecost choral festival in Heilbronn, for example, drew twelve hundred singers from across southern Germany, and its success was a source of great pride to the city's residents.

Even more impressive was the gymnastic festival of 1846. It was the first of its kind that attracted national attention. Besides team and individual competitions, the festival featured a march through the city and debates on such questions as whether *Turnverein* members should address one another with the familiar *du* form. Adolf Cluss later recalled the festival: "Following my encouragement, a group of twenty-eight gymnasts from Mainz decided to attend the festival. My parents invited this whole bunch to stay at our place and to treat our big house as their own during the festival."[30] Cluss also described the journey of a number of the festival participants to the home of the poet Justinus Kerner in Weinsberg (fig. 10): "When we arrived at the house of Kerner, Germain Metternich introduced the old poet J. K. from a platform that had been prepared specifically for this purpose. From the throats of two thousand young gymnasts, he was greeted enthusiastically with his song: 'Wohlauf noch getrunken' [Come On, Let's Drink]. The old man was completely overcome with emotion." The festival was also a political gathering. Among the gymnasts were many young men with pronounced democratic and revolutionary views; the Germain Metternich Cluss mentioned, for instance, was to be a prominent leader of the 1848 revolution in Mainz.

1848 in Heilbronn

Heilbronn was considered one of the strongholds of the democratic revolution in Württemberg. There was broad support in the city for the revolutionary movement. The local *Turnverein* converted itself into a militia and played an active part in the events of 1848.

Adolf Cluss seems to have been involved in the revolutionary events taking place in his home town. In February 1848, pamphlets addressed "To Our Brothers, the German Proletariat" began to circulate in Heilbronn and Weinsberg,

Fig. 10. The Heilbronn *Turnfest* (Gynmanstics Tournament) of 1846: the *Turner* serenade the poet Justinus Kerner. This is the scene Cluss described in a letter many years later. Illustration from Ludwig Kies, *Album des Heilbronner Turnfests.* Badische Landesbibliothek Karlsruhe.

causing an uproar among the authorities in the Heilbronn region.[31] The pamphlets had appeared earlier in Mainz and Hanau; in Mainz, the "mechanic" Adolf Cluss was suspected of distributing revolutionary writings such as these.[32]

A second possible indication of Adolf Cluss's involvement in the political upheaval in Heilbronn is a "personal letter from Mainz" published in the *Heilbronner Tagblatt*. The letter detailed the bylaws of the Mainz Workers' Club; since Adolf Cluss was the secretary of the club, it seems likely that he was also the author of this "personal letter."[33]

The political situation in Heilbronn turned volatile in March 1848. There were numerous public meetings and raucous protests. The situation reached its high point when the revolutionaries succeeded in winning over the Württemberg regiment stationed in Heilbronn. This mutiny was, however, short-lived. The insurgents were quickly disarmed and led away by the state authorities. The revolutionary climate in Heilbronn thereupon cooled down noticeably.

Heilbronn and Adolf Cluss

Nineteenth-century Heilbronn was characterized by a pronounced intellectual openness that is evident in the city's dynamic industrial, architectural, technological, and social development. This dynamism rested, in turn, on the prevailing liberal climate of opinion rooted in the city's enlightened Protestant tradition.

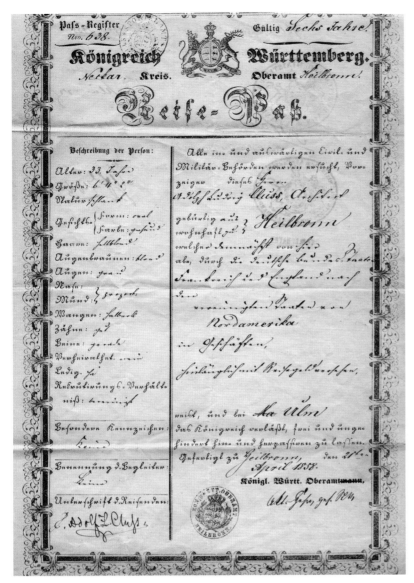

Fig. 11. Adolf Cluss's passport allowed him to travel "through the German states, France, and England to the United States of North America on business" in April 1858. Cluss Papers, Smithsonian Institution Castle Collection, Gift of William S. Shacklette.

Adolf Cluss returned to Heilbronn twice after his emigration. Following the death of his father on June 22, 1857, he came back to the city in the spring of 1858 to claim his inheritance (fig. 11). His father's considerable property had already been auctioned off in September 1857 to facilitate the transfer of the inheritance. During this visit, Adolf Cluss applied for a passport from the Württemberg authorities; on his return trip to Washington, he stopped in London for what was to be his last contact with Karl Marx.

Adolf Cluss remained in contact with family members in Heilbronn. His correspondence with them was initially sporadic but increased noticeably beginning in the 1890s. In

1891, Hugo, the son of Henriette Cluss, visited his uncle in Washington.[34] In 1898, Adolf Cluss made a final visit to Heilbronn, and afterwards his siblings still living and many of his nieces and nephews sent a steady stream of letters to him in America.

In his last letter to his family in Heilbronn, Adolf Cluss wrote on July 9, 1905: "It always makes me sad to reflect that father and mother Christine and Mine, and all the children, with the exception of Pauline and me, have long since shaken off the dust of mother earth. These years at the end of one's life are simply more beautiful in a poetic sense than one is accustomed to assume."[35]

NOTES

1. Birth notice in the Evangelical registry of baptisms in Heilbronn.
2. Peter Wanner, "Hans Seyfer, Johann Lachmann und Adolf Cluss: Das Steinkreuz vor dem Sülmertor und der Christuskopf aus der Klostergasse," in *Heilbronnica 2*, ed. Christhard Schrenk and Peter Wanner, Quellen und Forschungen zur Geschichte der Stadt Heilbronn, vol. 15 (Heilbronn, 2003), 163–78.
3. Adolf Cluss to Joseph Weydemeyer, 16 April 1852, International Institute of Social History Amsterdam (hereafter IISH), Weydemeyer Archives, No. 24.
4. Karl Marx and Friedrich Engels, *Briefwechsel September 1852 bis August 1853*, Karl Marx Friedrich Engels Gesamtausgabe (MEGA), part 3, *Briefwechsel*, vol. 6 (Berlin 1987), 251.
5. Adolf Cluss in a letter to his family from 5 July 1901; cited in Werner A. Cluss, "Die Geschichte der Familie Cluss," (unpublished typescript, 1932; copy on deposit in the City Archives of Heilbronn), 5.
6. On the history of Heilbronn in the nineteenth century, see: Helmut Schmolz and Hubert Weckbach, *Heilbronn. Geschichte und Leben einer Stadt in Bildern*, 2d ed. (Weissenhorn,1973); Christhard Schrenk et al., *Von Helibrunna nach Heilbronn*, Veröffentlichungen des Archivs der Stadt Heilbronn, vol. 36 (Stuttgart, 1998); Christhard Schrenk, "Schock und Chance. Die Mediatisierung der Reichsstadt Heilbronn," in *Alte Klöster, neue Herren. Die Säkularisation im deutschen Südwesten 1803*, ed. Hans Ulrich Rudolf, Begleitbücher zur grossen Landesausstellung Baden-Württemberg 2003 in Bad Schussenried, vol. 2.1 and 2.2: Essays (Ostfildern, 2003): 749–58.
7. City Archives of Heilbronn, Council Proceedings of 17 November 1843.
8. City Archives of Heilbronn, PKR E 005-1, 3a–5, 1845.
9. City Archives of Heilbronn, Council Proceedings of 10 August 1843; City Archives of Heilbronn, Proceedings from the Examination of Building Permits, 1840–1843, 520b and 526b, 9 August 1843.
10. City Archives of Heilbronn, PKR E 005-1, 3a–5, 1845.
11. *Heilbronner Intelligenzblatt*, 24 January 1835.
12. City Archives of Heilbronn, Council Proceedings of 1832, 526b and of 1833, 44; advertisements in the *Heilbronner Intelligenzblatt*, 5 July 1834 and 9 June 1835.

13. *Heilbronner Intelligenzblatt*, 12 May 1847.

14. City Archives of Heilbronn, "Organization and Statutes of the Fire Extinguishing and Rescue Department," 1847.

15. City Archives of Heilbronn, CP 1826/27, 237b–238a.

16. Gustav Rümelin, *Verhandlungen der Versammlung deutscher Wein- und Obstproducenten zu Heilbronn am Neckar* (Heilbronn, 1847), 418.

17. IISH Amsterdam, Joseph Weydemeyer Archives, 20 September 1854.

18. State Archives of Ludwigsburg, F 173, fasc. 47.

19. City Archives of Heilbronn, Council Proceedings 1827, 364, #1436.

20. Cluss 1932, II, 8.

21. *Heilbronner Intelligenzblatt*, 20 February 1844.

22. City Archives of Heilbronn, excerpts from the proceedings of the Foundation Council, vol. 10, 338.

23. City Archives of Heilbronn, decree of 9 July 1827.

24. IISH, Adolf Cluss Archives, No. 8, letter to Weydemeyer, 11 January 1852.

25. Karl Marx and Friedrich Engels, *Briefwechsel Januar bis August 1852*, Karl Marx Friedrich Engels Gesamtausgabe (MEGA), part 3 *Briefwechsel*, vol. 5 (Berlin 1987), 487–91; IISH Amsterdam, Joseph Weydemeyer Archives No. 28a, letter to Weydemeyer, 2 January 1852.

26. Adolf Cluss to his family in Heilbronn, 9 July 1905: quoted from W. Cluss, *Die Geschichte der Familie Cluss*, 1932, II, 13.

27. See Ute Grau et al. *Revolution im Südwesten. Stätten der Demokratiebewegung 1848/49 in Baden-Württemberg*, (Karlsruhe 1997), 257.

28. Quoted in Achim Frey, "Ein Mord, ein Schriftsteller und ein Architekt. Lokalbezüge zu Heimito von Doderer," *Historischer Verein Heilbronn, Veröffentlichung* 33 (1994): 219–24.

29. City Archives of Heilbronn, Council Proceedings of 14 March 1844.

30. Copy of a letter by Adolf Cluss, 14 September 1904, private archive.

31. State Archives of Ludwigsburg, E 173-I fasc. 482; E 146 fasc. 4827.

32. Heinz Monz, *Die Verbindung des Mainzer Paul Stumpf zu Karl Marx und Friedrich Engels. Zugleich ein Beitrag zur Geschichte der Mainzer Arbeiterbewegung*, Hessische Beiträge zur Geschichte der Arbeiterbewegung, vol. 5 (Darmstadt, 1986), 241; Eckhart G. Franz, *Die hessischen Arbeitervereine im Rahmen der politischen Arbeiterbewegung der Jahre 1848–1850*, Hessische Beiträge zur Geschichte der Arbeiterbewegung, vol. 1 (Darmstadt, 1975), 172.

33. *Heilbronner Tagblatt*, 9 and 16 April 1848.

34. Hugo Wolf, *Briefe an Hugo Faisst*, ed. Joachim Draheim and Susanne Hoy. (Tutzing, 1996), 246.

35. Quoted from W. Cluss, *Die Geschichte der Familie Cluss*, 1932, II, 13.

BIBLIOGRAPHY

Die Geschichte der Familie Cluss. Parts 1 and 2 [Werner A. Cluss]. Typescript [Heilbronn 1932]. [Part 3] manuscript by Eugen Cluss.

Franz, Eckhart G. *Die hessischen Arbeitervereine im Rahmen der politischen Arbeiterbewegung der Jahre 1848–1850*. Hessische Beiträge zur Geschichte der Arbeiterbewegung, vol. 1. Darmstadt, 1975.

Frey, Achim. "Ein Mord, ein Schriftsteller und ein Architekt. Lokalbezüge zu Heimito von Doderer." *Historischer Verein Heilbronn, Veröffentlichung* 33 (1994): 219–24.

Grau, Ute et al. *Revolution im Südwesten. Stätten der Demokratiebewegung 1848/49 in Baden-Württemberg*. Arbeitsgemeinschaft hauptamtlicher Archivare im Städtetag Baden-Württemberg, ed. Karlsruhe, 1997.

Marx, Karl, and Friedrich Engels. *Briefwechsel Januar bis Dezember 1851*. Karl Marx Friedrich Engels Gesamtausgabe (MEGA), Abteilung 3: Briefwechsel, vol. 4. Berlin, 1984.

Marx, Karl, and Friedrich Engels. *Briefwechsel Januar bis August 1852*. Karl Marx Friedrich Engels Gesamtausgabe (MEGA), Abteilung 3: Briefwechsel, vol. 5. Berlin, 1987.

Marx, Karl, and Friedrich Engels. *Briefwechsel September 1852 bis August 1853*. Karl Marx Friedrich Engels Gesamtausgabe (MEGA), Abteilung 3: Briefwechsel, vol. 6. Berlin, 1987.

Marx, Karl, and Friedrich Engels. *Briefwechsel September 1853 bis März 1856*. Karl Marx Friedrich Engels Gesamtausgabe (MEGA), Abteilung 3: Briefwechsel, vol. 7. Berlin, 1989.

Monz, Heinz. *Die Verbindung des Mainzer Paul Stumpf zu Karl Marx und Friedrich Engels. Zugleich ein Beitrag zur Geschichte der Mainzer Arbeiterbewegung*. Hessische Beiträge zur Geschichte der Arbeiterbewegung, vol. 5. Darmstadt, 1986.

Rümelin, Gustav. *Verhandlungen der Versammlung deutscher Wein- und Obstproducenten zu Heilbronn am Neckar*. Heilbronn, 1847.

Schmolz, Helmut, and Hubert Weckbach. *Heilbronn. Geschichte und Leben einer Stadt in Bildern*. 2d ed. Weissenhorn. 1973.

Schrenk, Christhard. "Schock und Chance. Die Mediatisierung der Reichsstadt Heilbronn." In *Alte Klöster, neue Herren. Die Säkularisation im deutschen Südwesten 1803*. Hans Ulrich Rudolf, ed., vol. 2, 749–58. Ostfildern, 2003.

Schrenk, Christhard, Hubert Weckbach, and Susanne Schlösser. *Von Helibrunna nach Heilbronn. Eine Stadtgeschichte. Mit einem Beitrag von Siegfried Schilling*. Veröffentlichungen des Archivs der Stadt Heilbronn 36. Stuttgart, 1998.

Wanner, Peter. "Kommunist der ersten Stunde und Baumeister Washingtons— Adolf Cluss (1825–1905)." In Christhard Schrenk, ed., *Heilbronner Köpfe II. Lebensbilder aus zwei Jahrhunderten*. Kleine Schriftenreihe des Archivs der Stadt Heilbronn 45, 21–36. Heilbronn, 1999.

Wanner, Peter. "Hans Seyfer, Johann Lachmann und Adolf Cluss: Das Steinkreuz vor dem Sülmertor und der Christuskopf aus der Klostergasse." In Christhard Schrenk and Peter Wanner, eds., *Heilbronnica 2. Beiträge zur Stadtgeschichte*. Quellen und Forschungen zur Geschichte der Stadt Heilbronn 15, 163–78. Heilbronn, 2003.

Wolf, Hugo. *Briefe an Hugo Faisst*. Joachim Draheim and Susanne Hoy ed. Tutzing, 1996.

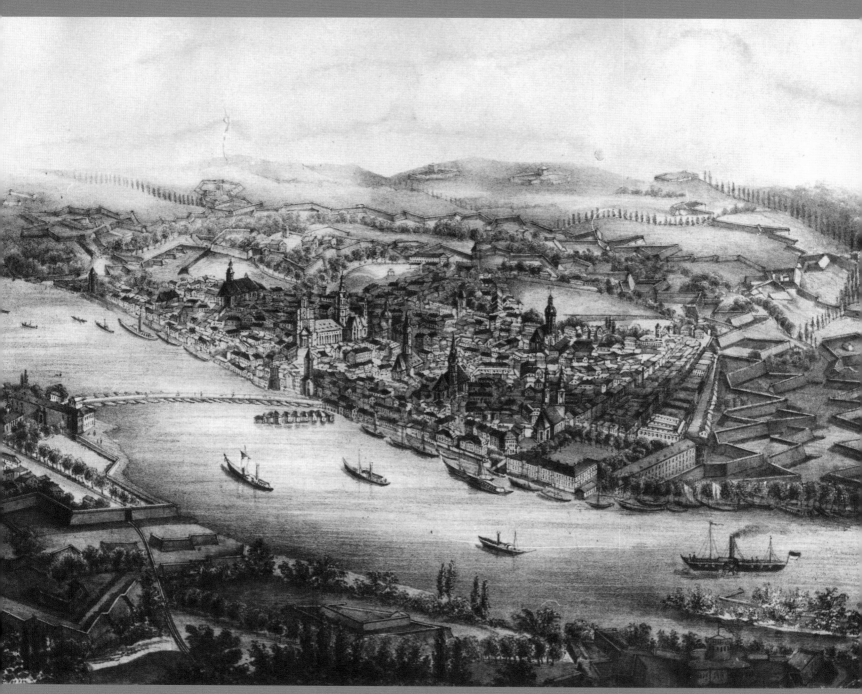

Mainz, a fortified town of the German Confederation, housed Austrian troops, as well as the Prussian troops whose clashes with citizen militias portended the suppression of the city's 1848 revolution. Courtesy Mainzer Stadtarchiv.

Years of Apprenticeship and Travel:
Adolf Cluss and the Revolution of 1848 in Mainz

SABINE FREITAG

ONE OF THE MOST notable aspects of Adolf Cluss's participation in the German Revolution of 1848 was his age. Cluss belonged to the young generation that had so far participated in political life only through extra-parliamentary agitation. Born in 1825, he knew nothing of life during the Napoleonic occupation or the Confederation of the Rhine, nor had he personally experienced the Wars of Liberation. From his own experience, he was familiar only with the relatively stable but politically unsatisfying conditions of the German Confederation. Although the provincial constitutions of the southwest German states were comparatively liberal, the public political sphere in the southwest was still strongly circumscribed by directives from the Bundestag in Frankfurt, which established an elaborate system of police control. Wayfaring journeymen in particular were subject to distrustful surveillance. The authorities suspected them of being members of secret foreign or underground organizations and of spreading revolutionary theories. In turn, the "restrictive practices of the authoritarian state . . . gave rise to a widespread hostility to the 'system' among journeymen."[1] Most of the founders and members of the workers' associations set up in Germany in 1848 to 1849 were journeymen. Among them was also Adolf Cluss, who possessed all the defining traits of the movement's intellectual leaders: "higher education, youthful age, and an uncertain job situation."[2]

Like many young men of his generation, Adolf Cluss was initially politicized through the gymnastics clubs (*Turnvereine*). Functioning as a kind of "substitute public sphere," these associations were of considerable importance in the formation of a German political public and in the emergence of opposition movements in the period leading up to the revolution in March 1848. Under cover of promoting nonpolitical activities such as singing, gymnastics, or reading, the *Turnvereine* and similar clubs promoted a latent politicization of their members, who came to question the state's monopoly on power and demanded expanded political participation. The *Turnvereine* were, along with singing clubs, the associations with the broadest impact. As a rule, they had a stronger urban focus than other clubs and had no class-based restrictions on membership. The majority of their members were employed in the craft trades, that is, chiefly as journeymen. The economic situation of journeymen was becoming increasingly precarious as a result of the onset of industrialization, the concomitant disintegration of the guild system, and the economic crises and price increases of the early 1840s. Given their social makeup, most gymnastics clubs were noticeably more radical than, for instance, the singing clubs, and in 1848 the political sympathies of most members of gymnastics clubs lay with the radical left, which was fighting for a democratic republic based on free elections and universal male suffrage.

What brought Cluss to Mainz in 1846 was not primarily political agitation, however, but rather his first serious job opportunity. He was hired as the "second architect" in the office of the Hessian Ludwigsbahn[3] and worked as a draftsman on the railroad's construction. The company had been in existence for only a short time when Cluss was hired, and the project was not to be completed until long after he had moved to the United States.[4] Everything we know about Cluss's work for the Ludwigsbahn comes from his own letters. His "unconditional" embrace of the workers' movement, which he told Karl Marx in 1852 had come during his years in Mainz, was probably the outcome of his contact with the workers building the railroad and his involvement in workers' education associations; he had spent his life in Mainz, as he told Marx, "largely among the working classes."[5]

For young Adolf Cluss, it was no contradiction to participate in the building of the railroad even though trains, along with steamships on the Rhine, threatened the existence of many traditional trades. In Mainz, for example, many coachmen and carters found themselves out of work because more and more freight was being shifted to the railways. Likewise, the Mainz *Voranzieher* (towmen), who pulled yachts and sailing ships from land, lost their customers. It was above all these men who vented their growing social fears—even before the 1848 revolution—through targeted actions such as smashing machinery or destroying railroad tracks.[6] Cluss himself witnessed such protest actions in Mainz and considered them wrong. One of his first lectures in the Mainz Workers' Education Association in the spring of 1848 dealt with the ambiguities of advancing industrialization and, in particular, with the concrete situation of the coachmen, day laborers, and bargemen in and around Mainz.[7] Cluss tried to make the workers and artisans understand that their goal could not be to stop progress by destroying modern technology simply because it led to short-term unemployment for a few. In the long run, he maintained, the revolution in the transportation sector would increase the need for labor many times over. Moreover, it was clear to him that trains and steamships would bring "infinite advantages" for each person, and that the accompanying improvements in "means of communication" would eventually provide many new jobs. It is

quite obvious that at this time he entertained the optimism about progress shared by many contemporaries, but he also linked it directly with the idea of a social redistribution of wealth. The community owed financial compensation to those who lost their jobs as a result of necessary progress. Only those who depended on their own labor for their living should have a claim to such compensation, however, not those who put their capital to work for them, that is, factory owners and entrepreneurs. Cluss nonetheless wanted to guarantee capitalists "protection of their property"—a very atypical position for a communist. One should not forget that socialist and communist ideas were still in their infancy at this time, showed a good deal of overlap with radical democratic thinking, and were still a long way from constituting a rigorous theoretical system.

In his youth, Adolf Cluss seems to have been quite attracted to radical political positions. From what we know about his family background, and in particular about his turbulent relationship with his father, he appears to have been a rebellious young man who did not want to follow family tradition and go into the family business. Looking back later in life, Cluss once explained that before coming to Mainz and making the acquaintance of leading communists, he had been under the influence of "Heinzean revolutionary slogans."[8] The ultra-radical Karl Heinzen, who called for armed revolution and regicide as means to create a federal republic, embodied the extreme left of the spectrum of radical thought. When Cluss, under the influence of Marx and Friedrich Engels, distanced himself from Heinzen in 1847, it was his first step in a "more moderate" direction. By the fall of 1847, Cluss had completely adopted the ideas of Friedrich Engels as his own. Engels, in a polemic against Heinzen in the *Deutsche Brüsseler Zeitung*, dismissed the idea of overthrowing the monarchy as a one-time act to restore social justice as naive and unrealistic; he placed his hopes instead in having the communists educate workers about the important role they were to play in the unfolding of history.[9] In a declaration from Paris dated October 24, 1847, and signed "C. Lange"—the alias he took probably on account of his height (one meaning of *lang* is "tall")[10]—Cluss defended Engels's stance and explained that Heinzen's pamphlets "contained

Mainz viewed from the Rhine, ca. 1845, the flourishing river port where the young architect Cluss encountered radical socialist ideas while working as a railroad draftsman. Courtesy Mainzer Stadtarchiv.

nothing more than a constant, senseless call to let the fists fly, with no indication what to do when the fighting is over."[11] It is possible, as Welta Pospelowa suspects, that Engels himself encouraged Cluss to write this article because he was so well versed in Heinzen's writings. It is equally possible, however, that Cluss had growing doubts about Heinzen's radical slogans, which were conceptually shallow and had little to say about how a democratic republic and greater social justice could be achieved in the long term.

The precise moment when Adolf Cluss made the acquaintance of Karl Marx and Friedrich Engels in Brussels is not known. In one of his letters, he speaks generally of the year 1847 and "the time of the Brüsseler Zeitung."[12] It does not seem improbable that Cluss's contact to Marx came about

with the help of three acquaintances in Mainz—Karl Wallau, Johann Schickel, and Friedrich Jakob Schütz—with whom he was to collaborate in the revolutionary activities of spring 1848. All three were members of both the Communist League and the Communist German Workers' Association (*Deutscher Arbeiterverein*), which was established in Brussels two months after the founding of the International League of Communists in London, on June 9, 1847.

In Germany, the league relied on fifteen local *Gemeinden* (chapters) that had to operate in secret; the Bundestag had outlawed all communist associations as of August 6, 1846.[13] A letter from the league's central office, dated September 14, 1847, mentioned that a second group was being set up in Mainz and that the endeavor was made more difficult by the

Ludwig Kalisch (1814–1882), editor of *Der Demokrat*, which regularly published Cluss's articles during the optimistic spring of 1848. Courtesy Mainzer Stadtarchiv.

police "constantly breathing down the necks of our brothers in M[ainz]."[14] By this time, the "brothers" included Adolf Cluss, whose activities were being monitored by the authorities. An Austrian informant's report of December 1847 states that Cluss was "allegedly" supporting the acquitted radical democrat Germain Metternich in his "subversive political activities."[15] In January 1848, both men were mentioned as the disseminators of the "lithographed Soldier's Catechism,"[16] the purpose of which was to spur the discontented Austrian troops stationed at the confederation's fortress in Mainz to mutiny. The following April, a letter from the Mainz chapter to the league's central office in Cologne mentioned that Cluss had "attracted the eagle eyes of the still somewhat clueless police as secretary of the Workers' Association."[17] However, the authorities' surveillance never reached a point where Cluss's activities in Mainz were seriously threatened. There is thus little reason to see it as the cause behind his hasty departure to America in late summer 1848.

News of revolution in Paris and the proclamation of a French republic on February 28 to 29, 1848 spread like wildfire in the German states. Mainz, which was located close to the French border, saw spontaneous gatherings as early as March 1. A hastily established citizens' committee formulated the so-called *Märzforderungen* (March demands). Like their counterparts elsewhere in Germany, the citizens of Mainz called for freedom of the press and of assembly, the right to petition, a *Bürgerwehr* (a city militia with free election of officers), an immediate oath of loyalty to the constitution from the military, free municipal codes, preservation of the existing legislation on the left bank of the Rhine (i.e., the special rights of the Code Napoleon), and a pan-German parliament.[18] The demands put forward in Mainz and elsewhere were restricted to the political realm; they did not touch upon urgent social and economic problems. Under pressure, the government of Hesse-Darmstadt granted all these demands on March 2.

In the following weeks, citizens of Mainz took advantage of the more liberal climate to create numerous new associations.[19] The *Turner* clubs, through which Cluss had contact to the democratic movement, combined to form the Democratic Gymnastics Club. That organization, in turn, had close contact with the Democratic Association, which was founded on March 11 under the leadership of the radical democrats Ludwig Bamberger, Franz Zitz, and Ludwig Kalisch.[20] Cluss, like all other members of the Communist League, joined the Democratic Association in accordance with the expressed wish of the communist leaders. They wanted their people to participate in the establishment of all political opposition associations in order to gain influence in them and thereby to use them to heighten the impact of their own movement.

Following the outbreak of revolution in France, Marx decamped Brussels on March 4 and traveled to Paris, where Engels had been since fall 1847. Marx and Engels entertained the not unjustified hope that the revolutionary spark would jump from France to Germany; it was decided, accordingly, to organize the return of German workers and artisans in Paris to Germany. The returning workers were supposed to establish workers' associations throughout their homeland. But they reached the German border in unorganized fashion, "each on his own, one by one, and in various locations."[21] The communist movement was far from united, let alone extensive.

Friedrich Karl Wallau (1823–1877), chair of the Workers' Association organized by Mainz communists during the 1848 Revolution. Like Cluss, Wallau gradually moderated his politics and as a liberal became Mainz's mayor in 1872. Courtesy Mainzer Stadtarchiv.

In late March 1848, the Mainz members of the Communist League—Karl Wallau, Paul Stumpf, Philipp Jakob, and Johann Schickel—returned to the city from Paris. Wallau immediately contacted Cluss and Gottfried Stumpf, Paul Stumpf's brother, to help organize the founding of an educational association for workers.[22] The provisional managing committee invited all interested parties to a meeting on March 27, during which a set of bylaws setting out the goals and organization of the association was adopted. According to the "Rules and Regulations of the Workers' Educational Association in Mainz," the purpose of the association was "to bring about the greatest possible improvement in the material, intellectual, and moral condition of the working classes, and in so doing to secure the producers of man-made products their proper place within human society." This goal was very much in line with the theoretical ideas of Marx and Engels, who were not looking for a quick revolutionary action—for revolution and military conflict—but rather were seeking to set in motion a necessary historical process by edu-

cating the working class. The association hoped to raise the educational level of the workers by providing lectures and talks in all fields of knowledge and by providing access to books and newspapers that "represent the interests of the working class." What the association had in mind was the transmission of knowledge and skills from more educated to less educated members; every member should, accordingly, promote the goals of the association to the best of his ability.[23]

The association's executive committee was made up of eleven members. Karl Wallau was elected chair and Gottfried Stumpf deputy chair; Adolf Cluss acted as secretary. His task was to "take care of all the written business of the association and to keep a record of all decisions made by the executive committee and the general assembly."[24] He not only managed the correspondence of the Workers' Association but also, in his capacity as *Beistand* (counsel) the correspondence of the Mainz cell of the Communist League. Cluss organized most of the lectures, which were always held on Wednesday evening at the general meetings of the association, and gave many talks himself. He wrote to headquarters in Cologne about the educational events that took place daily in addition to the Wednesday lectures: "Among the subjects of instruction we have included writing, arithmetic, drawing, stylistics, and exercises in impromptu speaking, in order to attract the great masses and to make them accessible and receptive to political and social questions through education. . . . Wednesday is meeting day with lectures and discussions about questions that have come in. I am writing this so that if any one of you who happen to be making the trip could perhaps work around this day."[25] Cluss was thus soliciting possible lecturers from other groups that might have members passing through Mainz.

Viewed from outside, the association at times appeared to be an elementary school for adults. Yet what may have seemed ridiculous to some was the real core of all the workers' associations founded in the years 1848 to 1849, namely a faith in the emancipatory power of political education. This faith differed but little from the nineteenth-century enlightened bourgeois concept of *Bildung:* "The great receptiveness that the associations encountered from artisans and day-laborers shows how widespread the notion of education was in these

Paul Stumpf (1826–1912), the Mainz radical who apparently sent the newly published *Manifesto of the Communist Party* to Cluss from Paris, before returning to join his town's revolution in March 1848. Courtesy Mainzer Stadtarchiv.

social strata as well."[26] The Mainz workers did not have to be persuaded of the importance of education; they displayed a strong "urge for continued intellectual education, which manifests itself almost impetuously among these workers often subject to the burden of physical exertion."[27] Most participants in worker-education programs were probably seeking to improve their chances on the job market, and the communists clearly hoped such programs would lead to the self-emancipation of the working class as a whole. There was, however, an unintended consequence of worker education as well: namely, it promoted a form of social discipline that assisted in integrating the working class into bourgeois society.

Young Cluss seems to have been inspired not only by an optimism about political, social, and technological progress that was typical of his time, but also by an enthusiasm for education that was shared equally by all classes of society. As other chapters in this volume argue, Cluss's participation in the construction of buildings serving the public good, such as schools and museums, demonstrates that his belief in the socially transformative and moral power of education remained central to his work during his years in the United

States. His buildings were intended to serve not the needs of a privileged few, but rather the welfare of the community.

At the same time that the illegal Mainz chapter of the Communist League had very few members—a total of only six—[28] the legal Workers' Education Association was flourishing. On April 23, 1848, Cluss was able to report to Marx and Engels: "The local workers' association has right around 400 members, though it is still growing robustly. We are represented on the executive board with three members of the League, and the majority will always vote with us, which means that the association should be considered as being run entirely in line with our ideas. The correspondence is in our hands, since the counsel [*Beistand*] of the league is the *same person* as the secretary of the workers' association."[29]

Together with Karl Wallau, Cluss signed an appeal on April 5 that called for a centralized network of workers' associations in Germany. This appeal was distributed as a flyer and published in several newspapers. Very much in line with Marx's directives, these associations would serve as forums "where our conditions are discussed, measures to change our current situation are proposed, representatives for the German parliament from the workers' class will be identified, elected, and all other steps will be taken that are necessary to preserve our interests."[30] The signatories believed that these associations should then establish contact with one another as quickly as possible and form a supraregional organization. Cluss and Wallau proposed that a temporary coordinating central office be established in Mainz. On April 7, two days after the appeal was drafted, Marx, Engels, Wilhelm ("Lupus") Wolff, and Ernst Dronke stopped in Mainz on their way to Cologne. This meeting was the beginning of a close friendship between Cluss and Wolff.[31] Wolff almost certainly brought the recently published *Promotion of the Communist Party in Germany* with him to Mainz for propaganda purposes. Cluss appears to have got hold of a copy of the *Manifesto of the Communist Party*, which had been published in London a month earlier, through Paul Stumpf, who had sent it to him from Paris even before Marx's departure from Brussels on March 4, 1848.[32] It was this booklet above all that provided Cluss with the basic Marxist ideas expressed in his lectures.

The opening of the Preliminary Parliament in Frankfurt, March 31–April 3, 1848, whose plans for a German National Assembly seemed too timid to the radical Cluss. Courtesy Institut für Stadtgeschichte, Frankfurt-am-Main.

Largely in response to the Mainz appeal of April 5, the following six weeks saw the establishment of workers' associations and workers' education associations in all the larger cities of the Rhine-Main region. But, unlike the Mainz workers' association, not all of them took a distinctly socialist or communist stance. The Mainz association was the most radical of all the Hessian workers' associations and the only one where Marxist views were programmatically set forth in lectures. Cluss played a major part in this. His lectures "Capital and Labor"[33] and "On the Origins and Nature of the Proletariat"[34] summarized Marxist views, describing the current human order as determined by "the rule of capital over human laborers without capital." He directed particular attention at the process of the alienation of labor, through which capital was increasingly concentrated in the hands of the owning classes while workers, dependent on wages, were

simultaneously falling into poverty. Unable to accumulate capital of their own, workers were thereby blocked from rising into the "class of independent citizens." But when Cluss spoke of the "division of labor" as the hallmark of industrial development, he was thinking less of English factory workers than of the journeymen of the Rhine-Hessian region; increasingly compelled by economic pressures to take factory jobs, they were losing their independence and were in danger of proletarianization. Yet none of these journeymen thought of themselves as communists. They continued to see themselves as practitioners of independent trades, which, in their eyes, gave them a certain standing in society.

With the appeal of April 5, the Mainz Workers' Education Association, and Cluss as the driving force behind it, had fulfilled the task of promoting legal workers' associations in exemplary fashion. The plan to centralize these asso-

Members of the *Turner* movement in white costume during the opening of the Preliminary Parliament at Frankfurt's Paulkirche. Courtesy Institut für Stadtgeschichte, Frankfurt-am-Main.

failed in large part as a result of resistance from the large associations in Cologne, where Marx was publishing the *Neue Rheinische Zeitung* as the central organ of the communist movement, and Berlin, where Stephan Born had assumed leadership of the workers' movement.

Between March 31 and April 3, 1848, Cluss participated in the deliberations of the Preliminary Parliament (*Vorparlament*) in Frankfurt.[36] The main business at hand was to settle on the procedures for electing the delegates to the National Assembly, and Cluss was undoubtedly interested in shaping the electoral law so that workers' representatives could be elected as parliamentary delegates. He was bitterly disappointed at the outcome of the Preliminary Parliament, which declined to institutionalize itself as an interim revolutionary center until the convening of the National Assembly. Worse still, it did not pass an electoral law that would have allowed poor men to be elected to parliament. An outraged Cluss wrote a short time later to the Cologne Workers' Association that even greater effort was now called for to guarantee workers their appropriate place in society: "The urge to escape the slavery in which we find ourselves [must] stir in everyone. If that were to happen, our enemies would no longer have the courage to exclude us millions from representation in the German parliament, as has happened in recent days, we will [then] send our men there and will be ready at any time to back up their words."[37]

When the first pan-German parliament was festively convened in the Paulskirche in Frankfurt on May 18, 1848, the bias in favor of property and education was evident: there was no workers' delegation in attendance. Just how ineffective the assembly in the Paulskirche would be became clear to Cluss and the Mainz populace a few days after it opened. On May 21, the tensions between Prussian soldiers and members of the Mainz city militia escalated into a bloody fight; when it was over, four Prussian soldiers lay dead and twenty-five were wounded. Five Mainz citizens were also wounded. In response, General von Hüser, the Prussian governor of Mainz, threatened to turn his cannons on the city, unless all civilian defense and gymnastics groups turned in their weapons immediately. Although the citizens of Mainz complied with this order, their aversion to the foreign troops

ciations in Mainz ran into difficulties, however, and eventually failed for lack of interest. It was Cluss who suggested that a congress of delegates from the associations be postponed in order to avoid the embarrassment of a very small turn-out. Instead, he recommended sending emissaries to southern Germany "since personal appearances and acquaintance with the brighter minds would be very useful."[35] By May 17, the name "Mainz Workers' Association as the Provisional Central Committee of the German Workers' Associations" had been abandoned. The Mainz initiative within the walls of their city intensified. At the request of the Mainz delegate Franz Zitz, a radical democrat, the Paulskirche assembly took up the incident on May 23, 1848. It did not, however, support the civilian side, but rather made some half-hearted recommendations and backed the governor's effort to restore order. The backing for the hated Confederation ruled out any chance that an unarmed revolt in Mainz might succeed. The democratic forces had suffered a stinging defeat in the very city where they were strongest. This incident must have forced the young Cluss to acknowledge by the end of May 1848 that the initial revolutionary enthusiasm had waned and that the revolution had entered a phase increasingly less favorable to the realization of leftist utopias.

Cluss may have been confirmed in this assessment of the situation by the first Democratic Congress of German Republicans.[38] The congress, which took place June 14 to 17, 1848, in Frankfurt, had been organized at the initiative of leftist delegates to the Paulskirche assembly. Politically, the congress represented the mobilization of all the forces that had not had a say in the National Assembly itself. Marx was represented by Andreas Gottschalk, Joseph Moll, and Karl Schapper, among others. Cluss and Gottfried Stumpf traveled to Frankfurt as delegates of the Mainz group.[39] Although the congress did not have substantial impact, it did succeed in establishing an umbrella organization for democratic associations. The delegates even agreed on a joint party program, which envisioned the transformation of Germany into a democratic republic.

The communists participating in the congress, including Cluss, had no problem supporting the call for a republic, since that would undoubtedly be the form of government best suited to their goals. But the national framework invoked in Frankfurt was irrelevant to the main goals of the workers' movement. The workers' movement had always had a supranational orientation; its political theory did not require the evocation of national pathos. The class that would, in its view, be politically victorious in the long run could be found in every country that had embarked on industrialization on the English model. A communist could thus pitch his tent in virtually any country where the alien-

The Deutscher Hof pub in Frankfurt, site of the Democratic Congress organized in June 1848 by leftists disappointed with the composition and proceedings of the ineffective National Assembly in the nearby Paulskirche. Courtesy Institut für Stadtgeschichte, Frankfurt-am-Main.

ation of labor was evident. Cluss had never mentioned the unification of Germany as one of the primary goals he was fighting for. Moreover, it appears that the very idea of a German nation unified on the basis of a common language and tradition never meant very much to him, nor did the idea of being a German.[40] Those who longed for German unification were driven by other political visions or by personal (e.g., economic) hopes. Another point must also have become clear to Cluss in Frankfurt: compared to the large number of ardent democrats and republicans, the communists were an exceedingly small group.

Perhaps it was this realistic assessment of the political situation coupled with an awareness of his own very limited prospects that made Cluss set out for America in late summer 1848. An external reason, such as persecution by the police, should be ruled out.[41] Despite his communist views, Cluss knew how to take a moderate stance in public, so that even his political opponents could be led to believe they were fighting for the same cause as he.

After leaving Europe via Le Havre, Cluss arrived in New York on September 15, 1848, aboard the *Zurich*. He truthfully gave Hesse as his last place of residence and "architect" as his profession. At the time of his arrival, he was twenty-three years old, but, for reasons unknown, he told the immigration officials that he was a year older.[42]

One may speculate why Cluss chose America rather than England as his new home. England was certainly a more advantageous location for communist agitation—if that were Cluss's main concern. It was the most advanced industrial country in Europe and already had its own workers' movement, which could have quickly established contacts with the German Workers' Association. Many communists, chief among them Karl Marx, would later choose England as their place of refuge almost as a matter of course. Another advantage was Britain's proximity to the European continent, which would have made a quick return to Germany possible if the course of events called for it.

Yet none of these considerations dissuaded Cluss from opting for America. His desire to leave Europe might have been stirred by the enthusiastic contemporary literature about the new democracy across the Atlantic and, perhaps, by his relations with his family. Curiosity about experiencing a working democracy might have been another reason for his choice of the United States. In the end, personal considerations were perhaps the decisive factor. If that was indeed the case, his subsequent career as Washington's master architect suggests he was not mistaken in his choice.

NOTES

1. Michael Wettengel, *Die Revolution von 1848/49 im Rhein-Main-Raum* (Wiesbaden, 1989), 124.
2. Wettengel, *Die Revolution*, 129.
3. Cluss to his niece Sofie de Millas, letter dated 14 September 1904, Stadtarchiv Heilbronn, Cluss Datenbank No. 28. I am grateful to Peter Wanner of the Stadtarchiv Heilbronn for making this letter and other materials available to me as well as for answering numerous questions.
4. Rosel Spaniol, *Eisenbahnen und Museen* (Karlsruhe, 1979), 5−6.
5. Adolf Cluss to Karl Marx, 30 September 1852; quoted in Welta Pospelowa, "Adolf Cluss—ein Mitglied des Bundes der Kommunisten und Kampfgefährte von Marx und Engels," *Marx-Engels-Jahrbuch* 3 (1980): 91.
6. On this see Karl Georg Bockenheimer, *Mainz in den Jahren 1848 und 1849* (Mainz, 1906), 25−27.
7. Cluss mentioned their situation explicitly in his lecture. See "Maschinen und menschliche Arbeitskräfte," signed "C," *Der Demokrat*, No. 2 (April 23, 1848), 10.
8. Adolf Cluss to Karl Marx, 20 September 1852; quoted in Pospelowa, "Adolf Cluss," 86.
9. Friedrich Engels, "Die Kommunisten und Karl Heinzen," *Deutsche Brüsseler Zeitung* (October 1847); quoted in Pospelowa, "Adolf Cluss," 87. Also in *Marx-Engels-Werke (MEW)*, vol. 4, 309−22.
10. At 6 ft. 2 in., Cluss was unusually tall. I am grateful to Sabina Dugan for suggesting this interpretation.
11. *Deutsche Brüsseler Zeitung*, 4 November 1847, signed "C. Lange, communist worker in the name of several communists, Paris, October 24, 1847"; quoted in Pospelowa, "Adolf Cluss," 88.
12. Adolf Cluss to Joseph Weydemeyer, 20 December 1851; quoted in Pospelowa, "Adolf Cluss," 87.
13. Veit Valentin, *Geschichte der deutschen Revolution von 1848 und 1849*, 2 vols. (Berlin, 1998), 1:312.
14. Speech by the central office of the Communist League to the league, 14 September 1847, in *Der Bund der Kommunisten*, 2 vols. (East Berlin, 1970), 1:534.
15. Summary report of 22 December 1847, Report of von Engelhofen to Prince Metternich, Österreichisches Staatsarchiv Wien, Haus-, Hof- und Staatsarchiv IB, ZIP, box 38.
16. Summary report of 26 January 1848. Report of von Engelhofen to Prince Metternich, Österreichisches Staatsarchiv Wien, Haus-, Hof-und Staatsarchiv IB, ZIP, box 38.
17. Letter from the chapter in Mainz to the central office of the Communist League in Cologne, 23 April 1848, *Der Bund der Kommunisten* 1970, 1:768.
18. A pamphlet that includes the list of demands from Mainz is given in *Mainz und die soziale Frage in der Mitte des 19. Jahrhunderts* (Mainz, 1977), 16.
19. See the essay by Friedrich Schütz, "Politische Vereine 1848," in *Mainz und die soziale Frage*, 19−22.
20. See Pospelowa, "Adolf Cluss," 90.
21. *Der Bund der Kommunisten* 1970, 1:749.

22. Heinz Monz, *Die Verbindung des Mainzer Paul Stumpf zu Karl Marx und Friedrich Engels* (Darmstadt, 1986), 241.

23. Facsimile reprint in *Mainz und die soziale Frage*, 23–26.

24. *Mainz und die soziale Frage*, 23–26.

25. Letter from the chapter in Mainz to the central office of the Communist League in Cologne, 23 April 1848, *Der Bund der Kommunisten* 1:766.

26. Wettengel, *Die Revolution*, 145.

27. *Der Demokrat*, No. 1 (16 April 1848); quoted in Wettengel, *Die Revolution*, 146.

28. Besides Cluss, the members were Gottfried and Paul Stumpf, Philipp Jakob Neubeck, Johann Schickel, and Germain Metternich.

29. Letter from the chapter in Mainz to the central office of the Communist League in Cologne, 23 April 1848, *Bund der Kommunisten* 1970, 1:766; emphasis in the original.

30. "Aufruf des Arbeiterbildungsvereins in Mainz an alle Arbeiter Deutschlands," printed in *Mainzer Zeitung* No. 102 (11 April 1848); quoted here from reprint in *Bund der Kommunisten* 1970, 1:751–52.

31. Pospelowa, "Adolf Cluss," 100; also Monz, *Die Verbindung*, 306.

32. See Monz, *Die Verbindung*, 240.

33. "Kapital und Arbeit," continuation of the essays "Maschinen und menschliche Arbeitskräfte, *Der Demokrat*, No. 4 (7 May 1848), 26–27.

34. "Üeber die Ursachen und das Wesen des Proletariats. Vorgetragen im Mainzer Arbeiter Verein von C-ss, 1/2. Juli" [On the Origins and Nature of the Proletariat. Presented at the Mainz Workers' Association by C-ss, July 1–2], *Der Demokrat* No. 6 (21 May 1848), 41–42.

35. Letter from the chapter in Mainz to the central office of the Communist League in Cologne, 23 April 1848, *Bund der Kommunisten* 1970, 1:767.

36. This fact can be deduced only indirectly from passages in later letters: Adolf Cluss to Karl Marx, Washington, 10 April 1853; Marx-Engels-Gesamtausgabe (*MEGA*) III/6, 432.

37. Letter of the Mainz Workers' Association as the Provisional Central Committee of the German Workers' Association to the Cologne Workers' Committee, 23 April 1848, *Bund der Kommunisten* 1970, 1:771.

38. On the congress, see Valentin, *Geschichte der deutschen Revolution* 2: 99–100; also Wettengel, *Die Revolution*, 188ff.

39. Rainer Wahl, "Der Arbeiterbildungsverein von 1848," in *Mainz und die soziale Frage*, 1977, 24.

40. Cluss did not choose—like so many other so-called Forty-eighters—to settle in one of the major centers of German American culture, such as St. Louis, Cincinnati, Milwaukee, or even Chicago. Being primarily interested in politics, he chose Washington for his new home, a city being characterized by the very absence of much "Germanness" as Kathleen Neils Conzen shows in her chapter in this volume.

41. That Cluss could return to Germany undisturbed by police persecution in 1857 to claim his inheritance would also support this view.

42. National Archives Microfilm Publications, List No. 1062, Film No. 75; a copy exists in the Stadtarchiv Heilbronn, Zs 6105.

BIBLIOGRAPHY

Brodhaecker, Michael, "Der 21. Mai 1848 in Mainz. Dokumentation der politischen und sozialen Unruhen in der Bundesfestung anhand der Quellen." *Mainzer Geschichtsblätter* 11 [Mainz und Rheinhessen in der Revolution von 1848/49] (1999): 20–37.

Der Bund der Kommunisten. Dokumente und Materialien, Band 1 (1836–1849). Publ. by the Institut für Marxismus-Leninismus beim ZK der SED und KpdSU. East Berlin, 1970.

Franz, Eckhart G., "Die hessischen Arbeitervereine im Rahmen der politischen Arbeiterbewegung der Jahre 1848–1850." *Archiv für Hessische Geschichte*, NF 33 (1975): 167–262.

Mainz und die soziale Frage in der Mitte des 19. Jahrhunderts. Zum 100. Todestag von Oberbürgermeister Wallau und Bischof Ketteler. Katalog zur Ausstellung im Rathaus-Foyer Mainz, 4. August bis 4. September 1977. Mainz, 1977.

Monz, Heinz, *Die Verbindung des Mainzer Paul Stumpf zu Karl Marx und Friedrich Engels. Zugleich ein Beitrag zur Geschichte der Mainzer Arbeiterbewegung*. [Hessische Beiträge zur Geschichte der Arbeiterbewegung 5]. Darmstadt, 1986.

Pauly, Herbert, "Zur sozialen Zusammensetzung politischer Institutionen und Vereine der Stadt Mainz im Revolutionsjahr 1848." *Archiv für Hessische Geschichte*, NF 34 (1976): 45–81.

Pospelowa, Welta, "Adolf Cluss—ein Mitglied des Bundes der Kommunisten und Kampfgefährte von Marx und Engels." *Marx-Engels-Jahrbuch* 3 (1980): 85–120.

Schütz, Friedrich, "Revolution 1848 in Mainz." In *Mainz und die soziale Frage*, 17–22.

Spaniol, Rosel, *Eisenbahnen und Museen. Frühe Eisenbahnanlagen in Mainz (einst und jetzt). Ein Beitrag zur Stadtgeschichte und-archäologie*. Karlsruhe, 1979.

Valentin, Veit, *Geschichte der Deutschen Revolution von 1848–1849*. 2 vols. Berlin, 1998.

Wahl, Rainer, "Der Arbeiterbildungsverein von 1848." In *Mainz und die soziale Frage*, 23–27.

Wanner, Peter, "Kommunist der ersten Stunde und Baumeister Washingtons—Adolf Cluss, 1825–1905." In *Heilbronner Köpfe*. Edited by Christhard Schrenk. Vol. 2. Heilbronn, 1999.

Wettengel, Michael, *Die Revolution von 1848/49 im Rhein-Main-Raum. Politische Vereine und Revolutionsalltag im Grossherzogtum Hessen, Herzogtum Nassau und in der Freien Stadt Frankfurt*. Wiesbaden, 1989.

Sozialdemokratische Bibliothek.

XXXIII.

Das

Kommunistische Manifest.

~~~~~~~~~~~

Fünfte autorisirte deutsche Ausgabe.

Mit Vorreden von Karl Marx und Friedrich Engels.

Berlin 1891.

Verlag der Expedition des „Vorwärts", Berliner Volksblatt.

(Th. Glocke.)

Adolf Cluss's copy of Karl Marx's *Communist Manifesto* (5th ed. 1891).
Cluss Papers, Smithsonian Institution Castle Collection, Gift of
William S. Shacklette.

Adolf Cluss: From German Revolutionary to Architect for America's Capital

SABINA W. DUGAN

That fellow is an invaluable agent.[1]

THE FAILED GERMAN 1848 revolution forced many to flee their homeland and emigrate to safer territories. Adolf Cluss was one of the earliest to leave. While it is unclear what his motives were for emigrating to the United States, his independent spirit and sense of optimism led him to cross the Atlantic to a distant land. The United States of America held a mythical connotation to Europeans. Not only was it perceived as the land of opportunity, but it was also seen as a symbol of democracy, where government officials were elected and held no hereditary titles.[2] To an ambitious and ideological young man such as Adolf Cluss, the United States offered freedom from oppression and the opportunity to observe how a free democracy functioned.

Adolf Cluss in America

Cluss arrived in New York City on September 15, 1848. He listed himself on the ship records as being an architect from Rhine-Hessen.[3] Indeed, his penchant for architecture and engineering led him to investigate "grandiose industrial enterprises and bold engineering projects"[4] shortly after he arrived. He spent six months improving his English language skills.

Political interests, however, soon returned to the forefront of Cluss's pursuits. By March 5, 1849, arriving in Washington, D.C., he witnessed the inauguration of President Zach-ary Taylor and settled in the nation's capital. His technical skills secured him employment with the U.S. Coast Survey, where he spent summer months surveying the coasts of Delaware, Maryland, and Virginia. During the slower winter months, while stationed at the Washington Navy Yard, he found time to attend congressional sessions to learn about the American political process.[5] The transitory and confining lifestyle of spending summers at sea, however, did not appeal to Cluss.

When Adolf Cluss turned twenty-five in July 1850, he began employment for the Ordnance Laboratory at the Washington Navy Yard, drafting gun designs and doing mathematical calculations.[6] While his choice of employment may seem unusual for someone with architectural ambitions, many technically trained immigrants followed a similar path, thereby fulfilling a demand by the U.S. Navy for skilled workers. At the time, Commander John A. Dahlgren was responsible for handling all ordnance matters at the yard and was intent on launching the first sustained weapons program in American naval history.[7] As Dahlgren's ideas took hold, the Navy authorized construction of facilities to handle the entire process for designing, testing, and manufacturing cannon. Cluss stated: "I wish to say that the furnaces by which all the brass cannon of the Navy are cast are of my own original introduction and construction."[8] Presumably he was also responsible for drafting plans for the new ordnance foundry, built in 1852 to 1854.[9]

By 1853, Cluss felt confident enough in his position to petition for higher wages: "I have just exercised loyalty and honesty in business diplomacy: I wrote a strongly fortified document to the Chief of the Bureau of Ordnance and Hydrography, U.S. Navy, entitled *Striking for Higher Wages.*"[10] Despite failure in this endeavor, he remained at the Ordnance Department through October 1855, and his departure prompted Commander Dahlgren to record in his diary: "Mr. Cluss, draughtsman, left my department—very sorry;—had been here five and a half years, and is always right."[11]

Adolf Cluss found it hard to adjust to Washington's provincialism. "In Washington I strongly feel a lack of appropriate companionship and am thus living a fairly withdrawn existence."[12] He longed for news from Europe and subscribed to the French publication *Voix du peuple* to keep himself informed of world events and often visited the Library of Congress to borrow books.[13] Cluss rented a small apartment to keep costs low and hired a maid from Bavaria to attend to his needs. "Life in Washington is more expensive than anywhere else in the U.S.; for room and board alone I have to pay $24 per month (without fuel or light). On the other hand, I have two rooms in a *remote* but healthy part of town, I live almost without furniture, unless you want to call one table and two chairs as furniture."[14]

By May 1852, Cluss felt restless and wanted to leave Washington. "I hope soon to get Washington's dust off my shoes, because I have reached the point at which I've had enough of it. . . . Perhaps I will go to Cincinnati after all." He felt unsettled and was searching for a new identity both professionally and personally. He considered becoming a book dealer in early 1852, while his father suggested he manufacture cement and tile ovens, which Cluss considered "too dirty." Cluss sought advice on opening a publishing house, but such a venture depended on paternal financial support, which was not forthcoming. None of his ideas seemed to work, so Cluss remained in Washington, employed at the Navy Yard. "I do not frivolously want to leave a position— even if I hate it; I won't foolishly trade a downpour for a leaking gutter. The demise of too many Germans' careers in America serves as an effective deterrent." Cluss also remained

Fig. 1. Karl Marx, London, May 1861. International Institute of Social History, Amsterdam.

hopeful of returning to a unified Germany, a hope which his friend Karl Marx shared. "In at least one year, I think, you will be here with us," wrote Marx (fig. 1).[15]

Reestablishing Contact with Fellow Communists

A year after settling in Washington, Adolf Cluss resumed regular correspondence with leaders of the Communist League who were living exiled in Great Britain. His earliest letters were sent to his old friend and ally of Marx, Wilhelm Wolff, whom he had met in Brussels. Cluss's letters reveal that he kept abreast of events in Europe and offered support to revolutionary causes. While he failed to secure funding from others, "the Germans here are in such poor shape that you would have difficulty imaging it,"[16] he continued to offer his own money to the cause. Cluss also studied Marxist writings to prepare not only for his eventual return to Europe, but also to be able to oppose political foes in the German American community.

German immigrant Gottfried Kinkel undertook a speaking tour of the United States during 1851 to raise funds for a second German revolution; he received a hero's welcome among German audiences in many U.S. cities, even though he was only able to raise a small amount.[17] Since Kinkel had gained a reputation for being weak and tending towards compromise, Marx and Friedrich Engels mocked him, thereby establishing divided allegiances among the German American political community. Cluss had no fondness for Kinkel and described him to Wolff in the following terms: "Kinkel strikes me precisely as you described him; he had no confidence in me, not least because of my clearly expressed adherence to Marx. . . . Kinkel is easy to defeat in debates, for his view of Germany's social requirements is really funny." One of Cluss's aims was to minimize the influence that Kinkel held over the German American community by denouncing him in the German American press. Cluss sought ammunition to counter Kinkel's hold over German Americans from his friends in London. To Wolff he wrote: "I was very happy to receive your letters. The information in them, as well as those which you and Marx sent to me in the first letter, are precious raw materials which will be converted into ammunition for ruining these democratic rascals, surreptitiously at first. . . . You cannot imagine how vigorously I am now pursuing this fellow [Kinkel], ever since I pulled the mask so decisively off his ugly patriarchal features. . . ."[18]

Adolf Cluss recognized the important role that newspapers played in American politics during the 1850s and upon which Kinkel relied heavily. In one of his earliest letters, Cluss reported that the most important American publication was the *New York Daily Tribune*, "the only effectual publication in the United States, which supports socialistic ideas." Indeed, under the direction of Horace Greeley, this daily newspaper had become the most prominent and influential newspaper in the United States. Cluss, intrigued by Greeley's endorsement of the French socialist Pierre-Joseph Proudhon and the antislavery party, declared Greeley "the most interesting American whom I have met so far." Greeley wrote to Karl Marx in July 1851, offering him the opportu-

nity to become a regular correspondent for the paper. Marx and Engels accepted the offer and submitted articles about revolutionary activities in Europe, which Cluss translated into English for publication.[19]

In November 1851, Joseph Weydemeyer, an ardent supporter of Marx, active in the 1848 revolution and coeditor of the *Neue Deutsche Zeitung* in Frankfurt (1849–50), emigrated to the United States.[20] Marx advised him to contact Cluss immediately upon arrival, since Cluss "is one of our best and most talented people, and he will be able to be of great use to you in general."[21] Cluss and Weydemeyer soon developed a close friendship and joined forces in combating the anticommunist factions in the German American community (fig. 2).

Weydemeyer, with his extensive publishing experience, organized the first U.S. Marxist newspaper, entitled *Die Revolution*. With full support from Cluss, Marx, and other communists, Weydemeyer's aim was to educate readers on industrial and commercial matters, class struggles, and the need for a revolution of equal rights. *Die Revolution* was meant to become the voice of communism in the United States, featuring articles by Marx, Engels, Wolff, and Ferdinand Freiligrath.[22] Cluss offered advice on content and cautioned Weydemeyer against attacking their adversaries too openly:

> Our party still has a very small base in America and therefore we must prevent an attack delivered too early, depriving the newspaper of support. . . . After all, the main reason we are known here at all is the constant denunciation by our opponents. In fact, to some extent we are feared. If your newspaper survives, even if only for a limited time—which I do not doubt at all—then we will soon have our own party, and will be able to present ourselves in a decisive and unified manner.[23]

Despite Cluss and Weydemeyer's enthusiasm and initiative, the lack of financial resources at their disposal meant that only two issues could be published. Three months later, Weydemeyer and Cluss instead published a series of pamphlets, using the material they had received from London, including Marx's *The Eighteenth Brumaire of Louis Bonaparte*,[24] in which Marx parodies Louis Bonaparte for proclaiming himself Emperor Napoleon III.

When Cluss and Weydemeyer met in New York City in February 1852, they discussed the importance of transplanting the Communist League to America. "The only way for us to gain influence here and to control all associations is to transplant the central organization to American soil. I have already arranged everything that is necessary with Cluss."[25] To test the success of such a venture, Weydemeyer organized a *Proletarierbund* (proletariat club) in June 1852, using Marx's *Manifesto of the Communist Party* as a guiding principle. Initially he could rely only on six members, including Cluss in Washington. Their goal was to destabilize other worker's associations, thereby minimizing the influence of other leftist parties on German Americans.

Ultimately, their efforts failed. While Marx and Engels encouraged the formation of socialist chapters in the United States, London continued to be the headquarters for all communist political activities and the *Proletarierbund* soon dissolved. Cluss considered it "an unfortunate attempt to keep the leaders of the local association together."[26]

During the early 1850s, many Forty-eighters (political refugees of the failed German revolution) joined local *Turnvereine* (gymnastic societies), since these German-language clubs helped bridge the gap between the old culture and the new. In a way, they became reservoirs for political refugees who were ready to organize the next German revolution.[27] Most *Turner* were also abolitionists and regarded slavery as unworthy of a republic and contrary to all concepts of freedom.[28]

Cluss became a founder of the *Sozialer Turnverein* of Washington on July 17, 1852, with members from the working class.[29] "I immediately let myself be elected secretary, mainly to gain influence with the *Turner*, but also to gain influence over my opponents. If that had not happened, I would have inadvertently given them ammunition that could have been used against me." Another motive was to use his position to exert influence on the national *Turnerbund*, which he was able to maintain through 1853.[30]

As secretary of the Washington *Turner*, Cluss "obtained carte blanche to act on behalf of the club"[31] and submitted monthly reports of their activities to the *Turn-Zeitung* (*Turner* newspaper) published in New York City. The pur-

Fig. 2. Joseph Weydemeyer, 1860s. International Institute of Social History, Amsterdam.

pose of the *Turn-Zeitung* was to educate its readers "intellectually and disseminate socialist ideas," while taking a favorable position to the emerging labor movement.[32] Cluss recognized its potential of reaching a large audience and explained to Marx that the *Turners* "have their own newspaper and a firm organization, as well as much influence on the radical petite bourgeoisie."[33] The *Turn-Zeitung* also was the only German American publication in 1852 that accepted articles for publication without censorship.[34] Cluss and Weydemeyer wielded extensive influence over the publication during 1852 to 1853; each submitted articles for fourteen of the fifteen issues published in 1852.

Two of Cluss's articles received special praise from his colleagues in London. The first, entitled "Material Criticism and the Moralizing Point of View" is a theoretical analysis of the political factions in the German American community. Marx thought it one of Cluss's most clever pieces. His wife wrote to Cluss: "Your essay in the *Turn-Zeitung* has been much applauded here. My husband thought it was first-rate and the style, in particular, exceptionally brilliant."[35] Seven months later, Engels applauded Cluss for lambasting his critics in an editorial commentary where Cluss wrote: "Through my own initiative I was able to achieve recognition among the best society and secure an independent position in my field as engineer. I am therefore justified in rejecting with contempt the allegations that I supposedly live a lie like so many other revolutionary agents do."[36] Engels marveled at Cluss's cunning tone. "The nobleman [August Willich] will have been surprised to find, among the uncouth 'agents,' a fellow who is so stylish, so clever, and so naturally offensive and, yet, who presents himself at the same time so unpretentiously noble."[37]

In September 1852, Cluss reported on the first *Turnfest* held in Baltimore, which was organized by the *Sozialistischer Turnerbund*. The Washington *Turner* elected Cluss as their delegate to the festival, which Cluss used as an opportunity to recruit new members to the Communist League. Furthermore, Cluss considered it an opportunity to exert pressure on the Marxist adversaries, such as Karl Heinzen, in order to weaken their influence over the radical petite bourgeoisie.[38]

The years 1852 and 1853 were Cluss's most active for writing propaganda articles for the Communist League. In addition to publishing in the *Turn-Zeitung*, many of his articles appeared in London's *The People's Paper* and *Die Reform* in New York. Ernest Jones, editor for the *People's Paper*, wanted to expose government corruption and "reveal the wrongs under which vast classes of this country are suffering."[39] Karl Marx was one of the paper's main supporters and contributors. It was upon his suggestion that Cluss was asked to submit regular reports from America for the publication. Cluss's articles, entitled "Our American Correspondence," covered topics ranging from economic development to U.S. policies both at home and abroad.[40] Often, Cluss used articles from the *People's Paper* for republication within the United States, thereby ensuring wider exposure.

In early March 1853, the newspaper *Die Reform* first appeared in New York and quickly gained prominence among German American workers. Among the many socialistic newspapers of the time, it became the leading voice for

the working class. Cluss and Weydemeyer openly endorsed the publication and, through their active contribution, became responsible for its proletarian-revolutionary voice. As Cluss wrote to Weydemeyer in April 1853: "We should focus our attention on *Die Reform* so that it will soon come into its own and so that our friends in London can see how we, through our own efforts, established a solid base for it."[41]

Weydemeyer and Cluss wrote articles for almost every edition of the publication. While Weydemeyer's expertise was to articulate Marx's ideas, Cluss focused on American political history, labor and immigration issues, and political commentary. His series entitled "Social History of America" demonstrates his knowledge of the U.S. economic situation and American capitalism.[42] Cluss was developing a fondness and expertise for American history: "I will certainly not become disinterested in American affairs." While Cluss recognized the progress he and Weydemeyer were making: "We are certainly on the way to becoming a significant power in the press, and it is to that end that our efforts must now focus"; he was also well on his way to becoming "Americanized."[43] Weydemeyer, acknowledging this change, explained it to Marx in the following terms: "Over there it makes less difference if there is one more measly person to make a difference, whereas it is important to have our party represented in this country, and really only Cluss and I are capable of doing that, which is why I don't even want to consider Cluss returning to Europe." At the same time, Weydemeyer mocked Cluss for his changed attitude. "Incidentally, accept the observation that you are well on your way to becoming an America-enthusiast."[44]

With his growing knowledge of America's past and present economic situation, Cluss became focused on labor issues specifically. "No one can feel more deeply than I that we must work with all our might for the cause of the 'Workers' Organization.'" Cluss chose to engage himself even more directly with laborers, observing how the growing industrialization was streamlining production, resulting in labor cuts and low pay for workers while capitalists reaped all the benefits. Cluss, like Marx, believed that such a situation could only lead to another revolution. "A crisis in America, with all of its upheavals of private fortunes, will generate an immense jolt in social development. The crisis will bring society forward in a revolutionary manner. . . . The skills of the American workers are first-rate, and there is no lack of mechanical devices to assist them."[45] In early March 1853, Cluss attended a labor strike in Baltimore hoping to find a burgeoning labor movement. Instead, he became frustrated by the workers' lack of leadership and focus. "These eternal celebrations have demoralized those fellows shamefully. In the beginning I had been assured by everyone that something could be made of the movement, but now it is clear that any agitation would only end in ridicule."[46] Cluss and Weydemeyer were learning that their European expectations were not easily adapted to the United States; different conditions required different approaches. "All of us came from a phase of the proletarian movement that differs from the American one. Therefore we have to abandon our own theory, or else risk overestimating our practical importance for the labor movement here."[47]

Cluss tried to rally workers in his immediate environment, namely the Washington Navy Yard. "As for me, I am currently looking for a powerful and good American labor movement, developing here among the workers at the Navy Yard, to link to *Die Reform*."[48] He approached laborers, introduced them to Marxist theories, and offered them subscriptions to *Die Reform*. He encouraged them to draft a leaflet outlining their situation, with a petition to fellow workers to unite to achieve reform:

> I just received the attached leaflet from one of our workers. The signers are all machinists; very nice fellows who are receptive to progressive ideas, which I have often observed in our conversations. The leaflet contains valuable material for *Die Reform*, because of its purely American origin, which will bring life to our German movement. I will approach these people at their association, which has around 160 members, show them *Die Reform* and thus bring them new courage.[49]

Despite his efforts, hope soon turned to discontent yet again, when Cluss realized how disorganized and disenfranchised the American labor movement really was. One of the biggest obstacles was the lack of communication between German laborers and those of other nationalities. When the German laborers in New York asked Cluss to translate one of

their letters into English for wider distribution, Cluss voiced his frustration to Weydemeyer:

> From the *National Advocate* you can see how our German movement is not seen as an American movement. How can those people act as the central committee for *American* workers when they are not even able to write a letter in English? . . . I have suggested to the local labor movement that they should get in contact with the people in New York and that they should unite the German, French and Irish workers and establish permanent contact with them.[50]

Cluss grew weary of the neverending problems and insurmountable obstacles to achieving the labor revolution that Marx had envisioned.

Severing the Tie to the Communist League

The friendship between Adolf Cluss and Karl Marx became strained towards the end of 1852 and the beginning of 1853. Their weekly correspondence dwindled to occasional letters, each accusing the other of being negligent and resorting to childish threats. In October 1852, Marx berated Cluss: "Your weekly letters have become such a necessity for me that I am not at all happy about your changed method [of corresponding]. Your silence has made me angry, for which reason I have remained silent too" (fig. 3). Five months later, Cluss had a similar complaint of Marx: "I marvel at my patience in constantly writing letters without ever getting an answer," to which Marx responded: "If you start writing again each week, be it much or little, I will reinstate our regular letter exchange."[51]

Part of the strain resulted from the difficulty of maintaining motivation, while witnessing few results. Cluss, ever the pragmatist, had warned Weydemeyer of this as early as February 1852: "It is unrealistic to expect that in America it will always be possible to get people who will do that kind of work solely because of dedication to the cause."[52] In addition, alliances between political interests kept shifting, which meant that publications that favored Marxist principles often changed their ideologies in response to new editors or lack of subscriptions. Even Marx complained: "The constant journalistic bickering annoys me."[53]

A pivotal moment came in early November 1853, when *Die Reform* experienced serious financial difficulties and the editors, Weydemeyer and Gottlieb Kellner, called upon Cluss to bail them out. While Cluss had supported the publication from the beginning, he became disgusted with its apparent mismanagement and refused to provide additional funds.

> I, without saying a word, step in to save the business, which was started by others and which has ever since then plagued me financially . . . you knew that starting a business required capital. If you started the business without considering all the necessary conditions, then you are simply guys who know very little about business matters, and whom I cannot trust to reflect upon such matters calmly and coolly. I have no doubt that the *Reform* must succeed; its demise would be a scandalous disgrace.[54]

Cluss felt betrayed by his close friend. He had given his all to *Die Reform*. He was one of its most prolific contributors and had promoted the paper among labor unions, secured new subscriptions, and repeatedly offered financial support. Finally, with no palpable results for his efforts, he had had enough. The experience caused him to reconsider his own financial situation and priorities. "I absolutely have to have a secure and constant financial reserve, and that, if possible, right here, because then I am master of my destiny—something I'm determined to be always—and not a servant, dependent on the caprices of these mariners."[55]

While Cluss's correspondence to Marx continued to taper through December 1855, his friendships with Marx and Weydemeyer effectively ended after the *Die Reform* fiasco in November 1853. Cluss formed a new friendship with the German physician Abraham Jacobi living in New York, who "now takes care of everything for me in New York," making Weydemeyer dispensable. By January 1857, Engels lamented that "actually we have not had one reliable person in all of America since Cluss became strangely silent."

Two years later, Marx wrote to Weydemeyer: "If we were vain, then we would have been very hurt to find out that a lunatic such as [August] Willich could lure away such an intelligent man as Cluss." Willich, a former Prussian officer and Marxist follower, had emigrated to the United States in

Fig. 3. Karl Marx's letter to Adolf Cluss, October 8, 1852 opens: "Dear Cluss! Your weekly letters have become such a necessity for me that I am not at all happy about your changed communication method. Your silence has made me angry, so I have remained silent too." International Institute of Social History, Amsterdam, Marx-Engels Collection, Sig. C 100.

1853 to organize political refugees for a military invasion of Germany in order to establish a republic. While Marx, who ridiculed Willich's plan, may have suspected a Cluss-Willich alliance, Weydemeyer disputed that claim. "You are mistaken in regards to Cluss: his behavior was a result of other things. Cluss inherited money upon the death of his father, and his true philistine nature—really, he has always been a philistine in disguise—has fully surfaced. He has long been in touch with Willich . . . there was never any talk of a closer connection."[56] Weydemeyer, in the end, seemed to understand his old friend best of all. Personal and political affiliations were not the only things that had changed in Cluss's life; the year 1855 became a turning point.

Adolf Cluss, the American

In 1855, Cluss became an American citizen, perhaps in response to a mandate from the *Turnerbund* for members to obtain citizenship in order to achieve voting rights.[57] Early in the year, he changed employment and became a draftsman for the Treasury Department. Ammi B. Young, Supervising Architect of the Treasury, wrote of his intention of hiring Cluss: "I would suggest whether I had not better set Mr. Adolf Cluss (formerly in the service of the Ordnance Office at the Navy Yard) at work upon trial; at least until we can do better." Young was the chief designer of all federal buildings that fell within the jurisdiction of the Treasury Department. Despite Young's early misgivings, Cluss proved skillful and remained at the department for three years. While it is not clear what Cluss's exact contributions were, he most likely assisted in preparing copies of written specifications and drawings for distribution to prospective contractors. He claimed to have "had charge of one room in the Supervising Architect's office."[58]

Later on, in March 1869, a curious publication by the American Institute of Architects (AIA) in New York appeared, entitled *The Office of the Supervising Architect: What It Was, What It Is, and What It Ought to Be*. Although it was simply signed "Civis," Cluss most likely wrote it, since the AIA retains a copy of the pamphlet with Cluss's handwritten signature. The pamphlet identified "the existing disorganization of that important branch of the Treasury Department," pointing out that the office lacked proper reference guides and tests "in the ascertainment of figures and facts for safe and proper construction." It recommended that government bureaus should "exercise the most beneficial influence" upon the architectural profession, specifically elevating the importance of heating and ventilation, engineering matters that later became benchmarks in Cluss's own architecture. Further reference to Cluss's future contributions can be found at the end of the pamphlet, when he anticipates the formation of a civic public works department: "The day cannot be distant when we shall have a department of public works. The appropriations for internal improvements of all kinds have steadily increased, and will continue to increase."[59]

Personal Developments

Upon the death of his father on July 22, 1857, Adolf Cluss received a substantial inheritance, which perhaps explains why he again became restless. Joseph Weydemeyer reported in a letter to Marx that Cluss traveled during this time to Milwaukee, Wisconsin, before embarking on an extended European trip in late April and May 1858.[60] In addition to visiting his relatives in Heilbronn, Cluss visited Paris and London, where he made a half-hearted, last attempt to contact Marx.

When Cluss returned to America, he settled in Philadelphia and founded a brewery with a friend named Fischer. This business venture was short-lived, but known to Weydemeyer, who offered the only known account of it in a letter to Marx: "The Fischer-Cluss enterprise meanwhile was dissolved because Mr. Fischer disappeared. Although business assets were seized by the sheriff, Cluss is said to have pulled out his capital in time."[61]

During this time, Adolf Cluss also made a proposal of another kind. On February 8, 1859, he married Rosa Schmidt in Baltimore.[62] He had met Rosa seven years earlier through Franz Arnold, one of Rosa's early suitors and a fellow immigrant from Cluss's hometown, Heilbronn. Cluss had enjoyed many engaging political discussions with the Schmidt family, émigrés from the Pfalz who were Heinzen supporters and held liberal views about religion and Germany's future government. In 1852, Cluss recounted his initial visit with the Schmidt family to Weydemeyer: "Tell Arnold that I have greatly amused myself with his 'ex-dulcinea' and her family. The young girl, who is an eager supporter of Kinkel, made sure, by whatever means, that I heard unpleasant things, such as that the old man wanted to beat me up if I showed up. That of course gave me my hoped-for motivation to deliver some bad jokes. That raised their fury to a peak, though the explosion came only after I had left."[63] Time apparently mellowed Adolf and Rosa's political differences. On their honeymoon, they traveled to Europe and later settled in Washington, living near the Capitol at 130 Second West Street (later changed to 413 Second, NW). Lillian, their first child, was born in January 1860, followed by two more daughters and four sons who were born between 1861 and 1874. Sadly, only the daughters survived; all four sons succumbed to illnesses.

The Civil War Years

As a married man, Cluss returned to the Navy Yard in April 1859, drafting for the Ordnance Department. Commander Dahlgren was designing different caliber rifles and testing pitches for the rifles, believing that rifled cannon would be the ordnance of the future.[64] Later, when secession threatened to divide the country, Dahlgren, a supporter of the Union, was put in command of the Washington Navy Yard. Adolf Cluss was entrusted with drafting Dahlgren's new gun designs, and the two formed a close bond. Robert Schneller, a naval historian and expert on Dahlgren, explained the Cluss-Dahlgren relationship in the following terms: "Dahlgren wanted to enthrall potential clients with beautiful drawings of his inventions. This is where Cluss would have played a crucial role. Dahlgren used the drawings as his main selling point."[65] In other words, Dahlgren relied upon Cluss's ordnance drawings to convince Congress to strengthen naval capabilities, a timely measure since civil war was imminent in spring 1861.

On April 6, 1861, only one week before the bombardment of Fort Sumter, Cluss wrote of an encounter, which demonstrates how important his work was to the Navy. He was approached at his home one evening by a draftsman from the Armory Department in Richmond, Virginia, who "had been secretly dispatched to this city" to obtain ordnance drawings from Cluss and "would pay any price that was asked for information and drawings." Cluss responded "evasively," stating that drawings could only be furnished if specific information were first provided of "a deckplan of the Steamer" and the proposed placement of the weapons on board.[66] In other words, by putting the man on the defensive, Cluss remained loyal to the Union and refused to leak information to a Southern sympathizer.

The Civil War years changed Washington. No longer simply a provincial backwater with lofty ambitions, the city became a bustling metropolis. Returning soldiers and freed slaves seeking opportunities contributed to the city's explo-sive growth. An urban infrastructure that included new housing, new government buildings, and an improved sanitation system was needed. The completion of the cast-iron dome for the Capitol in 1863 became a symbol of the era's new optimism, attesting "to faith in the permanence of the United States of America and its capital on the Potomac."[67] Adolf Cluss, recognizing the advantages of the sudden boom, seized the opportunity to found his own architectural firm in 1862, while still employed at the Navy Yard. He formed a partnership with Joseph W. von Kammerhueber, a fellow German immigrant who worked as an assistant draftsman for the Ordnance Department. They advertised their services as "architects and civil, mechanical and naval engineers."[68] While some of their earliest commissions were for the military, they built Washington's first pubic school building, the Wallach School, followed by many other civic and private buildings, applying a social consciousness to urban improvement. Although their partnership dissolved in 1868, it launched Cluss's career as a prominent Washington architect.

Cluss had become a well-known personality in his adopted city. His architectural practice flourished, he befriended many prominent citizens, and he participated in a growing number of civic events. He had joined the *Sängerverein* (German men's choir) upon its founding in 1859 and participated in committees for the German Relief Association. Cluss, like so many fellow *Turner*, joined the new Republican Party sometime between 1855 and 1860, when it was still largely ostracized in Washington for its antislavery stance.[69] In January 1861, he published a satirical commentary in the *Evening Star*, urging the German Republicans to remain loyal to the Republican Party, putting aside their dispute over representational power in the party.[70] In 1871, he assumed a leadership role among the German Republicans when he was elected president of the organization.[71] Even towards the end of his career, friends and colleagues remembered him as a "pronounced Republican."[72] Adolf Cluss, the former communist sympathizer and exiled revolutionary, had become a respected member of the Washington community, channeling his socialist ideals into support for the Republican Party of his adopted homeland and transforming the infrastructure of the nation's capital.

NOTES

Abbreviations

BBAW   Berlin-Brandenburgische Akademie der Wissenschaften
FES   Friedrich Ebert Stiftung in Bonn
IISG   International Institute of Social History in Amsterdam
MEGA   Karl Marx–Friedrich Engels Gesamtausgabe
MEW   Karl Marx Friedrich Engels Werke
RGASPI Russian Center for the Preservation and Study of Records of Modern
        History, Moscow

1. Friedrich Engels to Jenny Marx, 14 January 1852, *MEGA* III/5 (Berlin: 1987),
   10–11.
2. Many travel books were written for German visitors to the United States. One
   such book which Cluss may have known was C. H. Collins, *Sichere Anleitung für
   Auswanderer und Reisende nach den Vereinigten Staaten von Nord-Amerika* (Heilbronn,
   1833).
3. Adolf Cluss was listed as passenger #211 on the ship *Zurich*, which had departed
   Le Havre, France, and arrived in New York City on September 15, 1848.
   National Archives, M237 Passenger List of Vessels Arriving at New York,
   1820–1897.
4. Adolf Cluss to Karl Marx, 30 September 1852. *MEGA* III/6 (Berlin: 1987),
   250–53.
5. Cluss recounted his early activities in three letters: Adolf Cluss to Wilhelm
   Wolff, 30 March 1850, Bestand: Adolf Cluss, No. 1, FES; Cluss to Wolff, 4–6
   November 1851, BBAW; Adolf Cluss to Karl Marx, 30 September 1852, *MEGA*
   III/6, 250–53.
6. Adolf Cluss to Joseph Weydemeyer, 1 July 1853, *MEGA* III/6, 612–13.
7. Edward J. Marolda, *The Washington Navy Yard: An Illustrated History*
   (Washington, 1999), 15.
8. *Affairs in the District of Columbia*, 43d Cong., 1st sess. (June 16, 1874), S. Rept.
   453, Testimony, 2049.
9. Plans and an 1860s Mathew Brady photograph survive of the Ordnance Foundry
   building at the Naval Historical Center. Edward J. Marolda, naval historian,
   attributes the building to Adolf Cluss.
10. Cluss to Marx, 13 November 1853, *MEGA* III/7 (Berlin, 1989), 292–93.
11. Madeline Vinton Dahlgren, *Memoir of John A. Dahlgren*, vol. 1 (New York,
    1891), 173.
12. Cluss to Wolff, 31 March 1850, FES.
13. *Voix du peuple* was published by Pierre-Joseph Proudhon in Paris; Cluss
    explained in his letter to Weydemeyer that the Library of Congress was the only
    place to borrow books, since the Smithsonian Institution only allowed access to
    their library during business hours and offered no borrowing privileges. Cluss to
    Weydemeyer, 17 March 1852, IISG, #18.
14. Cluss to Weydemeyer, 22 April 1852, IISG, #25.
15. Cluss to Weydemeyer, 16 August 1852, *MEGA* III/5, 552–58; Cluss to
    Weydemeyer, 27 February 1852, IISG, #14; Cluss to Weydemeyer, 10 March
    1852, IISG, #16; Cluss to Weydemeyer, 8 January 1853, IISG; Marx to Cluss,
    25 March 1853, *MEGA* III/6, 142–44.
16. Cluss to Wolff, 31 March 1850, FES.
17. A. E. Zucker, *The Forty-Eighters, Political Refugees of the German Revolution of 1848*
    (New York, 1950), 311.
18. Cluss to Wolff, 4–6 November 1851, BBAW; Cluss to Wolff, 27/28 December
    1851, BBAW.
19. Cluss to Wolff, 31 March 1850, FES; In 1851, 15,000 copies were printed,
    growing to 50,000 by the end of 1852. Three years later, in 1855, readership
    was up to 190,000, far exceeding any other publication in the United States.
    "Werke, Artikel, Entwürfe, Juli 1851–Dezember 1852," *MEGA* I/11.2 (Berlin,
    1995), 574; Cluss to Wolff, 31 March 1850, FES; The original letter with
    request has been lost, however Marx wrote to inform Engels about it on 8–14
    August 1851, *MEGA* III/4 (Berlin, 1985), 170; They submitted fifteen articles
    for publication in 1852 and another seventy-five during 1853. "Marx/Engels,
    Werke, Artikel, Entwürfe Januar–Dezember 1853," *MEGA* I/11.2 (Berlin,
    1995), 669.
20. Hermann Schlüter, *Die Anfänge der deutschen Arbeiterbewegung in Amerika*
    (Stuttgart, 1907), 158–59.
21. Marx to Weydemeyer, 19 December 1851, *MEGA* III/4, 276–77.
22. The weekly *Die Revolution* first appeared on January 6, 1852 and the second,
    and final, edition appeared on January 13, 1852, Karl Obermann, *Joseph
    Weydemeyer: Ein Lebensbild 1818–1866* (Berlin, 1968), 245; Weydemeyer to
    Engels, 9 February 1852, *MEGA* III/5, 245–46; "Werke, Artikel, Entwürfe,
    Juli 1851–Dezember 1852," *MEGA* I/11.2, 614–15.
23. Cluss to Weydemeyer, 12 January 1852, IISG, Adolf Cluss, #9.
24. "Werke, Artikel, Entwürfe, Juli 1851–Dezember 1852," *MEGA* I/11.2, 618.
    Publishing the pamphlets also proved unsuccessful, prompting Cluss to advise
    Marx to redirect all future articles to other publications. Cluss to Weydemeyer,
    30 May 1852, *MEGA* III/5, 527–29.
25. Weydemeyer to Engels, 9 February 1852, *MEGA* III/5, 245–46.
26. Cluss to Marx, 6 January 1853, *MEGA* III/6, 357–60.
27. Ralph Wagner, "Turner Societies and the Socialist Tradition," ed. Hartmut Keil,
    German Workers' Culture in the United States, 1850 to 1920 (Washington, D.C.,
    1988), 225.
28. Minutes of the National Convention at Philadelphia, October 1851, in Heinrich
    Metzner, *Jahrbücher der Deutsch-Amerikanischen Turnerei*, vol. 1 (New York,
    1892–1894), 80.
29. Cluss to the *Turnerbund*, 20 July 1852, published in *Die Turn-Zeitung*, No. 11
    (New York), 1 August 1852; Adolf Cluss and Joseph Gerhardt, "Der sociale
    Turnverein von Washington an den Vorort des socialistischen Turnerbundes,"
    Die Turn-Zeitung, No. 20 (New York), 1 February 1853.
30. Cluss to Marx, 22 July 1852, *MEGA* III/5, 444–46; Weydemeyer to Marx, 13
    August 1852, *MEGA* III/5, 467–69.
31. Cluss to Marx, 20 January 1853, *MEGA* III/6, 368–70.
32. Preface, *Die Turn-Zeitung*, No. 1 (New York), 15 November 1851.
33. Cluss to Marx, 16–18 September 1852, *MEGA* III/6, 228–32.
34. "Werke, Artikel, Entwürfe, Juli 1851–Dezember 1852," *MEGA* I/11.2, 620.
35. Adolf Cluss, "Material Criticism and the Moralizing Point of View," *Die Turn-
    Zeitung*, No. 13 (New York), 1 October 1852; Jenny Marx to Cluss, 28 October
    1852, *MEGA* III/6, 560–62.
36. Adolf Cluss, "To the Editors of the New-Yorker-Criminal-Zeitung,"
    Belletristisches Journal, No. 10 (New York), 20 May 1853.
37. Friedrich Engels to Marx, 6 June 1853, *MEGA* III/6, 185–91.
38. Cluss to Marx, 1 September 1852, *MEGA* III/5, 476–83. Also, Cluss to Marx,
    5 August 1852, *MEGA* III/5, 457–60; Cluss to Marx, 16–18 September 1852,
    MEGA III/6, 228–32.
39. Advertisement for *The People's Paper*, *MEGA* I/2 (Berlin: 1995), 597.
40. *The People's Paper*, No. 21 (London), 25 September 1852.
41. Cluss to Weydemeyer, 27 April 1853. SIIG.

42. Adolf Cluss, "Sociale Skizzen über die Geschichte Amerikas," *Die Reform*, Nos. 35, 37, 38, 39 and 40 (New York), 30 July 1853; 6, 10, 13, and 17 August 1853.

43. Cluss to Weydemeyer, 10 March 1852, IISG, #16; Cluss to Weydemeyer, 7 December 1853, *MEGA* III/7, 576–78.

44. Weydemeyer to Engels, 2–6 May 1853, RGASPI; Weydemeyer to Cluss, 26 December 1853, *MEGA* III/7, 581–82.

45. Cluss to Weydemeyer, 26 March 1853, *MEGA* III/6, 580–84; Cluss to Weydemeyer, 17 February 1853, *MEGA* III/6, 574–77.

46. Cluss to Weydemeyer, 7 March 1853, SIIG.

47. Cluss to Weydemeyer, 26 March 1853, *MEGA* III/6, 580–84.

48. Cluss to Marx, 31 March 1853, *MEGA* III/6, 421–25.

49. Cluss to Weydemeyer, 28 March 1853, SIIG.

50. Cluss to Weydemeyer, 19 April 1853, SIIG.

51. Marx to Cluss, 8 October 1852, *MEGA* III/6, 37–39; Cluss to Marx, 6–8 March 1853, *MEGA* III/6, 402–6; Marx to Cluss, 25 March 1853, *MEGA* III/6, 142–44.

52. Cluss to Weydemeyer, 14 February 1852, *MEGA* III/5, 493–95.

53. Marx to Cluss, 15 September 1853, *MEGA* III/7, 11–12.

54. Cluss to Weydemeyer, 16 November 1853, SIIG. The second half of the quote comes from Cluss's letter to Weydemeyer and Gottlieb Kellner, 25 November 1853, SIIG.

55. Cluss to Weydemeyer and Kellner, 26 November 1853, IISG.

56. Cluss to Marx, 25 May 1854, *MEGA* III/7, 377–81; Engels to Marx, 22 January 1857, *MEGA* III/8, 74–75; Marx to Weydemeyer, 1 February 1859, *MEW* 29 (Berlin, 1980), 570–73; Weydemeyer to Marx, 27 March 1859, *MEGA* III/9, 367–68.

57. Cluss became a U.S. citizen on June 5, 1855. National Archives, Register and Indexes for Passport Applications, 1898. *Turnerbund* mandates are discussed in: Horst Ueberhorst, *Turner unterm Sternenbanner* (Munich, 1978), 45.

58. RG 121, Records of the Public Building Service, Box 1, Vol. 1, 186–87, National Archives; Antoinette J. Lee, *Architects to the Nation: The Rise and Decline of the Supervising Architect's Office* (New York, 2000), 48–49; Congressional testimony given by Adolf Cluss, May 20, 1874, 2049.

59. Civis, *The Office of the Supervising Architect: What It Was, What It Is, and What It Ought to Be* (New York, 1869), 3, 5–6, 8.

60. Weydemeyer to Marx, 27 March 1859, *MEGA* III/9, 367–68.

61. Ibid.

62. Zion Church of Baltimore Register, #11–1859.

63. Cluss to Weydemeyer, 25 May 1852, *MEGA* III/5, 525–26.

64. Robert J. Schneller Jr., *A Quest for Glory: A Biography of Rear Admiral John A. Dahlgren* (Annapolis, 1996), 171–72.

65. June 15, 2000 interview with Robert Schneller by author at the Washington Navy Yard.

66. Cluss to the Washington Navy Yard. Library of Congress, Manuscript Division, Dahlgren Collection, Box 4.

67. Constance McLaughlin Green, *Washington*, vol. 1 (Princeton, 1962–63), 200.

68. RG 21, Records of the Public Building Service, Box 120, Equity Case 2072, National Archives.

69. Lewis Clephane, *Birth of the Republican Party, with a Brief History of the Important Part Taken by the Original Republican Association of the National Capital* (Washington, D.C., 1889), 5, 8.

70. Adolf Cluss, "Breaker's Ahead: Fatherland and Other Lands on the 'Qui Vive,'" *Evening Star* (Washington) 10 January 1861, 3.

71. "German Republicans: Ratification Meeting," *Evening Star* (Washington) 14 April 1871.

72. Letter from J. M. Wilson to the Honorable William Windom, Secretary of the Treasury, 12 June 1889. RG 42, Records of the Office of Public Buildings and Public Parks of the National Capital, Entry 87, 651, Box 29, National Archives.

Die Residenzler: German Americans in the Making of the Nation's Capital

KATHLEEN NEILS CONZEN

Mid-nineteenth-century Washington with its radial avenues and sleepy economy may have been an anomaly within urban America's rectilinear bustle, but to German Americans it occupied familiar conceptual space. It was, they were prone to point out, essentially a *Residenzstadt*—like Darmstadt, Friedrich Kapp suggested, "or some other boring two-bit prince's residence."[1] It shared with the capitals of small German principalities its state-oriented Baroque plan, pompous edifices, limited self-governance, and economic dependence on the seasonality and fickleness of government demand. A *Residenzstadt* required artisans to build and maintain its grand structures, service workers to care for its officials, clerks and courtiers to conduct the business of governance, artists and scholars to glorify and edify the state.[2] Many German immigrants almost instinctively sought analogous opportunity in America's seat of government.

But Washington, they found, was a *Residenzstadt* with a difference. In even a third-rate German *Residenz*, as an 1860 St. Louis visitor noted, "art plays its modest role alongside politics and parade ground; there's usually a court poet and a certain supply of learned wigs and bluestockings; a theater

with at least one hero of distinction and a tasteful princess in distress; a few congenial places where you can sit together as cozily as in any beer garden in an Odenwald village; where you can find a good glass of wine and a laughing barmaid, a cheerful red-nosed parson, and an organist who knows how to finger a Bach fugue."[3] But with no aristocracy, a poorly paid president, and elected officials living bachelor lives without the taste, means, or continuity in office to support a finer culture, without even the spendthrift officers of a garrisoned army, Washington could be only a social and cultural desert, exhibiting all the intrigues of a court but none of its brilliance.[4] *Residenz* soon became German Washingtonians' ironic shorthand for the odiferous cultural wasteland in which they found themselves, and *Residenzler* their facetious name for themselves.[5]

Adolf Cluss was among the Germans oriented to state service who gravitated to this peculiar American *Residenzstadt* at mid-century. Unlike many, he found real opportunity here and remained to play a central role in the re-creation of post–Civil War Washington as a true national capital. Any attempt to understand his role has to take into account the distinctive character of the broader German immigrant community of which he was a part—a community that was uniquely shaped by, and in turn helped reshape, Washington's *Residenzstadt* milieu. Cluss and his German contemporaries formed in Washington a distinctive ethnic culture that, owing to the nature of the city itself, the kinds of Germans

Seventh Street, NW, a major corridor for German life and German-owned businesses in 19th-century Washington. The buildings are decorated for the 1881 inaugural of James Garfield, the ball for which took place in Cluss and Schulze's new National Museum building. Photograph. Historical Society of Washington, D.C.

who were drawn to it, and their vision of what a real *Residenz* could be, was paradoxically both less encompassing and yet more broadly influential than its counterparts elsewhere in America.[6]

The Distinctive Contours of Washington's German Community

When Cluss arrived in Washington in the spring of 1849, he became part of a German population shaped by three factors: the city's location in the Philadelphia-Baltimore hinterland, its southern character, and above all its status as a federal city. These factors influenced the size of the city's German population, its regional origins, its religious affiliations, its occupational structure, and the kind of community it formed. Washington's German-born population was a relatively small one. Its size reflected the limited economic opportunities of a slowly growing nonindustrial city with a significant African American workforce. With only 1,257 German-born in 1850, at a time when New York already counted more than 55,000, Baltimore almost 20,000, and even infant Milwaukee over 6,000, the District of Columbia's immigrant profile resembled that of other southern cities in its small immigrant population and its low German-Irish ratio. In 1850 Germans were only 2 percent of its total population and 29 percent of its immigrants. The German-born population grew by more than two and a half times between 1850 and 1860, to 3,254, then increased again by half to 4,918 in 1870, before virtually leveling off for the remainder of the lifetime of Cluss and his immigrant generation. German proportions within the District's population also remained remarkably steady. Germans in 1870 were still only 3 percent of its total and 30 percent of its foreign-born population, and 2 percent of its total and 29 percent of its foreign-born by 1890, when another 11,824 native-born District residents belonged to the maturing second generation.[7]

The community was unusually cohesive in its German regional origins, reflecting the continuing influence of migration chains from southwestern Germany to Pennsylvania and Maryland reaching back to the late seventeenth century. Washington's earliest German-speaking residents probably

drifted in from these older German areas, attracted like other Americans to the new city's opportunity. Newer immigrants arriving through Baltimore or Philadelphia followed in their footsteps. The District's federal census returns for 1860 show that some 81 percent of the 1,445 Germans who specified their state of birth (44 percent of the total) came from the southwestern German states of Baden, Württemberg, Hessen-Darmstadt, and Bavaria (usually Rhenish Bavaria). Later-arriving Prussians were far less evident than they would have been in northern or western cities by 1860.[8]

Washington's *Residenzstadt* economy created an equally distinctive occupational profile. The District's 1860 census listings suggest three main groupings among its German-speaking breadwinners and their families. First were the "old Washingtonians," born perhaps in America or arrived as children, some of them long-settled farmers and gardeners on the city's fringes, others craftsmen who moved from older communities to the new federal city. Often with American-born spouses, they tended to own property, lived scattered throughout the city, and showed every demographic sign of integration into the city's broad middling sector. Younger, more recent immigrants, products of the great immigration wave of the 1840s and early 1850s, formed the second major element. They congregated in heavily German neighborhoods, including the major corridor along Seventh Street, NW, and shared with older immigrants their craft and service occupations. Bakers, butchers, shoemakers, carpenters, cabinet makers, smiths, tailors, painters, brewers, cigarmakers, builders—these were classic German occupations in Washington as elsewhere in urban America, often practiced within traditional households of family members, apprentices, and employees sharing a single roof. Equally prominent were service occupations, like restaurant and tavern keepers, innkeepers, barbers, grocers, storekeepers and merchants, hucksters and rag dealers. Comprising the third and smallest element were teachers, attorneys, clerks, clergymen, government employees, architects, draftsmen, engineers—in short, educated men like Cluss, and like him more likely to have emigrated for political than economic reasons after Europe's 1848 revolutions. They were relatively young, often single on arrival, with diverse German origins and less clustered Washington residences.[9]

Three classes of occupations were in short supply in contrast with other cities: there were virtually no German laborers, few draymen and carters, very few servants—the *Residenzstadt* lacked the usual bottom of the German American occupational hierarchy. This occupational profile remained remarkably persistent. By 1880, still only 3 percent of Washington's employed Germans were laborers, compared with 12 percent in nearby Baltimore, while 20 percent of Washington's Germans were in professional and service occupations but only 8 percent in Baltimore.[10]

Without a large working class, German Washington's religious profile was equally distinctive. Protestants probably formed a larger part of Washington's German population, and Catholics a smaller one, than in many American cities. The city's German Catholics were numerous enough to separate from their Irish coreligionists only in 1845, and a second German Catholic parish was not formed until 1868; by 1892, the first church, St. Mary's on Fifth Street, NW, had an exclusively German membership of 250 families, but St. Joseph's on Second Street, NE, numbered only twenty German among eighty African American and three hundred English-speaking families.[11] By contrast, the first German Protestant church, Concordia, dated to 1833, and by 1894 fifteen Lutheran and Reformed churches could be found in the District.[12] Even more distinctive, as the city's German newspaper noted in 1860, was the "very large portion of the local German population" that was Jewish. Jews were present in Washington almost from its founding, and by 1847 some twenty-five Jewish names could be found in city directory listings. The first Hebrew Congregation was formed in 1852, and by 1865 the Jewish population numbered perhaps three hundred families. They came mainly from the same areas of southwestern Germany as the city's other Germans, and with similar occupations, though with greater commercial concentration; most had initially settled elsewhere in the United States. Their numbers and increasing prosperity meant that Jews would play important roles in shaping Washington's German community both when they chose to participate and when they refrained.[13]

But the most distinctive among the *Residenzler* were the government employees. The antebellum federal government's small size, relative inactivity, and patronage system generated few of the court-related positions, whether in luxury trades or in artistic, administrative, or scientific endeavors, that Germans expected in a *Residenzstadt*. But there was always some social life, a certain level of administrative activity requiring specialized knowledge, and a small body of government-sponsored research that attracted a highly qualified group of cultured Germans to the city in slowly growing numbers before the Civil War.

The United States Coast Survey, for example, where Cluss found initial Washington employment, provided opportunity for other educated Germans as well. The Swiss origins of the survey's long-time superintendent, Ferdinand Rudolph Hassler, may have made it particularly open to foreign-trained engineers, scientists, and technicians, but so too did the specialized needs of the ambitious survey itself. After Hassler's 1843 death, his successor, Benjamin Franklin's West Point–trained, great-grandson Alexander Dallas Bache, sustained and expanded the survey to match the country's own dramatic geographical expansion, turning it into one of the prime centers of America's emerging scientific community. Two German visitors in 1852 confessed that "we secretly took national pride . . . in seeing Germans employed as the most skilled draftsmen and engravers" in the survey.[14] By September 1855, thirty-seven of the survey's 135 civilian employees were foreign-born, twenty-five of them German, and their presence and large salaries were attracting nativist complaints; German numbers increased to thirty-four in an 1860 count. Like Cluss, many spent summers working in the field but often returned to Washington in the winter to put down roots in its German community.[15] One of their number, Julius E. Hilgard, would become the survey's chief in 1881.[16]

Other government agencies provided similar specialized opportunities for educated German speakers. As early as 1825, a Swiss visitor found a skilled mechanic from Schaffhausen supervising the Patent Office's collection of models.[17] Louis Schade, a Berlin law student who arrived as a political refugee in 1851, found a job as an assistant librarian at the Smithsonian Institution before moving to the Census

Bureau and then to the State Department as a translator and statistician. Subsequently admitted to the bar in Iowa, he returned to Washington in 1859, where his most notorious later client was William Wirz, the Swiss-born Confederate commandant at Andersonville.[18] Theodor Poesche, a Halle philosophy student and revolutionary, gained notoriety after his 1854 arrival with a coauthored book on America as the new Roman empire, but it was his statistical flair that brought him first to the Internal Revenue and then to the Census Bureau, where he played an important role in improving statistics on immigrant stock in the U.S.[19] Not all educated immigrants made as smooth an adjustment. Joseph Gerhardt, who studied at the Bonn Polytechnikum and led a battalion during the Baden revolution, before the Civil War was able to advance through menial jobs only to the dignity of innkeeper.[20] Nevertheless, by 1860, Germans could count seven of their number with Patent Office jobs, eleven with professional positions in the Treasury, and five in the General Land Office, while four others worked alongside Cluss in the Navy's Ordnance and Hydrographic Bureau.[21] Although foreign-born applicants were at a disadvantage in federal patronage, official records show a steady increase in the number of Washington Germans working for the government, from forty in 1859, to 187 in 1869, to 276 by 1879, when the Treasury, Interior, War, and the Coast Survey led the list.[22]

Building an Ethnic Community

Educated immigrants like these quickly gave new texture to German ethnic life in Washington, but over time also challenged its boundaries. A German visitor to Washington in the mid-1840s found few Germans of public prominence; the tone of German life was set by its artisans, he observed, who maintained a clubhouse and a "fröhliche Gemeinschaft" among themselves.[23] The city's oldest German organization was reputedly its *Wohltätigkeits-Verein*, a mutual benefit society dating to about 1836. Conrad Finkmann from Osnabrück, who arrived in Washington as a twenty-five-year-old in 1839, was probably typical of the community's early leaders. He kept what was for many years the city's only German

hotel, the Franklin on Pennsylvania between Twelfth and Thirteenth streets, built the city's first German hall, was an active member of the *Deutsche Jäger*, a militia company dating from the early 1850s, and helped establish one of the first two singing societies in 1851.[24] That date is significant; it marks the appearance on the Washington German scene of men like Cluss, and the transformation in its leadership and institutions that they stimulated. The petty bourgeois organizational world created by Germans like Finkmann in the 1840s continued, embedded in growing numbers of church and craft-linked mutual benefit societies, lodges, and building societies, but alongside it would flourish a new set of cultural and reform associations that came to embody the ethnic group's communal self-image.

Cluss, like others of his kind, first suffered in Washington from the lack of "suitable society" and then set out to do something about it.[25] The first of the new *Vereine* were the *Social-demokratischen Turnverein*, the liberal gymnastics organization that he helped found in 1852, its *Liedertafel* in which he sang, and the long-lived Washington *Sängerbund*, whose 1851 origins derived from the choir of the *Concordiakirche*.[26] By the end of the decade, German Washington finally supported a regular weekly German-language newspaper buoyed by ads for the halls, taverns, beer gardens, and private parks that hosted German conviviality. Its pages chronicled a full calendar of concerts, balls, picnics, *Volksfeste*, gymnastics, and singing competitions, and a major campaign to memorialize Baron von Steuben. Excursions across the Potomac to the dance pavilion erected by George Washington's stepson, Parke Custis, on his Arlington Springs estate became highpoints of each summer season. Serenades for local notables and visiting dignitaries were frequent, and Prospect Hill Cemetery, founded in 1858 by the *Concordiakirche*, became a broader German community project.[27]

Political divisions soon paralleled these social divisions. In city elections most Germans supported whichever candidate seemed least tainted by nativism, particularly after anti-immigrant violence and deaths scarred the 1857 election.[28] But the emergence of the anti-slavery Republican Party in the 1856 presidential campaign (Washingtonians campaigned, even if they couldn't vote) divided the German

A gathering at the park run by Washington's popular *Schützen-Verein*, whose banquet hall Cluss designed in 1873. Photograph undated, ca. 1890. Historical Society of Washington, D.C.

community, creating a split in the *Turner* that was not mended until late 1859, and division returned as national passions heightened at decade's end. Festivals that once drew Germans together now became sources of contention. The *Jäger* survived a threatened dissolution and reorganized as the Washington Rifles under new officers in early summer of 1860, a new German Republican Club with Cluss among its activists sought to rally Germans to the Union cause, and by early 1861, the winter season's balls and masquerades were punctuated by the earnest drills of the Rifles and a new *Turner* militia company. At the outbreak of war, they, along with another *Turner* company, formed part of the Eighth Battalion of D.C. Volunteers that helped hold the city for the Union; two of their number killed at Great Falls would be honored as the city's first battle casualties.[29]

The Civil War brought major transformations to German Washington. With numerous German-speaking soldiers regularly encamped about the city, and Germans from around the country among the hordes descending on Washington to pluck the plums of wartime opportunity, German became an everyday sound on the city's streets, and its German community gained new numbers, prosperity, and visibility. Germans, Mayor Richard Wallach would note in 1866, had contributed more to the growth and welfare of the District than any other group.[30] The wartime city could now support commercial German opera and vaudeville, while Washington's lively *Vereinswesen*, temporarily eclipsed at the outbreak of war, swung back into high gear by late 1863. Familiar groups like the *Turner* and singers again filled the social calendar with balls and *Carneval* masquerades, German Republicans rallied again for the 1864 presidential campaign, and a new weekly, the *Columbia*, reported community doings.[31] The Washington Literary and Dramatic Association, a Jewish group with roots in the mid-1850s, established a broader community presence with its major lecture series that winter. The most significant new organization was the *Washingtoner deutschen Hülfsgesellschaft für verwundeten und kranken Soldaten*, which began by aiding German-speaking soldiers in

Washington's numerous military hospitals, and soon extended its assistance into the field.[32] Its great benefit festivals were high points of wartime summer seasons, while its postwar reorganization helped spawn three major new societies: the *Deutsche Gesellschaft*, which combined charity with elite socializing, the *Frauen-Wohltätig-keitsverein* to assist widows and orphans, which built on the self-confidence German women gained from wartime aid experience, and the *Schützen-Verein*. While target shooting had long been popular among Washington Germans, only in the wake of the great post-war *Schützenfest* in Baltimore did they organize the society that became the focal point for German communal life for decades to come.[33] Germans prided themselves on their tasteful illuminations for the city's victory celebration in mid-April 1865 and marched as a large contingent in Lincoln's sad funeral procession a week later. The *Sängerbund* sang at Lincoln's bier in the Rotunda, although Cluss may not have sung with them that day.[34]

Cluss and his wife certainly remained among the tone-setters of postwar German Washington. He served on the planning committee for the Relief Society's summer 1865 Peace Festival, and undoubtedly belonged to the elite *Deutsche Gesellschaft*, since Mme. Cluss was one of the stars of its charity benefit concert the following spring. She also conferred a flag "in the name of Washington women" on the *Schützen-Verein* at its first *Schützenfest*, and was rewarded with a *Sängerbund* serenade that evening for the grace with which she handled her task. Cluss naturally was a *Schützen-Verein* member.[35] But his gradual fading from reports of ethnic activities in the German-language press is one clue to the broadened horizons that he shared with many other *Residenzler* of his kind. By the 1870s, his name more often appeared as a public official than as a community member. Only occasionally did his professional capacity bring him back into the ethnic context, as when he drew up plans for a new hall in the *Schützen-Verein*'s popular park in 1873. At the same time, he and other Germans made ever more frequent appearances in the new society columns of the city's English press.[36]

If wartime activities helped draw older German residents like Cluss into the mainstream of Washington public life, the city's patronage-linked opportunity almost by definition

Simon Wolf (1836–1923), the lawyer and insurance agent born to a Jewish family in a small town in the Palatinate. Wolf became a central figure in both Washington's German community and its interethnic professional life. Goethe-Institut Washington.

attracted German newcomers who already possessed well-developed links to the broader society. Thus Carl Roeser, a Forty-eighter who settled in Manitowoc, Wisconsin, to edit a German newspaper in 1853, claimed a clerk's job in the Treasury Department as reward for his 1860 Republican Party service. The novelist Reinhold Solger, among the most distinguished of the Forty-eighters, also landed what he considered a soul-destroying patronage appointment in the wartime Treasury.[37] Simon Wolf, destined to become German Washington's most prominent spokesman, failed in his 1862 quest for a patronage appointment, instead founding the highly successful law firm that became his springboard to later public office; a Rhenish Bavarian Jew, he had arrived in small-town Ohio at age twelve with his grandparents in 1848.[38] After the war, each new election brought renewed tides of such office-seeking Germans along with other Americans to Washington. The expensive trip might be in vain, as one embarrassed Wisconsin party stalwart discovered when what he thought was a lucrative official appointment turned out to be merely the examination for a minor clerical position.[39] But successful job hunters strengthened both the community's integration into national German American circles, and its local linkages to the emergent nonethnic society of Gilded Age Washington.[40] At a time when German communities elsewhere were receiving massive infusions of industrial laborers, it was aspiring bureaucrats who swelled Washington's German ranks.

The postwar appearance on the Washington scene of small but growing numbers of German-born congressmen, and Carl Schurz's presence first as Senator from Missouri and then in 1877 as Rutherford B. Hayes' powerful Secretary of the Interior, further bolstered the self-assurance of the German community while facilitating its role as a congressional lobbying platform for national German American interests. First visible during the Civil War, this role would gain in importance as pressures built for congressional action on issues like temperance, Sunday observance, and an amendment defining America as a Christian nation—all issues to which most Germans passionately objected.[41] The continued expansion of government-supported science also meant the continued arrival of German scientists like Ferdinand Kampf, an East Prussian mathematician recruited in 1872 from the polytechnic school in Tilsit to participate in the Transit of Venus project at the Naval Observatory, only to lose his life on the Wheeler Expedition in 1877.[42] One final element in shaping Washington's unique post–Civil War German community was the greater prestige of Germany itself following the Franco-Prussian War and the unification of the German Empire. The newly prominent German (and Austrian) diplomatic presence lent aristocratic cachet to major community events.[43]

The Quest for Public Influence

Washington's federal status also shaped the German community's wider civic presence. As Washington during the territorial period (1871–74) sought to refashion itself into a capital worthy of the newly reunited nation and a city worth living (and speculating) in, *Residenzler* flirted with electoral power like Germans elsewhere. But when the city's democratic moment passed, they had to fall back on the courtier's option of access to the prince's ear—in American terms, Congress and the administration. They were enthusiastic contributors to the city's physical improvement. Cluss, associate of "Boss" Alexander Shepherd, profited mightily from the development boom while helping lend the city at long last true *Residenzstadt* elegance.[44] Other Germans shared the benefits, whether they were quarry operators like Nickolas Acker, brewers slaking the thirsty throats of workers like Christian Heurich, or the craftsmen whose own homes, bought with the help of ever-multiplying building societies, spread through the city's expanding neighborhoods.[45] But a parallel crusade for Washington's moral improvement through temperance and Sunday blue laws quickly clashed with the *Residenzlers'* vision of public sociability and provoked efforts of defensive organization that ultimately only underlined German vulnerability.

Territorial Washington's three leading German foci remained the *Columbia-Turn-Verein* (the less radical successor to the city's socialist *Turner* of the 1850s), the *Schützen-Verein*, and the long-established *Sängerbund*. The Columbia's *Turnhalle* housed not only gymnastics, balls, and other social events, but also the city's only regular amateur German theater and night school classes in English and technical drawing for workingmen. Other gymnastics organizations included the *Pyramiden und Pantomimen-Club* and the Georgetown *Turnverein*.[46] The *Schützen-Verein's* elaborate park up Seventh Street was German Washington's main communal gathering place for great ethnic festivals, sporting events, and convivial Sunday strolls. A pillar crowned with Steuben's bust greeted entering visitors, the Marine Band played on Sunday afternoons, and by the early 1870s American families also were venturing inside this privately maintained but publicly accessible parkland; even a delega-

Dietz's Rathskeller, an example of the beer halls at the center of local German social life and targeted by Washington's temperance reformers. Historical Society of Washington, D.C.

tion of visiting Indians in 1873 tried their hands at target shooting and bowling in the park.[47] The *Germania Schützenverein* also maintained a park, theirs in Gales Wood, as did the marksmen and anglers of the wonderfully named *Treffdusia*.[48] The *Sängerbund*, too, was joined by other musical groups, including the very active *Arion Quartette-Club* founded in 1867, the *Frohsinn Quartett-Club* organized by young single members of the *Sängerbund* in early 1874, and groups within various fraternal lodges. In the early spring of 1874, *Sängerbund* members formed a joint-stock company to construct a fitting hall for their performances.[49] Other types of associations also flourished, including groups like the Washingtoner Boat-Club, a Deutsche Fishing Club, a *Gambrinus Verein*, and new groups based on German origin like the *Verein Baden* or the *Schwaben Verein*, which held its first *Schwaben-Kirbe* in the autumn of 1873.[50]

This is an impressive tally for a relatively small German community, a fact the city's German daily acknowledged when it hired a special correspondent to report on Washington's *Vereinsleben* in 1873.[51] But equally notable is what is missing. An only slightly larger, and considerably more

impoverished, German population in frontier Milwaukee before the Civil War, for example, seems to have supported a much richer musical, theatrical, and intellectual scene than did Gilded Age Washington.[52] It was hoped that a new debating club formed in Swampoodle in 1873 would meet a long-felt need, but the *Schiller-Bund*, with its literary aspirations, would require a second founding in late 1877, before it awakened to a real community role.[53] Scientific lectures had perennial difficulty attracting audiences.[54] The liberal German-English school established in 1859 apparently collapsed in the postwar period, and only in 1873 would the city's educated Germans, under the leadership of Robert Reitzel, the later notorious pastor of the Independent Protestant (free-thinking) Congregation, again organize a nonsectarian German-American school; Milwaukee's analogous German and English Academy was organized in 1851 and by the 1870s was a flourishing leader in American education.[55] Fraternal lodges and mutual benefit societies continued to prosper, joined now by a *Deutsche Veteranen-Bund* to provide benefits for Civil War veterans and their widows and orphans, but postwar charitable societies were less in evidence. The central focus of Washington's *Vereinswesen* was recreational; German ethnicity in Washington seemed defined almost exclusively by its festive culture.[56]

Hence the German concern when the year 1873 opened with two ominous developments: a new Evangelical Temperance Alliance against the sale of intoxicating beverages in the city and stepped-up police enforcement of Sunday closing laws. War, or so it seemed, had been declared against the mainstays of German culture.[57] Response followed quickly. Why, wondered one of the city's two German newspapers, had Washington Germans not organized like compatriots elsewhere to make their political weight felt? Washington, the editor observed, probably had proportionally more intelligent, capable, and respected German citizens than any other city in the Union, yet they held almost no public offices, and those who did, largely acquired those offices through personal contacts—he may have had Cluss in mind, and Wolf, then recorder of deeds—and not through the influence of their countrymen.[58] As the sense of crisis grew with stepped-up blue-law enforcement, the German newspapers merged in late March to better focus community defense; proposals circulated for a new umbrella organization to coordinate efforts of the city's German associations, and in late May, while the rest of the city gathered at Arlington, Germans conspicuously held a separate Memorial Day ceremony of their own in Prospect Hill Cemetery.[59] Then in July appeared the *Sentinel*, a new, English-language newspaper edited by Louis Schade and subsidized by the nation's brewers to represent German antiprohibition interests in the nation's capital. The "Beer Bung Starter," as it was dubbed by English-language competitors, gave assimilating Washington Germans an English voice that compatriots elsewhere could only envy.[60]

Finally, with autumn elections for District delegate approaching, the *Columbia-Turn-Verein* sponsored a series of mass meetings that at long last sparked a popular German electoral movement to recommend and blacklist candidates and get out the vote. When the results came in, the *Journal* was able to triumph: "*Sieg. Sieg! Ein Sedan für die Temperenzler. 18 unserer Candidaten gewählt. Temperance Laws played out. Ehrlich währt am Längsten!*" Only in three or four districts

were their hopes dashed. Some might think that other issues, such as race, were central to the election, but Germans knew that antiprohibition explained the outcome.[61] In the euphoria following the election, delegates from the various election districts finally met to form a permanent organization, the *Deutsch-amerikanisches Repräsentativ-Komitee des Distrikts Columbia*, to defend their interests against "all puritanical, temperance, or other religious or political infringements," with Simon Wolf as its president.[62]

The committee aggressively addressed a range of issues, from tax exemption for church property and racial integration in the public schools (both of which it opposed), to patronage for Germans in District government, railroad rights-of-way in residential neighborhoods, denial of liquor licenses, German-language publication of official notices, care for German speakers in the city's Central Dispensary, and German-language instruction in public schools. The campaign for German in the schools met with success in April 1874, but the struggle against the rising tide of liquor license denials was less satisfactory. By late spring 1874, with the scandals of District government taking central stage, and Germans squirming in ethnic embarrassment for the apparent disgrace of Cluss's congressional testimony, popular support for the committee dissipated.[63] By 1877, when the new Hayes administration again emboldened prohibitionists, it was clear that Washington's new commission form of government offered no scope for mass electoral action. By default, Washington Germans had to rely on interest representation by leaders defined more by personal than group access to the city's centers of power, and on the newer possibilities of directly lobbying German and other sympathetic members of Congress.[64]

The Germans' quest for unity and influence shattered on the rocks of the District's altered government but also, as editor Koch charged, on the political indifference and lukewarm loyalties of "older residents" and government employees. But perhaps the quest itself was part of the problem. Germans, Koch, and even Schade included, always seemed a little embarrassed that the only cause for which they were willing to battle was beer. Even their demand for a "just" share of offices was less about patronage spoils than about controlling instruments that could be used to attack the sociable habits and rituals of German associational life. Like German Americans elsewhere, they defended their position in terms of personal liberty and the democratic right of the group to its own culture, and pointed to the class injustice of laws that criminalized public but not private consumption and barred public Sunday socializing for people without large homes and gardens of their own.[65] But it took the more reputable goal of commemorating the 1883 bicentennial of German settlement, led by the city's German Civil War veterans, to produce a quasi-permanent central organization that all of the community could support. In 1890 it evolved into the United German Societies, charged with coordinating annual German Day celebrations and other community projects, including the 1910 dedication of a statue of Steuben on Lafayette Square.[66] Charitable institutions like the German orphanage founded in 1879 and the later old people's home also attracted broad support.[67]

The great Steuben festival with its presidential dedication and massive parade was a classic *Residenzler* triumph (Congress funded the statue) but also their final sunset glory. The United German Societies was always more an antiprohibition lobby than an expression of ethnic fellowship, while the forty-three German societies of 1883 declined to twenty-four by the eve of the Great War. New, high, liquor-license fees that year endangered even their survival and provoked serious proposals to merge all remaining German activities in Washington into a single clubhouse.[68] As early as 1891 Germans lost their prime festival grounds to developers when special liquor zoning forced closure of the *Schützenpark*.[69]

Integration and Transfiguration

Therein lay real irony. German Washington, uniquely shaped by the kind of migrant the capital attracted, not only offered but almost demanded equally distinctive trajectories of integration into the broader nonethnic society. It was not only the money to be made in Washington, and the social openness of a parvenu society that permitted men like Heurich to erect mansions alongside American-born neighbors; it was their American connections that brought so many partially

assimilated Germans to the capital in the first place, the jobs that demanded English, the stimulating engagement in the broader business of the city and nation rather than the narrow group, however sociable that group might be. But this was an integration made easier by the fact that Washington, too, was a *Residenzstadt* now changed, made more cultured and livable, by among others the Germans themselves.

In the 1850s, Cluss helped create a simulacrum of the small-city social world he knew from *Vormärz* Germany. By the 1870s, he was part of Washington's power structure, his children were in public schools, his daughters would "finish" at an elite convent, and they and their mother—and occasionally Cluss himself—soon took their places in society-page reports of dances, evening excursions on the Potomac, New Year receiving rituals, and musical soirees.[70] As he later commented, "While I am a native of Germany, I have been living here for forty years; and I hold in higher regard the United States than I do my birth-place."[71] But he and his wife also continued to appear at *Sängerbund* carnival balls and receptions for distinguished German guests, and Mme. Cluss headed the ladies' committee for the German Orphans' Fair.[72] Theodore Poesche, the noted statistician, was another who was as readily found on the Yankee as the German social circuit, accompanied by his talented wife Rosa, authoress and president of the very active German Dramatic Club of the 1890s.[73] Even Simon Wolf, long-time president of the *Schützen* and omnipresent in just about every major German or Jewish organization in the city, was equally prominent in nonethnic civic, philanthropic, and social circles.[74]

Ethnic lines were readily crossed in this open society, and ethnic influence thereby diluted but also extended. As in other American cities, the everyday constitution of Washington's German world went on, largely unreported, in the neighborhoods, workplaces, churches and synagogues, taverns, and lodge meetings of the community's ordinary working- and lower-middle-class members. But they were never numerous enough to create the vital German workers' culture that a city like Chicago could support.[75] Nor with its peculiar opportunity structure could Washington attract the more recent and nationalistic immigrants who formed the backbone of the assertive German ethnicity flourishing elsewhere at this time. The older Pennsylvania German stock, counted by the community if not the census-taker as among its members and sharing its social habits, evidently had little interest in supporting more formal ethnic organization. Thus cultivation of formal German identity in Washington, even more so than in other American cities, rested primarily on the shoulders of the merchants, bureaucrats, and professionals who made up its increasingly second-generation middle class—precisely the ones with easiest entrée to other circles as well. The 1873 campaign for German political organization found a telling culmination in spring 1874 in the founding of a new organization with an English name, the Osceola German American Association. Its purpose was "to foster brotherly sentiments among young Germans and Americans."[76]

The *Residenzstadt* society that German Washingtonians created was as unique among the constellation of America's urban German communities as was the city itself. The peculiarities of its opportunity structure, the resulting selectivity of its migration, the distinctiveness of its governmental system, left Washington's German residents without the incentives, numbers, or means to support the political organization so central to German community formation elsewhere. This absence may have meant that Germans in Washington could never make their influence felt as a group. But they gained a platform from which to lobby for national German American interests and the temporal space in which to amplify their vision of a sociable urban community amid the churning, striving ostentation of Gilded Age Washington. In reshaping a city "suitable" for themselves, in which they could lead integrated, bicultural lives as the Cluss family so obviously did, the *Residenzler* also helped realize a more cosmopolitan vision for their new nation's capital. ✣

NOTES

1. Friedrich Kapp, *Aus und über Amerika*, 2 vols. (Berlin, 1876), 2:191.

2. Cf. *Die Residenzstadt Karlsruhe, ihre Geschichte und Beschreibung* (Karlsruhe, 1858).

3. *Das Washingtoner Intelligenzblatt*, Washington, D.C. (hereafter WIB), 7/21/1860.

4. Theodor Griesinger, *Land und Leute in Amerika: Skizzen aus dem amerikanischen Leben* (Stuttgart, 1863), 518, 521; Samuel Ludvigh, *Licht- und Schattenbilder republikanischer Zustände* (Leipzig, 1848), 318.

5. E.g. *Columbia*, Washington, D.C. (hereafter WC), 10/17/1863; 1/9, 12/24/1864; 1/14, 7/22, 9/23, 10/28, 12/18/1865; 2/3, 3/10/1866.

6. German Washington has received little scholarly attention; for helpful overviews see Klaus G. Wust, "German Immigrants and Their Newspapers in the District of Columbia," *Society for the History of Germans in Maryland, Reports* 30 (1959), 36–65; Mona E. Dingle, "Gemeinschaft und Gemütlichkeit: German American Community and Culture, 1850–1920," in *Urban Odyssey: A Multicultural History of Washington, D.C.*, ed. Francine Curro Cary (Washington, D.C., 1996), 113–34.

7. J.D.B. DeBow, *Statistical View of the United States: Compendium of the Seventh Census* (Washington, D.C., 1854), 200, 201, 399; Joseph C. G. Kennedy, *Population of the United States in 1860, Compiled from the Original Returns of the Eighth Census* (Washington, D.C., 1864), xxix, xxxii, 587, 589; Francis A. Walker, *Ninth Census, Volume I: The Statistics of the Population of the United States* (Washington, D.C., 1872), 336–42; United States Census Office, *Statistics of the Population of the United States at the Tenth Census* (Washington, D.C., 1883), 480, 492–95; U.S. Census Office, *Report on the Population of the United States at the Eleventh Census: 1890, Part I* (Washington, D.C., 1895), 395–96, 606–9; 684. For the sake of comparability, I have used figures for the District of Columbia, rather than for the city of Washington itself.

8. Kennedy, *Population of the United States in 1860*, 589.

9. These generalizations are based on rough tabulations from microfilms of the 1860 federal manuscript census for the District of Columbia; for further discussion of German occupational and residential patterns in nineteenth-century Washington, see Dingle, "Gemeinschaft."

10. Department of the Interior, Census Office, *Statistics of the Population of the United States at the Tenth Census* (Washington, D.C., 1883), Table XXXVI: Persons in Selected Occupations in Fifty Principal Cities.

11. Dingle, "Gemeinschaft," 116–17, 124; Johannes Nep. Enzlberger, *Schematismus der katholischen Geistlichkeit deutscher Zunge in den Vereinigten Staaten Amerikas* (Milwaukee, 1892), 25. German Catholic immigration was minimal until the 1830s, when it became an increasingly larger proportion of the total immigration for the next couple decades before Protestant proportions probably increased once more; western cities settled during this period, like Cincinnati, often had high German Catholic proportions. See Kathleen Neils Conzen, "German Catholics in America," in *The Encyclopedia of American Catholic History*, eds. Michael Glazier and Thomas J. Shelley (Collegeville, Minn., 1997), 571–72.

12. Dingle, "Gemeinschaft," 115, 124.

13. *Die tägliche Metropole*, Washington, D.C. (hereafter TM), 11/17/1860; Hasia R. Diner and Steven J. Diner, "Washington's Jewish Community: Separate But Not Apart," in Cary, ed., *Urban Odyssey*, 136–37; Robert Shosteck, "The Jewish Community of Washington, D.C., during the Civil War," *American Jewish Historical Quarterly* 56 (1967): 319–47; 1860 federal manuscript census, District of Columbia.

14. Frederic Trautmann, "Washington through German Eyes: A Visit by Moritz Wagner and Carl Scherzer in 1852," *Records of the Columbia Historical Society of Washington, D.C.* 52 (1989): 89.

15. Florian Cajori, *The Chequered Career of Ferdinand Rudolph Hassler, First Superintendent of the United States Coast Survey: A Chapter in the History of Science in America* (Boston, 1929); Sally Gregory Kohlstedt, *The Formation of the American Scientific Community: The American Association for the Advancement of Science 1848–60* (Urbana, 1976); Hugh Richard Slotten, *Patronage, Practice, and the Culture of American Science: Alexander Dallas Bache and the U.S. Coast Survey* (Cambridge, 1994), statistics 170; TM 10/12/1860.

16. Hilgard, eleven years old when his prominent liberal father brought his Rhenish Bavarian family to a frontier Illinois farm in 1836, came to the survey in 1847 after engineering study in Bache's home city of Philadelphia; Kohlstedt, *Formation*, Appendix; *Washington Post* (hereafter WP), 5/9/1891. Most of Cluss's German colleagues, however, were, like him, German-trained; stereotypes of Germans as given to drink and favoring their own seemingly played a role in the 1885 scandals that removed the elderly Hilgard from his superintendency; WP 8/7, 9/5, 9/14/1885.

17. Christian F. Feest, translator and editor, "Lukas Vischer in Washington: A Swiss View of the District of Columbia in 1825," *Records of the Columbia Historical Society of Washington, D.C.* (1973–74): 78–110.

18. Alexander Schem, *Deutsch-Amerikanisches Conversations-Lexicon*, 11 vols. (New York, 1869–74), 9:46.

19. A. E. Zucker, ed., *The Forty-Eighters: Political Refugees of the German Revolution of 1848* (New York, 1950), 326–27; WIB 7/14/1860.

20. Zucker, *Forty-Eighters*, 296.

21. TM 10/12/1860. One of Cluss's Naval colleagues, a Silesian Forty-eighter named Hermann Diebitsch, would go on to a long career at the Smithsonian; his daughter Josephine accompanied her husband, Admiral Robert E. Peary, in his polar expeditions and became a noted author in her own right; Corina Tanguay, "Josephine Diebitsch Peary," Women and the American Experience Web site, http://www.une.edu/mwwc/ams308/peary.htm (December 31, 2004).

22. Cindy S. Aron, *Ladies and Gentlemen of the Civil Service: Middle-Class Workers in Victorian America* (New York, 1987); U.S. Department of State, *Register of Officers and Agents, Civil, Military, and Naval, in the Service of the United States on the Thirtieth of September, 1859* (Washington, D.C., 1859); Department of the Interior, *Register of the Officers and Agents, Civil, Military, and Naval, in the Service of the United States, on the Thirtieth September, 1869* (Washington, D.C., 1870); *Official Register of the United States . . . Thirtieth of June, 1879; Vol. I: Legislative, Executive, Judicial* (Washington, D.C., 1879).

23. Franz von Löher, *Geschichte und Zustände der Deutschen in Amerika* (Cincinnati, 1847), 316.

24. *Washingtoner Journal* (hereafter WJ), 11/23/1877; Wust, "German Immigrants," 44.

25. Haila Ochs and Sabina Wiedenhoeft, "Einsichten in die amerikanische Gastgesellschaft: Die Briefe des Architekten Adolf Cluss," in *Politische Netzwerke durch Briefkommunikation: Briefkultur der politischen Oppositionsbewegungen und frühen Arbeiterbewegungen im 19. Jahrhundert*, eds. Jürgen Herres and Manfred Neuhaus (Berlin, 2002), 179.

26. Helmut Strauss, "Turner Movement in Washington," Research Report, German Historical Institute, Washington, D.C., 2004; Dr. Chr. Strack, "Geschichte des 'Washington Sängerbund,'" Deutsche Historische Gesellschaft für den District Columbia, *Berichte* 2, no. 1 (April 1906): 34–46.

27. WIB, April 1859 through March 1860; Strack, "Geschichte des Washington Sängerbund (Schluss)," *Berichte* 2, no. 2 (July 1906): 11–13.

28. TM 5/26, 5/29/1860; Wust, "German Immigrants," 44–45.

29. Strauss, "Turner Movement"; Wust, "German Immigrants," 46–48; WIB 9/17, 10/1/1859; 4/21, 4/28, 5/5, 6/9/1860; TM 10/15, 10/29, 11/1, 11/17, 12/31/1860; WJ 5/31/1873.

30. Kapp, *Aus und über Amerika*, 287–92; *Washington during the Civil War: The Diary of Horatio Nelson Taft, 1861–1865*, Library of Congress, American Memory Web site, http://memory.loc.gov/ammem/tafthtml/tafthome.html (December 31, 2004); Heinrich Börnstein, *Fünfundsiebzig Jahre in der Alten und Neuen Welt: Memoiren eines Unbedeutenden*, 2 vols. (Leipzig, 1884), 2:338–42; WC 6/2/1866.

31. WC 10/17, 12/19, 12/26/1863; 1/24, 1/30, 2/6, 6/18, 9/24, 11/15/1864. The successor to the *Washingtoner Anzeiger* of 1859, Werner Koch's *Intelligenzblatt*, subsequently renamed the *Metropole*, suspended publication in June 1861 when Koch, a printer from Hesse who had emigrated in 1853, left for military service; after his discharge he and Louis Schade published an unsuccessful paper aimed at German soldiers serving in the area, and then Koch became the printer for Max Cohnheim's new literary, humor, and political weekly, the *Columbia*. Cohnheim, a New York journalist first brought to Washington for war service, was a veteran of the Baden revolution who supported *Columbia* with a Treasury job for more than three years, until Schade denounced his anti-Johnson jibes, and he was forced to resign, fold his paper, and move to San Francisco; Wust, "German Immigrants"; Shosteck, "Jewish Community," 336–38; WC 3/6, 3/31, 4/7/1866; http://www.dmna.state.ny.us/historic/reghist/civil/infantry/41stInf/41stInfMain.htm.

32. Shosteck, "Jewish Community," 326–27, 329, 337; WC 11/28, 12/19, 12/26/1863; 1/9, 2/18, 6/4, 11/24/1864; 2/18, 4/2/1865.

33. WC 6/23, 7/2/1864; 6/17, 6/27, 7/22, 9/2, 11/11, 11/25, 12/2, 12/9, 12/16/1865; 2/17, 3/10, 4/7, 5/26/1866.

34. WC 4/15, 4/22/1865; Strack, "Washington Sängerbund," 2, no. 2:13.

35. WC 6/17, 12/18/1865; 3/31, 6/2/1866.

36. *Washingtoner Anzeiger* (hereafter WA), 1/31/1873. His firm would also design a new hall for the *Schützen-Verein* in 1879, after a fire destroyed the old facilities; WP 7/7, 11/15/1879; 5/9/1880.

37. Zucker, *Forty-Eighters*, 331, 343–44.

38. *Eminent and Representative Men of Virginia and the District of Columbia of the Nineteenth Century* (Madison, Wisc., 1893), 357–60; Esther L. Panitz, *Simon Wolf: Private Conscience and Public Image* (Rutherford, N.J., 1987).

39. WJ 3/31/1873.

40. On this new society, see Kathryn Allamong Jacob, *Capital Elites: High Society in Washington, D.C., after the Civil War* (Washington, D.C., 1995).

41. WJ 11/17/1877; Jörg Nagler, *Fremont contra Lincoln: Die deutsch-amerikanische Opposition in der Republikanischen Partei während des amerikanischen Bürgerkrieges* (Frankfurt am Main, 1984); Gaines M. Foster, *Moral Reconstruction: Christian Lobbyists and the Federal Regulation of Morality, 1865–1920* (Chapel Hill, N.C., 2002).

42. WJ 4/1/1878.

43. E.g., WJ 5/26/1873.

44. Alan Lessoff, *The Nation and Its City: Politics, "Corruption," and Progress in Washington, D.C., 1861–1902* (Baltimore, 1994), 48–49, 51, 62.

45. WJ 10/29, 1/20, 2/21/1877; Candace Shireman, "The Rise of Christian Heurich and His Mansion," *Washington History* 5 (1993): 4–27.

46. WJ 3/8, 2/25/1873.

47. WJ 6/9, 10/24/1873; WP 5/20/1890.

48. WJ 4/12/1873; 4/25/1874.

49. WJ 2/8, 2/25/1873; 2/24, 3/19/1874.

50. WJ 4/2, 8/22, 5/19, 5/27, 10/3/1873.

51. WA 1/21/1873.

52. Compare Kathleen Neils Conzen, *Immigrant Milwaukee, 1836–1860: Accommodation and Community in a Frontier City* (Cambridge, Mass., 1976). Nearby Baltimore, of course, offered many of the German cultural opportunities that Washington could not support; cf. Dieter Cunz, *The Maryland Germans: A History* (Princeton, N.J., 1948).

53. WJ 10/27/1873; 12/19/1877.

54. WJ 1/13/1873.

55. WIB 4/23, 6/18, 6/25, 11/3/1859; WC 5/6/1865; WJ 8/20, 8/21, 9/9/1873; Conzen, *Immigrant Milwaukee*, 182. Reitzel, a Baden immigrant, soon became too radical for even his free-thinking congregation, supported himself as a widely traveling lecturer and writer on free thought, and beginning in 1884 published *Der arme Teufel*, an idiosyncratic radical weekly, in Detroit. He gained national notoriety for his support of the Haymarket defendants in 1887, but Louis Schade reassured Washingtonians that "those who know Reitzel know he is perfectly harmless. It will be a long time before Mr. Reitzel has courage enough personally to shed one drop of any man's blood. But as long as the newspapers are willing to make his harangues conspicuous he will be willing to harangue. If the newspapers would ignore the anarchists they would soon shut up." WP, 11/18/1887. On Reitzel, see Richard Oestreicher, "Robert Reitzel, *Der arme Teufel*," in *The German-American Radical Press: The Shaping of a Left Political Culture, 1850–1940*, eds. Elliott Shore, Ken Fones-Wolf, and James P. Danky (Urbana, Ill., 1992), 147–67, and Reitzel's own delightful autobiography, *Adventures of a Greenhorn: An Autobiographical Novel by Robert Reitzel*, Jacob Erhardt, trans. (New York, 1992).

56. Cf. Kathleen Neils Conzen, "Ethnicity as Festive Culture: German America on Parade," in *The Invention of Ethnicity*, ed. Werner Sollors (New York, 1989), 44–76.

57. WA 1/11, 1/16/1873; WJ 6/20/1873.

58. WA 2/8/1873.

59. WA 2/25/1873; WJ 3/25/, 5/31/1873. Koch took over the *Columbia* after Cohnheim's departure, while N. H. Miller, a Berlin-born lawyer, established the daily *Anzeiger* as a Republican campaign journal in spring 1871; with the *Anzeiger* apparently in financial difficulty, and Miller distracted by his office of Assistant Attorney for the District, he was glad to sell out to Koch, who would edit the merged *Washingtoner Journal* for the next thirty-eight years. WJ 3/25/73; U.S. manuscript census, 1870, Georgetown; WP 4/14/1909; 3/9/1911.

60. WJ 6/7, 7/7/1873; WP, 8/10/1880.

61. WJ 9/10, 9/15, 9/18, 10/7, 10/8, 10/10, 10/11, 10/14, 10/16/1873.

62. WJ 11/12/1873.

63. WJ 11/27, 12/2, 12/4, 12/9, 12/12, 12/15, 12/16, 12/29/1873; 2/25, 4/7, 4/15, 7/17, 4/21, 5/1/, 5/21, 5/25/1874.

64. WJ 11/17/1877; 6/21, 7/10/1878.

65. E.g. WJ 3/8, 5/5, 5/31, 6/20, 7/3/1873; 3/22, 6/27/1877.

66. WP 10/4, 10/9, 10/10/1883; 10/7/1890; 10/3/1891; 10/18/1892; 10/16/1900; Dingle, "*Gemütlichkeit*," 128.

67. Dingle, "*Gemütlichkeit*," 124–25.

68. WP 9/17/1883; 6/22, 6/24/1914.

69. WP 3/27/1891.

70. WJ 6/9/1873; WP 6/28/1879; 2/21/1878; 7/29/1881; 12/31/1882.

71. WP 1/21/1889.

72. WP 6/27, 10/23, 11/29/1881; 2/16/1886.

73. WP 4/29/1883; 10/29/1888; 4/7/1889; 9/5/1895.

74. WP 1/18/1878; 10/2/1911; 10/12/1913.

75. Cf. Hartmut Keil, ed., *German Workers' Culture in the United States 1850 to 1920*, (Washington, 1988).

76. WJ 3/20/1874.

PHOTO ESSAY The Washington Cluss Found, the Washington Cluss Made

JOSEPH L. BROWNE, SABINA W. DUGAN, *and* HARRIET LESSER

If an ideal lies dormant deep in the heart as a guiding star from the remote future, and if a passionate man makes it his life's task to smooth the path to that ideal stone by stone, then someone with limited vision will see only the effort required for the next item in such action, and seeing no end in this small goal, shall denounce the hale and hardy worker. . . . But the wise person will recognize the work of an artist who, even in the rough beginning, is already pursuing the glimmering goal of the consummated idea. . . .

—*Der Demokrat*, Mainz, 1848

1. *Adolf Cluss*, 1880.
Photograph.
Smithsonian Archives,
Smithsonian Institution.

From Heilbronn to Washington

2. *German Confederation*, 1848. Gene Thorp, Cartographic Concepts, Inc., 2005.

In Cluss's boyhood years, the center of Heilbronn, flanked on the west by the Neckar River, contained a series of small streets with half-timbered houses organized around a few centers of activity: the Market Place, Kilian's Church, and the impressive buildings of the Teutonic Knights. A freie Reichstadt or free imperial city until 1803, its walls and social conventions were being gradually breached by an expanding middle class, industrialization, technologies that allowed faster communication and travel, and ideas and people from beyond the city walls.

—William Gilcher, Goethe-Institut, 2002

3. *Postcard of Heilbronn*, 1830s. Private collection.

4. *View from Capitol*, ca. 1863. The Smithsonian Castle is in the background and the notorious Washington Canal is to the right. Photograph. Library of Congress, LC-USZ62-127632.

My first impression of the political capital of the great American Republic was rather dismal. Washington looked at that period [1850s] like a big, sprawling village consisting of scattered groups of houses which were overtopped by a few public buildings—the Capitol, only what is now the central part was occupied; the Treasury, the two wings of which were still lacking; the White House; and the Patent Office.

—Carl Schurz, politician, 1906

5. *Patent Office and Neighborhood*, 1846. Photograph. Smithsonian Archives, Smithsonian Institution.

Major Peter Charles L'Enfant . . . was the author of the picturesque plan of Washington.

—Adolf Cluss, 1876

6. *Washington*, 1850. Lithograph. Historical Society of Washington, D.C.

7. *Patent Office, G Street, NW*, ca. 1856. Lithograph. Washingtoniana Division, D.C. Public Library.

8. *Smithsonian Institution, National Mall*, 1850s. Lithograph. Washingtoniana Division, D.C. Public Library.

Ordnance and Architecture—Cluss Begins His Career

9. *Admiral John Dahlgren*, 1840s. Painting. Edward Marolda, *Washington Navy Yard*, 1999.

Mr. Cluss, draughtsman, left my department—very sorry; had been here five and a half years, and is always right.

—Commander John A. Dahlgren, private journal entry, October 10, 1855

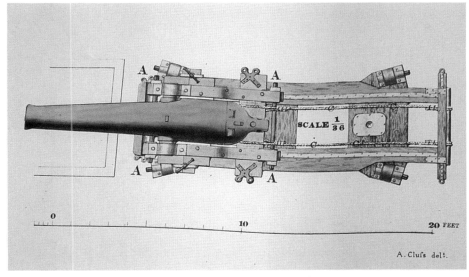

10. Adolf Cluss, *Eleven-Inch Swivel Gun*, ca. 1860. Painting. Naval Historical Center.

11. *Washington Navy Yard*, 1860s. Lithograph. Edward Marolda, *Washington Navy Yard*, 1999.

12. *Ordnance Foundry, Washington Navy Yard, 1860s.* Edward Marolda, *Washington Navy Yard*, 1999.

13. *Gun Park, Washington Navy Yard, 1840s.* Edward Marolda, *Washington Navy Yard*, 1999.

Forts bristled above every hill-top. Soldiers were entrenched at every gate-way. Shed hospitals covered acres on acres in every suburb. Churches, art-halls and private mansions were filled with the wounded and dying of the American armies. The endless roll of the army wagon seemed never still. The rattle of the anguish-laden ambulance, the piercing cries of the sufferers whom it carried, made morning, noon and night too dreadful to be borne. The streets were filled with marching troops, with new regiments, their hearts strong and eager. . . . But the streets were filled no less with soldiers foot-sore, sunburned, and wary, their clothes begrimed, their banners torn. . . . Every moment had its drum-beat, every hour was alive with the tramp of troops going, coming.

—Mary Clemmer Ames, journalist, 1874

14. *Camp Fry, near Washington Circle,* ca. 1863. Photograph. Historical Society of Washington, D.C.

Civil War and the Changing Face of the City

15. *Camp of Thirty-first Pennsylvania Infantry, near Washington, 1862. Photograph.* Library of Congress, LC-B8171-2405 L0T 4172.

16. *Oxen with Cannon, Fifteenth Street and Pennsylvania Avenue, NW, ca. 1861–65. Photograph.* Historical Society of Washington, D.C.

17. *President Lincoln's Last Reception, White House, 1865. Photograph.* Library of Congress, LC-USZC4-2438.

Here [at Murder Bay] crime, filth, and poverty seem to vie with each other in a career of degradation and death. Whole families are crowded into mere apologies for shanties. . . . During storms of rain or snow their roofs afford but slight protection. . . . In a space of about fifty yards square I found about one hundred families composed of from three to ten persons each. . . . There are no proper privy accommodations.

—A. C. Richards, Superintendent of the Metropolitan Police, 1866

18. *Shanties at Murder Bay, South of Pennsylvania Avenue, NW*, 1860s. Photograph. Historical Society of Washington, D.C.

19. *Tiber Creek, between North Capitol and First Streets, NW*, ca. 1870. Print. Washingtoniana Division, D.C. Public Library.

20. *Construction of Washington Aqueduct*, 1858. Army engineer Montgomery Meigs, who later worked with Cluss on the National Museum, stands at the center. Photograph. Historical Society of Washington, D.C.

21. *Streetcar and Train, near Capitol,* 1866. Lithograph. Historical Society of
Washington, D.C.

*. . . it ought to be appreciated that the luxurious life of the
higher classes depends upon the strength and activity of
the children of the industrious classes. . . .*

—Adolf Cluss, 1875

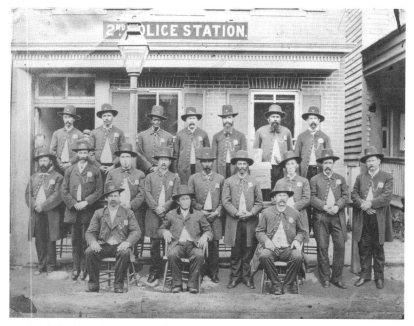

22. *Second Ward Police Station,* 1878. Photograph. Historical Society of Washington, D.C.

23. *Edward F. Droop Music Store, 925 Pennsylvania Avenue, NW,* ca. 1875. Droop was Cluss's brother-in-law. Photograph.
Washingtoniana Division, D.C. Public Library.

The style [of the Agriculture Department building] leans to French Renaissance with mansard roof. The conservatories are kept in light Moresques forms.

—Adolf Cluss, 1876

24. *Agriculture Department, National Mall*, ca. 1870. Lithograph. Washingtoniana Division, D.C. Public Library.

25. *Calvary Baptist Church, Eighth and H Streets, NW*, 1860s. Photograph. Calvary Baptist Church.

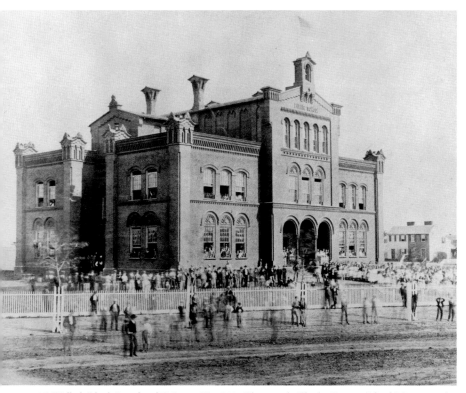

26. *Wallach School, Seventh and D Streets, SE*, 1870s. Photograph. Charles Sumner School Museum and Archives.

There were obvious symbolic ways the schools were speaking to local residents. These were model schools, not just your typical neighborhood schools, they tower over the skyline . . . they were supposed to inspire, uplift, and educate.

—William J. Reece, Professor of History, 2003

27. *Stickney Residence, Sixth and M Streets, NW, 1920.* Photograph. Historical Society of Washington, D.C.

It is well to emphasize that there is an indissoluble connection between truth and beauty, between prose and poetry, between science and fine art. One is simply the anti-thesis of the other.

—Adolf Cluss, 1898

28. *Masonic Temple,* ca. 1866. Drawing by Adolf Cluss shows proposed mansard roof. Historical Society of Washington, D.C.

29. *Masonic Temple, Ninth and F Streets, NW, ca. 1881.* Photograph. Historical Society of Washington, D.C.

A mansard roof [for the Masonic Temple] remains unfinished for want of funds.

—Adolf Cluss, 1876

Alexander Shepherd . . . hoped to restructure Washington's economy and politics after the model of northeastern cities. . . . His program of public investments on roads, bridges, sewers, and water lines was intended to give Washington an up-to-date infrastructure comparable to that of New York or Philadelphia.

—Carl Abbott, *Political Terrain: Washington, D.C., from Tidewater Town to Global Metropolis*, 1999

30. *Alexander R. Shepherd*, ca. 1871. This portrait by Henry Ulke, the German American who also painted the portrait of Rosa Cluss on page 96, hangs in the District Building. Reproduction courtesy Historical Society of Washington, D.C.

31. *Ulysses S. Grant*, ca. 1870. President Grant was a strong advocate of modernizing Washington. Photograph. Library of Congress, LC-USZ62-79351.

32. *Street Grading*, ca. 1873. Lithograph. Washingtoniana Division, D.C. Public Library.

Washington is fast becoming one vast garden in which the boundary line between city and county is almost entirely wiped out. . . . This parking, with its variously shaped terraces, now forms one of the most prominent, pleasing, and distinguishing features of our national capital. . . .

—Adolf Cluss, 1873

33. *Tree planting, Connecticut Avenue, North of Farragut Square, NW*, ca. 1874. Photograph. Historical Society of Washington, D.C.

34. *Reception for President Grant, Alexander Shepherd's House*, 1876. Lithograph. Library of Congress, LC-USZ62-4522.

35. *Shepherd's Row, designed by Cluss on the fashionable Farragut Square.* Lithograph. *New Harper's Monthly*, April 1875.

From the Renaissance, this golden age of art in Italy springs from the pervading spirit of the design of Franklin School Building. . . . [It will] diffuse good taste among the people at large, but pre-eminently among the growing generation.

—Adolf Cluss, 1869

36. *Franklin School, Thirteenth and K Streets, NW,* 1871. Lithograph. Historical Society of Washington, D.C.

37. *Alexander Graham Bell,* testing a device called a photophone at Franklin School, 1879. Lithograph. Charles Sumner School Museum and Archives.

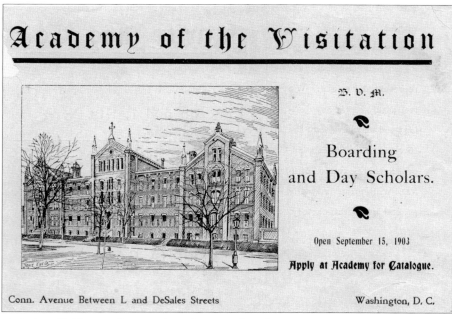

38. *Academy of the Visitation, Connecticut Avenue between L and DeSales Streets, NW,* 1903. Advertisement. Historical Society of Washington, D.C.

39. *Franklin Terrace Row Houses, K Street, between Thirteenth and Fourteenth Streets, NW, 1890.* Photograph. Historical Society of Washington, D.C.

41. *Varied Modes of Transportation, 1890.* Watercolor. Historical Society of Washington, D.C.

[Cluss] has done more than anyone else to foster an improved style of private architecture in the Nation's Capital.

—*New York Daily Tribune,* October 26, 1876

40. *Spencer F. Baird Residence, 1445 Massachusetts Avenue, NW, ca. 1925,* photograph. Historical Society of Washington, D.C.

42. *Market Place and Center Market, Pennsylvania Avenue between Seventh and Ninth Streets, NW, ca. 1885.* Photograph. Washingtoniana Division, D.C. Public Library.

Pennsylvania Avenue in the nineteenth century became the "nation's main street." . . . Significantly, at 8th Street was the Center Market, an imposing Victorian public building that gave that section of the Avenue the feeling of a bazaar every day.

—Robert A. Peck, Member, Commission of Fine Arts , 1995

43. *Center Market Vendor, Constitution Avenue, NW,* 1903. Lithograph. Historical Society of Washington, D.C.

44. *Railroad Station, Sixth Street, SW,* 1880s. Photograph. Library of Congress, LC-USZ62-7160.

Cluss at the Height of His Career

A modernized, Romanesque style of architecture was adopted for the new building in order to keep up a relationship with the Smithsonian building. . . . The external architecture is based upon the general arrangement of the interior, and shows plainly the prominence of the four naves and the careful management of the light for the central portion of the building.

—Adolf Cluss, 1880

45. *Building Committee for the National Museum at Construction Site, National Mall*, 1880. Photograph. From left to right: General Montgomery Meigs, General William T. Sherman, Peter Parker, Secretary Samuel F. Baird, Adolf Cluss, William J. Rhees, and Daniel Leech. Smithsonian Archives, Smithsonian Institution.

46. *President Garfield's Inauguration Ball, National Museum*, 1881. Sketch. Library of Congress, LC-USZ62-7160.

47. *Dance Card, President Garfield's Inaugural Ball Program*, 1881. Papers of William M. Evarts, Manuscript Division, Library of Congress.

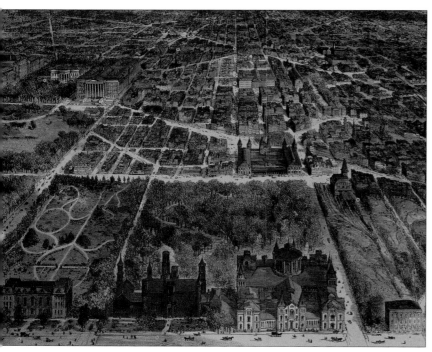

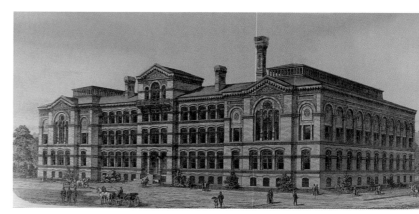

49. *Army Medical Museum and Library*, 1886. Photograph. *American Architect and Building News*, January 18, 1886.

48. *View of the National Mall*, 1881. Three of Cluss's major buildings are visible: the Agriculture Department (front left), the National Museum (front right), and Center Market (middle right). Cluss also oversaw renovation work to the Smithsonian Castle (front center). His Army Medical Museum would be built five years later at the site on the far front right. Lithograph. Albert Small Collection.

As a practitioner, Adolf Cluss had an enviable record. Few other architects have had a comparable, let alone a greater impact, on the shape and character of Washington. Certainly no architect has made an equivalent contribution in both the federal sphere and the local one—the latter encompassing public and private-sector buildings alike.

—Richard Longstreth, Professor of American Studies, 2005

50. *Telegraph Room, National Museum*, 1886. Photograph. Smithsonian Archives, Smithsonian Institution.

51. *Portland Flats, Thomas Circle*, 1950s. Photograph. Historical Society of Washington, D.C.

City Expansion: Suburbs, Parks, and New Technologies

52. *Construction of the Library of Congress*, 1880s, architects Smithmeyer and Pelz. Photograph. Library of Congress, LC-USZ62-73540.

53. *Sun Building, F Street between Thirteenth and Fourteenth Streets, NW*, 1887, architect Alfred B. Mullett. Washingtoniana Division, D.C. Public Library.

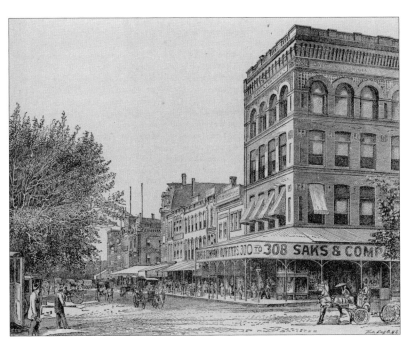

54. *Seventh Street at Pennsylvania Avenue, NW*, 1890. Etching. Washingtoniana Division, D.C. Public Library.

55. *Major Christian Fleetwood and Family*, ca. 1908. Photograph. Washingtoniana Division, D.C. Public Library.

Architecture is defined as the material expression of the wants, facilities, and sentiments of its age. . . . A return to the unarticulated mode of expression resorted to in the earliest stages of society would be a declaration of bankruptcy on the part of the taste of the age.

—Adolf Cluss, 1876

56. *Connecticut Avenue Residences between N Street and Dupont Circle, NW, 1890s.* Lithograph. Washingtoniana Division, D.C. Public Library.

57. *Pebble Arch Bridge, Rock Creek Park, 1902.* Photograph. Commission of Fine Arts.

58. *View of East Potomac Park toward Hain's Point, 1902.* Cartoon. Washingtoniana Division, D.C. Public Library.

59. *Anacostia Suburban Houses, 1885.* Photograph. Historical Society of Washington, D.C.

[The future leads to] a destiny which is determined by the progressive spirit of the age, and which cannot be retarded for any length of time; it involves the interests of all, both high and low.

—Adolf Cluss, 1875

60. *Pennsylvania Avenue near Fifteenth Street, NW, ca. 1900. Photograph. Washingtoniana Division, D.C. Public Library.*

61. *First Automobile in Washington, Pennsylvania Avenue at Twenty-first Street, NW, 1896. Photograph. Historical Society of Washington, D.C.*

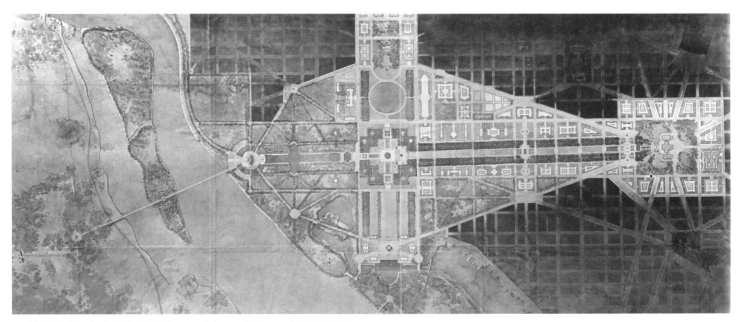

62. *McMillan Plan for the Mall, 1902. Drawing. Library of Congress, LC-D4-33481.*

63. *Federal Triangle, between Pennsylvania and Constitution Avenues, NW, ca. 1950.* Photograph. Washingtoniana Division, D.C. Public Library.

64. *Portland Flats, Thomas Circle, 1880–1962, replaced by nondescript, contemporary buildings as shown below.* Photograph. Historical Society of Washington, D.C.

65. *Residence Inn, Thomas Circle, 2004.* Photograph by Sabina W. Dugan.

66. *Aerial View of Thomas Circle, 1980s.* Photograph. Library of Congress, LC-HABS-640-2.

The work accomplished by Adolf Cluss . . . is doomed to disappear before long, all the more because it is mainly to be found in Washington, and for the most part, ill accords with the monumentally architectural character that the city is so rapidly acquiring.

—*American Architect and Building News,* August 5, 1905

67. *Army Medical Museum and Library, National Mall*, 1886–1969. Photograph. National Museum of Health and Medicine.

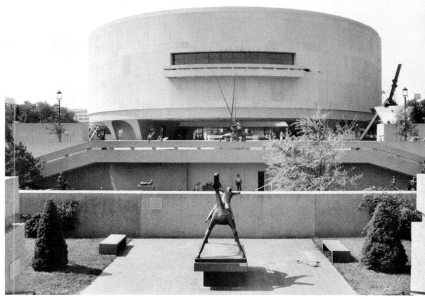

68. *Hirshhorn Museum, National Mall*, in 1986. Built in the early 1970s, the museum replaced Cluss's Army Medical Museum at left. Photograph. Smithsonian Archives, Smithsonian Institution.

69. *Agriculture Department, National Mall*, 1867–1921. Photograph. Washingtoniana Division, D.C. Public Library.

70. *Agriculture Department, National Mall*, 1980s. These buildings replaced Cluss's old Agriculture Building at left. Photograph. Library of Congress, LC-USZ62-22791.

I have always thought and am borne out by plenty ancient and modern precedents, that it is appropriate to study the progress of taste in a nation by the monuments and edifices we leave to succeeding generations.

—Adolf Cluss, 1879

Preservation

Buildings are among the most valuable records of a culture. If the play of history is to be seen as continual change, then individual buildings provide physical records—or at least significant clues—that can help us understand something of those who came before us. In turn, what we do to a building will help those who come after to understand us.

—Hugh Howard, *The Preservationist's Progress*, 1991

71. *Great Hall, Charles Sumner School*, 1979. Photograph. Charles Sumner School Museum and Archives.

72. *Charles Sumner School, Seventeenth and M Streets, NW*, 1986. The building was renovated for use as a museum and archives in the 1980s. Photograph. Charles Sumner School Museum and Archives.

73. *Fate of Nineteenth-Century Townhouses, Cluss's old neighborhood, Second Street, NW, 1980.* Photograph. Historical Society of Washington, D.C.

What one never finds in a nineteenth-century city is evidence of attempts to obliterate the past entirely and proceed as if the world had been created yesterday, like our recent efforts at comprehensive development.

—Donald J. Olsen, *The City as a Work of Art*, 1986

The current mood of reactionary preservationism . . . makes us better able to enter into the thought processes of the builders and designers of cities before 1914. We are discovering that they knew how to create not only a more beautiful, but a more livable, urban environment than we can today.

—Donald J. Olsen, *The City as a Work of Art*, 1986

74. *Restored Row Houses, Mintwood Place, NW, 2005.* Photograph by Joseph L. Browne.

ADOLF CLUSS A Family Album

JOSEPH L. BROWNE, SABINA W. DUGAN, *and* HARRIET LESSER

1. The Cluss Family, unidentified woman holding the Cluss's son Adolph S., Rosa and Adolf Cluss with their two daughters, Lillian and Anita, ca. 1864.

Lillie Cluss, geb. Jan. 13 1860.
Photogr. 1871.

2. Lillian Cluss, first daughter of Adolf and Rosa, 1871.

Carl Cluss, geb. Aug. 1865
Photo. 1871.

3. Carl Cluss, second son of Adolf and Rosa, 1871.

4. Rosa Schmidt Cluss, wife of Adolf, 1872.

5. Adolph S. Cluss, first son of Adolf and Rosa, 1871.

6. Anita Cluss, second daughter of Adolf and Rosa, 1871.

7. Flora Cluss, third daughter of Adolf and Rosa, with unidentified woman, possibly a nanny, 1871.

8. Anita Cluss, Washington, 1890.

9. Carl Cluss, Washington, 1893.

10. Adolph S. Cluss, Washington, 1885.

11. Lillian Cluss Daw, Washington, 1890.

12. Henriette de Millas, her mother Sophie de Millas, Adolf Cluss, Julie de Millas, and Adolf's nephew, Hermann de Millas, Heidelberg, 1898.

13. Flora Cluss Lathrop and her husband Henry Lathrop, Japan, 1905.

14. Carl de Millas (Adolf Cluss's nephew), his daughters Sophie and Anna, and a family friend, Switzerland, 1902.

5. House of Henriette Cluss Faisst, Heilbronn, 1900.

16. Henriette Cluss Faisst, Adolf's sister, Heilbronn, 1900.

7. House of August Cluss, Heilbronn, 1910.

18. August Cluss, Adolf's brother, Heilbronn, before 1887.

19. Cluss Brewery, owned by Adolf's brother, August, ca. 1900. Postcard.

20. Sons of August Cluss and nephews of Adolf: Alfred Cluss, Eugen Cluss with his wife Ottlie and their son Werner, and Adolf Cluss and his wife, Elizabeth, Heilbronn, ca. 1903.

Photographs 1–3 and 5–7, 14, and 21,
Stadtarchiv Heilbronn, courtesy of Rudolf
de Millas; no. 4, oil on canvas by Henry Ulke,
1872, photographed by Hugh Talman, 2004,
courtesy Smithsonian Institution;
nos. 8–13, courtesy William S. Shacklette;
nos. 15, 17, and 19, Stadtarchiv Heilbronn;
nos. 16, 18, and 20, Stadtarchiv Heilbronn,
courtesy Peter Cluss.

21. Adolf Cluss, Washington, 1900.

PART 2 An Architect of Modern Washington

Adolf Cluss, the World, and Washington

RICHARD LONGSTRETH

As a practitioner, Adolf Cluss had an enviable record. Few other architects have had a comparable, let alone a greater impact on the shape and character of Washington. Certainly no architect has made an equivalent contribution in *both* the federal sphere and the local one—the latter encompassing public and private-sector buildings alike. Cluss was also the consummate survivor. Many architects who secured contracts for major federal buildings during the nineteenth century endured savage assaults on their professional integrity, sometimes to the detriment of their careers. George Hadfield, Robert Mills, Thomas Ustick Walter, and Smithmeyer & Pelz were all subjected to such humiliation. Cluss's reputation remained unscathed during the nearly thirty years he engaged in independent practice, despite involvement in a government scandal. As an architect and public servant, he played a key role in transforming Washington during the Gilded Age. Cluss operated in a fluid, international framework, drawing from a range of past and present European as well as American sources. Yet the local context is as important as an international one in understanding his legacy. The nation's capital helped shape Cluss,

just as he brought a fresh, vigorous approach to recasting its environment.

When Cluss came to Washington in 1849, the city was not quite a *tabula rasa* but was still in embryo, with a primitive infrastructure, a weak and seasonal economic base, meager amenities, and few legal means of self-determination. Moreover, Washington lacked an established corps of locally oriented professionals, including architects. On the other hand, professional expertise could be found to a considerable degree in various agencies of the federal government, which made the city a training ground that had few rivals on this side of the Atlantic before the Civil War. Cluss soon became a part of this sphere, first with the U. S. Coast Survey, the oldest scientific agency in the federal government and the locus for attaining an accurate picture of the nation's topography. Cluss then worked in the ordnance laboratory at the Navy Yard, another important center for precision engineering. In 1855, he joined the Treasury Department's Bureau of Construction under the aegis of architect Ammi Young, where he appears to have been responsible for overseeing the design of federal buildings that were among the country's most technologically advanced in their use of structure and systems.[1] Coupled with his training in Germany, Cluss's Washington experiences made him unusually well prepared for his field at that time. In Washington, almost no architects outside the federal sector were practicing in the 1850s.[2] Cluss may have secured government employment out of necessity, but he

Phillips Row, 1302–1314 Connecticut Avenue. Designed in 1878 by Cluss with his partner Paul Schulze, these fashionable rowhouses set a tone and precedent that less well-known Washington builders emulated throughout the city. Photograph, ca. 1929. Washingtoniana Division, District of Columbia Public Library.

could have moved to any number of other cities where the opportunities were far greater in the private sector. Washington may have indeed been Cluss's choice of an adopted city because of the expertise he could gain there in pertinent technical realms. Cluss considered himself both an architect and an engineer. The technical realm was a major concern in itself, not just a means by which to realize an abstractly conceived design, but as a basis for design development and resolution. This outlook reflected the way in which architecture was taught in Germany but also was consistent with the approach taken with one of the first professional architects to work in Washington, Benjamin Henry Latrobe, who, Cluss took pains to mention, "was educated in Germany."[3]

At the outset of his practice in the early 1860s, Cluss was in an unusual position. He was in certain respects a "pioneer" architect—the first well-trained professional in the community focusing on local work. Previously, most buildings in Washington designed by architects came from those who had moved to the city under federal contract, such as Latrobe, Mills, and Walter, or by others who received commissions locally, while maintaining their office elsewhere, most notably James Renwick of New York. Army engineers also had prepared plans for some buildings and other structures. The majority of the city's fabric, however, was conceived as well as executed by builders.[4] Cluss's emergence as an architect in private practice thus paralleled the establishment of Gideon Shyrock in Louisville, Kentucky (1835), Charles Heard in Cleveland (1847), John van Osdel in Chicago (1837), George I. Barnett in St. Louis (1839), or Asa B. Cross in Kansas City (1858)—all of whom made major, sustained contributions to their respective cities.[5] Most such pioneers grew out of the artisan tradition. With over fifteen years of education and experience, Cluss was unusually well prepared to work on his own in the 1860s. Not until the mid-1870s did a critical mass of well-trained architects establish a permanent beachhead, and not until the following decade was the profession firmly ensconced in Washington.[6] Even then, no other locally based architect came close to matching Cluss's imprint on the fabric of the burgeoning capital.

During much of his career, Cluss secured associates who bolstered his practice's stature. He entered into partnership with another German émigré, Joseph W. von Kammerhueber, who had worked on the Capitol extensions under Walter, but had to leave practice in 1868 owing to personal problems. To enter the competition for the Library of Congress, Cluss associated with the New York–based Schulze & Schoen, which had placed in competitions for the federal building in New York and the state house in Albany. Following Schoen's death, the German-born, Viennese-trained Paul Schulze allied with Cluss in a partnership that lasted from April 1878 until June 1889. Schulze was somewhat mercurial in temperament and an artist in inclination, complementing his more even-handed, technically prone partner.[7] Even at an early stage of his independent career, Cluss's standing is suggested by his election in 1867 as a "Fellow"—then the designation for senior members—of the American Institute of Architects (AIA), concurrent with its reorganization to address the cause of professionalism nationally. Cluss took an active role in the AIA, whose membership was concentrated in larger cities. As late as 1881, he was one of only three Washington architects to belong. Six years later, he joined a few colleagues to establish the Washington chapter of the AIA, serving as its second president.[8]

As Washington's pioneer professional architect, Cluss enjoyed unusual opportunities for patronage. In contrast to most cities where major architectural commissions were closely tied to the business community, in Washington the major client, directly or otherwise, remained the federal government. While Cluss was never a federal architect per se, he received numerous commissions for municipal buildings, which fell under congressional purview, as well as for a growing array of specialized federal buildings. During the territorial government of 1871 to 1874, Cluss exercised considerable influence through the Board of Public Works. Combined with other prominent residential and institutional projects, this output had a decisive role in the transformation of Washington into an urban center of consequence during the decades after the Civil War.

Washington's rise as a city was closely tied to the Republican commitment to ensuring it would remain the nation's capital and be developed as a model city.[9] Richard Wallach Jr., a political independent who was mayor from

1861 to 1868, provided an important foundation for this effort when he instituted professional fire and police departments and measures for a much-improved public school system. For the first time, substantial investments began to be made by Congress in long-neglected municipal facilities. Cluss launched his career with what was later named the Wallach School (1862–64), first product of the mayor's reorganized educational system.[10] Between 1869 and 1875, Cluss designed seven other schools, creating a citywide network in the process. His services were also secured for rebuilding Center Market (1871–78) into an immense compound capable of addressing the needs of the swelling population and for the new Eastern Market (1872–73) as a model facility for another rapidly expanding residential area.

When President Ulysses S. Grant appointed Cluss to the Board of Public Works in October 1872, that body was fully engaged in its spectacularly ambitious program of transforming Washington into a modern city under the aegis of Alexander Shepherd, who spearheaded the board and later became governor in the territorial regime Congress had instituted in June 1871. Street grading and paving, the extension of water and sewer lines, the establishment of comprehensive building regulations, and the planting of street borders and other public spaces were all undertaken by the new territorial government. Work performed could be as poorly executed as it was swift, yet the ultimate change was remarkable by any standard of the day and created a matrix upon which the city would continue to grow for decades. What had been frequently derided as one of the least prepossessing centers in the nation was now beginning to seem more like a capital.[11] Cluss's responsibilities expanded two months later when he was made chief engineer of the city. Although he was dismissed from the board eighteen months later, following his congressional testimony on the Shepherd regime's overspending and misappropriation of funds, Cluss appears to have had a significant impact on public works while on the board. He took pride in clarifying the intent and in enforcing the provisions of the city's first comprehensive building regulations, which had been adopted just before his appointment. He worked energetically on other aspects of Shepherd's plan as well.[12]

Cluss also was proud of the appearance of the board's improvements. In his 1873 report to Congress, he expressed enthusiasm for the "verdure-bordered footways by the sides of the wide streets . . . [that have] been developed to such an extent that Washington, beyond its business streets, is fast becoming one vast garden, in which the boundary line between city and country is almost entirely wiped out. . . . This parking [i.e., the planted space between the curb and building line], with its variously shaped terraces, now forms one of the most prominent, pleasing, and distinguished features of the national capital."[13]

The effect was distinctly urban, conceived by Army engineer Montgomery Meigs and inspired by the Unter-den-Linden in Berlin and Champs-Élysées in Paris.[14] Like Meigs and his colleagues in the Army Corps of Engineers, Cluss viewed technical and aesthetic improvements as going hand-in-hand. The Germanic origins of the scheme, at least in part, were no doubt also a source of satisfaction. In fact, ongoing civic projects in central European cities appear to have been just as important a source for recasting Washington as the often celebrated transformation of Second Empire Paris. No other city in the United States could boast of a more sweeping plan or body of technicians to implement it. In Chicago, the extensive park and boulevard system begun before and accelerated after the great fire of 1871 covered more extensive territory, but did not permeate the city's fabric the way Washington's did. The contemporaneous development of Boston's Back Bay was far more ambitious from a technical standpoint, but limited to a single sector.[15] In Washington, the matrix had been provided citywide by the L'Enfant Plan of 1791; the challenge lay not in breaking from the existing pattern, but in realizing its potential.

Cluss pursued stylishness along with technical proficiency. Residential work undertaken while he was on the Board of Public Works and thereafter helped set the tone for buildings commensurate with the new landscape. Cluss's lavish house (1873) facing Dupont Circle for Senator William Morris Stewart, who was a key backer of Shepherd in the quest for public improvements, helped set the tone of the new mansions that were emerging along Connecticut Avenue northwest from Lafayette Square (see page 125). An equally

Fig. 1. Row houses, 1500 block T Street, NW, Washington, ca. early 1880s. Photograph by author, 1970.

potent symbol of new residential development was the contemporaneous row of three grand dwellings Cluss designed for Shepherd, Hallet Kilbourn (a Shepherd associate heavily engaged in real estate speculation), and himself close to the southeastern end of Connecticut at K Street (see page 81).[16] Both buildings were pronounced departures from the boxy massing that had previously characterized most residential architecture, introducing turrets, multistoried bays and, in the case of Shepherd's Row, a suave three-dimensional plasticity quite in keeping with work of the period in major European centers. Having promulgated the city's new building regulations, which restricted the use of projecting bays, Cluss now aggressively took advantage of the exceptions for which that document provided, creating an important precedent for local building in the process.

Perhaps even more influential was the speculative row of seven houses (1878) for attorney Samuel L. Phillips on Connecticut Avenue between Stewart's and Shepherd's piles (see page 102). The idea of a range of narrow unit fronts broken into a rhythmic sequence of intricately molded parts was

not entirely new. Grant's Row, constructed seven years earlier on East Capitol Street, had wide projecting fronts from which extended angled bays.[17] But Cluss fashioned the four-story bays of Phillips Row in a far less brittle way, taking full advantage of the variations in form that brick construction permitted, making the material itself an essential contributor to the decorative effect. The prominence of Phillips Row, and perhaps the prestige of its architect, appear to have made it influential in the evolving vernacular of middle-class row houses in Washington. Largely the creation of small-scale, speculative builders, this work began to show a decisively more sculptural manipulation of form through the use of full-height brick bays by 1880 (fig. 1).[18] In the new precincts, especially, this astylar mode, bereft of overt historical references, at once decorative and appearing to be rational as expression, gave the urban landscape a vibrant character that was particularly responsive to the spaces created by the diagonal intersections of the L'Enfant Plan, but was also effective along the many blocks of uninterrupted grid in between. Cluss not only helped implement the new infrastructure that distinguished Reconstruction Washington, but set the tone for many of the dwellings that now fronted the streets.

An agenda of transformation was equally evident in Cluss's public buildings. Toward that end, he exhibited a penchant for responding to new or changing functional needs commensurate with the swift evolution of the modern metropolis and in so doing helped set new standards nationally as well as locally. Schools were central to this contribution. In his design for the Wallach School, Cluss went beyond the institutional norm—established to a significant degree in the 1850s by Philadelphia architect Samuel Sloan—to create a building that at once had more of a civic presence and was more commodious in terms of light, ventilation, acoustics, and space (see page 78).[19] A few years after the school's completion, educators on a reconnaissance tour from Boston, the epicenter of the then still nascent quest for comprehensive public education, pronounced it as the handsomest they had seen, while the projected Franklin School (1864–69), "promises to be unsurpassed in the country." Strategically sited, facing the square from which it got its name, Franklin School at once became a source of municipal pride and a destination for visitors (fig. 2). In a rare account of his own work, Cluss noted that the exterior "assumes an air of importance not commonly accorded to brick buildings," adding that "the pervading spirit of the design" springs "[f]rom this golden age of art in Italy [i.e., the Renaissance]." Much of its effect, he continued, emanates from "a wise sobriety . . . in the use of modest, severe, and delicate ornaments, coupled with a scrupulous care to attain that seemly comeliness, that elegant exterior, which is powerful to . . . good taste among the people at large."[20]

While not as ambitious as Franklin, Cluss's other school buildings were consistent in their decorous appearance and state-of-the-art facilities.[21] The architect's concern with economy—in cost, but also in design resolution, where every component served a clear purpose, where utilitarian and expressive qualities were integrated—was fully evident in these buildings, which often stood in sharp contrast to the small, sometimes poorly kept, wood-frame houses around them (see page 152). Equally striking was the Sumner School (1871–72), the flagship of new instructional centers for blacks (fig. 3).[22] A byproduct of an unfortunate separate-but-equal approach to education, the building nevertheless was probably the most distinguished example of its kind in the country for many years, one to which some supporters hoped both races would wish to attend.

Center Market—a business venture that involved Shepherd, but one enabled by Congress—likewise propelled the capital city from having one of the most antiquated public markets to enjoying one of the most advanced in the United States (see page 84). The building was conceived to be unrivaled in size and amenities, with extensive provisions for wholesale as well as retail concessionaires. Once in operation, Center Market indeed became a symbol nationally of the regeneration of the public market during the Gilded Age.[23] Just as with his schools, Cluss was careful to ensure that the satellite unit he designed, the municipally owned Eastern Market, upheld the same high standards. Eastern Market featured abundant light and ventilation and flexible space. Light-weight iron bar trusses spanned the roof clear across (see page 166).

Matching his accomplishments in the public realm was the scheme Cluss prepared for the first major apartment building in Washington, the Portland (1880–83) (fig. 4). Built for a New York investor, it hardly resembled counterparts there or elsewhere in the United States. Sited on a gore lot, facing Thomas Circle in a prestigious residential area, the plan was wholly oriented to the open spaces beyond the lot's perimeter. Contemporary accounts emphasized how it lacked the usual light courts and airshafts; all thirty-nine of its copious apartments boasted sweeping external views.[24] To enhance those prospects, Cluss relied on multistoried window bays, just as he had done at Phillips Row, but here more ornate and culminating in a tower at the apex. The result was a lavish integration of form and embellishment on a scale seldom matched locally or elsewhere in the country.[25] As a maverick advancing change in architectural program, Cluss somewhat paralleled Richard Morris Hunt in New York, who during the same years set important precedents in the design of libraries, apartment houses, and other building types.[26] But Cluss had the advantage of securing work of exceptional prominence in a much smaller city. Moreover, he had few

Fig. 2. Franklin School, 13th and K streets, NW, Washington, 1867–69, Adolf Cluss, architect. Photograph by author, 1994.

Fig. 3. Sumner School, M and 17th streets, NW, Washington, 1871–72, Adolf Cluss, architect. Photograph by author, 2004.

serious competitors, while enjoying exposure to an international audience of both inhabitants and visitors.

At an early date, Cluss seems to have been aware of the broader implications his distinctive buildings could possess. He pursued an approach in which image no less than accommodations might set a new course for architecture. His first major federal commission, housing the recently formed Department of Agriculture (1867–68), was an emphatic deviation from the monumental classicism that had characterized all previous work of comparable stature in Washington (see pages 78, 91). The Agriculture building's soft tapestry of ornamentation, with seemingly unstructural brick, was also a rejection of the plain, solid masonry masses of federal buildings nationwide on which he had worked under Young's direction (fig. 5). The edifice also could not have been more different in effect than that of the equally eclectic, yet some-

what mechanical, interpretation of Second Empire classicism that Alfred Mullett was developing as a new paradigm for large public buildings, most conspicuously with the State, War, and Navy Building (1871–88) a few blocks away (fig. 6).[27] Budgetary constraints may have contributed as well. But within the context of Cluss's architectural endeavors citywide over a number of years, nurturing new expressive forms for federal architecture—one that carried no overtones of the monarchal power that he had spurned in the 1840s—appears to have been the underlying motivation. Some precedent existed for his endeavor with Renwick's Corcoran Gallery of Art (1859–61), prominently situated near the White House (fig. 7). Yet the effect Cluss attained is quite different, with a more fluid manipulation of surfaces in contrast to the rather stiff application of ornament found on the gallery. Subsequently, Cluss became more rigorous and robust

Fig. 4. The Portland apartment house, Vermont Avenue and 14th Street, NW, Washington, 1880–81, 1882–83, Cluss & Schulze, architects; demolished 1962. From *American Architect and Building News* (April 12, 1884), plate.

Fig. 5. U.S. Customhouse and Post Office, Market and 16th streets, Wheeling, West Virginia, 1856–59, Ammi B. Young, architect. Photograph by author, 1995.

in his modeling of form, yet the idea of an intricate, often polychromatic, layering of brick, augmented by picturesque silhouettes anchored by symmetrical compositions, remained characteristic to his work.

A decade later, Cluss & Schulze won the competition to design the National Museum (now the Arts and Industries building), which would relieve the overcrowded Smithsonian of its exhibits and add new ones brought from the recent Centennial Exposition in Philadelphia (fig. 8).[28] When it opened in 1881, the museum ranked among the first purpose-built, fully realized, permanent facilities of its kind in the United States. The closest counterpart was Hermann Joseph Schwarzmann's Art Gallery (Memorial Hall) (1874–76), built for the Centennial and one of the most fully developed Beaux-Arts institutional buildings in the country at that time (fig. 9). The pursuit of national collections of art had been developing for some years abroad and, without success, at home, but the function of the new Washington establishment came closer to that of a natural

history museum, such as those at Oxford (1855–60) and Edinburgh (1861–89) and planned for London and New York.[29] Cluss no doubt looked to these sources and many others as well, but his scheme represented a significant departure in concept and execution, integrating an innovative plan with sophisticated technical solutions and arresting expressive qualities to create what was arguably the capstone of his career.

For the museum's layout, Cluss adapted a Beaux-Arts, cross-in-square plan that by then was a mainstay in the planning of major governmental and institutional buildings internationally, including the two most ambitious museum projects in this country, Memorial Hall and the approximately concurrent plan for the American Museum of Natural History in New York, designed by Calvert Vaux and Jacob Wrey Mould. Cluss's decisive break from such precedent was to connect all the encompassed spaces. Generally, the "residue" spaces of these overlapping geometries were left outside as sources of light and ventilation, as with the largely

Fig. 6. State, War, and Navy Building (Old Executive Office Building), Pennsylvania Avenue, 17th and E streets, NW, Washington, 1871–88, Alfred B. Mullett, architect. Photograph by author, 2001.

Fig. 7. Corcoran Gallery of Art (Renwick Gallery, Smithsonian Institution), Pennsylvania Avenue and 17th Street, NW, Washington, 1859–61, James Renwick, architect. Photograph by author, 1970.

unrealized plan for the Natural History Museum. At Memorial Hall, on the other hand, Schwarzmann treated the front wings as open arcades, while minimizing spatial connections within to create extensive wall areas for the display of paintings. The pervasive openness of the National Museum internally is more akin to that of exhibition buildings, including the Crystal Palace in New York (1853), which Schulze had designed with a previous partner, and Schwarzmann's Main Exhibition Building and Machinery Hall at Philadelphia (figs. 10, 11).[30] Yet the pervasive use of exposed iron structure and glazing in such temporary shelters created a very different atmosphere than that which Cluss pursued on the Mall, where fireproof walls were a paramount concern. Cluss also eschewed the prevailing trend in British natural history museums, where skylights enveloped

Fig. 8. National Museum (Arts and Industries building, Smithsonian Institution), Independence Avenue between 8th and 10th streets, SW, Washington, 1879–81, Cluss & Schulze, architects. Photograph by author, 1970.

Fig. 9. Art Gallery (Memorial Hall), Centennial Exposition, North Concourse at 42d Street, Fairmont Park, Philadelphia, 1874–76, Hermann Joseph Schwarzmann, architect. Photograph by author, 1985.

nave- or gallerylike spaces. Instead, he pursued a balance, using clerestory and monitor windows to flood the exhibition spaces with diffused natural light, further tempered by double glazing with etched exterior panes.

In its character, the sequence of space possesses a clear hierarchy and a dynamic tension. The once lavishly polychromed rotunda exudes basilican grandeur, tying the array of spaces at the core (fig. 12). From this massive centerpiece extend arms more suggestive of utilitarian halls—a great market or railroad shed, perhaps (fig. 13). Both allusions are evoked in the spaces beyond, the ensemble unified not only by the omnipresent parade of masonry arches, varying in size, but also by the parasol-like, light-weight iron trusses and roofs above. Throughout, the interaction of art and industry—both of which the building was to display—is at once subtly and dramatically conveyed. This duality is evident on the exterior as well, where motifs associated with traditional religious architecture are organized in a manner that is both a rationalist reflection of internal needs and a vibrant mural of particularized elements, as if a giant machine had been frozen into art.

Fig. 10. National Museum, architects' rendering of interior, 1878; modified in execution. Smithsonian Institution.

Fig. 11. Main Exhibition Building, Centennial Exposition, Main Concourse at 42d Street, Fairmount Park, Philadelphia, 1874–76, Hermann Joseph Schwarzmann, architect; demolished 1877. Interior view. From *Frank Leslie's Historical Register of the United States Centennial Exposition*, 1876, 120–21.

The aplomb with which Cluss used a spectrum of historical and contemporary sources at the National Museum reflects the fact that, like most architects of his generation, he considered a wide range of precedent as a point of departure for developing his designs. During the initial years of practice, he worked in numerous popular modes, drawing from examples in France and England as well as from various German states and his adopted country. Soon, however, his

Fig. 12. National Museum, rotunda. Photograph by author, 2004.

Fig. 13. National Museum, west arm. Photograph by author, 2004.

approach became more synthetic and tied to expressing functional attributes of the scheme. Yet he resisted formulas. The model exhibition galleries of the rebuilt Patent Office Building (1878–79, 1883–85), for example, while ostensibly similar in purpose to those of the National Museum, were imbued with a far more ceremonial character, perhaps in deference to the neoclassical exterior, which Cluss admired (fig. 14).[31] Even in his schools, there is a refusal to rely on standardization, then common for that building type, and a method to which he had gained considerable exposure while working on the design of federal buildings at the Treasury Department.[32] The development of a strong personal style does not appear to have been as important as refining a rationalist approach. Sound construction, abundant natural light, state-of-the-art building systems, good acoustics, and a clear, purposeful disposition of space consistently seem to have been the basis upon which a design was generated,

however varied the mode or extravagant the appearance. In this regard, his German training was probably reinforced by the writings of Gottfried Semper, whose *Der Stil* (1860, 1863) had an enormous influence on many German American as well as other architects of the era.[33]

Throughout his work, Cluss avoided monumentality and mannerism—both common traits among contemporaries. If in eschewing the former he was rejecting the mode that Mullett propagated as a paradigm for major public buildings nationwide, in spurning the latter, he defied the more characteristically English pursuit of willful expression, which was developed with particular intensity by Frank Furness in Philadelphia but was also pursued by prominent architects in New York, Boston, and other major cities.[34] Cluss was selective, while looking to the world, as it were, for inspiration, and it was no doubt on the international stage that he wished to be judged. He was proud of his German background and

Fig. 14. United States Patent Office Building (National Museum of American Art and National Portrait Gallery, Smithsonian Institution), F, G, 7th and 9th streets, NW, Washington, rebuilt exhibition galleries, 1878–79, 1883–85, Cluss & Schulze, architects. Photograph by author, 1984.

continued to be influenced by the concrete examples and theoretical postulations of German colleagues. Yet rather than considering himself a German architect or a German American architect, Cluss more likely saw himself as a *modern* architect, employing the best ideas and technologies Western culture had to offer, creating an architecture appropriate to an advancing, but still adolescent, democracy. Washington was the optimal place to so practice because it was the nation's capital, but especially because it was, itself, a new, struggling place, bereft of strong traditions, in contrast to larger East Coast cities—a place where a new, modern architecture could take hold and flourish.

By 1888, Cluss probably had more experience in designing museums than any other American architect. Besides the National Museum was his reconstruction work on the

Smithsonian Building (1865–67, 1883–84, 1887–88), the Army Medical Museum (1885–88) (see pages 86, 91) and the extensive exhibition spaces in the Agriculture building as well as those of the reconstructed Patent Office building.[35] Only Robert Mills rivaled the extent of his imprint on the federal presence in Washington. No designer since L'Enfant and prior to the members of the Senate Park Commission had greater impact on shaping the National Mall. Cluss not only participated in the transformation of the city's infrastructure, he set important standards for its mansions and more pervasive row houses, whose neighborhoods were punctuated by his schools. To this repertoire were added numerous churches, commercial buildings, and other edifices of almost every type. Locally he had pioneered in almost every conceivable realm of his field.

Cluss's imprint on Washington was omnipresent at a formative stage of the city's development, but was also remarkably short-lived. It was not his kind of rationalism that endured, but rather that rooted in French academic practice, which first gained widespread acceptance in the United States through the brilliantly original interpretations of Henry Hobson Richardson. In 1890, when Cluss retired from practice and the Richardson legacy was at its peak, the former's recent work must have seemed a bit stodgy. Within a few years, as a new generation embraced a more formal, classically inspired historicism, the Cluss portfolio would seem unfortunate. Not only had taste in architecture markedly changed, so too had many programmatic demands and technology. The museums, schools, apartment houses, and other building types he had taken pride to develop in the most up-to-date fashion now had substantially different sets of requirements. The authors of the Senate Park Commission Plan (1901–2) called for the eradication of four of Cluss's major buildings as well as the original Smithsonian building. With that plan, Washington became a national focus for a very different kind of architecture and urbanism—one generated by designers in New York, Chicago, and Boston and avidly supported by colleagues on the local front.[36] Following Cluss's death in 1905, a lengthy lead editorial in the *American Architect and Building News* was respectful, but fell far short of a tribute. The legacy of Cluss and other architects of his generation was "doomed to disappear before long" in large part "because the artistic worth of the work itself cannot compare with the work that can now be done by better-trained successors."[37] The editors had known Cluss since their magazine's founding almost thirty years before, and they thus especially regretted his passing. They no doubt felt their remarks to be charitable toward a career that yielded what many readers would have by then considered the nadir of taste. The pioneer architect had fallen far to the rear of his profession.

In the progressive era, the red-brick city of Cluss's era was a thing to be purged and replaced by a white city of marble and limestone. That view persisted into the mid-twentieth century. Only in the past few decades has the earlier legacy of Washington become appreciated. Most of Cluss's work has gone. The central areas where these buildings lay began to succumb to the pressures of denser development at an early stage. Yet a number of the most important examples of his output survive and are remarkably intact. That they are now carefully preserved and interest in them continues to rise is an encouraging sign. Cluss's distinctive and rather personal approach to recast Washington as a great city of the world is part of a multifaceted inheritance, the value of which we are only beginning to understand.

NOTES

I am grateful to Christoph Mauch, director of the German Historical Institute, for inviting me to prepare this essay and to John Cloud, Cynthia Field, James Goode, Isabelle Gournay, Harriet Lesser, Alan Lessoff, and Pamela Scott, as well as Judy Capurso of the Charles Sumner School Museum and Archives and Nancy Hadley of the American Institute of Architects Library and Archives, for their insights and assistance.

1. Tanya Edwards Beauchamp, "Adolph Cluss: An Architect in Washington during the Civil War and Reconstruction," *Records of the Columbia Historical Society* (hereafter *Records*) 48 (1971–72): 340–41; Antoinette J. Lee, *Architects to the Nation: The Rise and Decline of the Supervising Architect's Office* (New York, 2000), 47–48. Cluss was one of seven on Young's design staff in 1856. Period sources on Cluss's career include Affairs of the District of Columbia, 43d Cong., 1st Sess., S. Rept. 453 (June 1874), Testimony, 2049; *National Cyclopedia of American Biography* (New York, 1897), 4:507; and "Adolf Cluss Passes Away," *Washington Post*, 25 July 1905, 2. Concerning the Coast Survey, see Albert E. Theberg Jr., "The Coast Survey, 1807–1867," at http://www.lib.noaa.gov/edocs/CONTENTS.htm (October 5, 2004).

2. Pamela Scott, "A Directory of District of Columbia Architects 1822–1960," 2d ed., Washington, D.C., June 2001, typescript, is an immensely valuable resource for examining the subject. Architects listed therein for the 1850s include Edward Clark, who worked with Walter on the Capitol, succeeding him in 1865; Charles Clusky, who had been prolific in Georgia, but appears to have had little success in Washington; Edward Donn, also working on the Capitol; William Elliott, employed at the Patent Office; Emil Friedrich and August Fusback, apparently two other German émigrés about whom little is known; John C. Harkness, who was previously listed as a "house carpenter"; August G. Schoenborn, another employee of Walter's; and Ammi Young.

3. Adolf Cluss, "Architecture and Architects at the Capital of the United States from Its Foundation until 1875," *Proceedings of the . . . Annual Convention of the American Institute of Architects* (hereafter, *Proceedings*), 1876, 38–44. The implication was wrong in that Latrobe, of course, did not receive his *professional* education in Germany, but Cluss's knowledge of the architectural development of Washington was impressive for its time and suggests he was very conscious of the need for design that was appropriate to the national capital.

4. As can be gleaned from Daniel D. Reiff, *Washington Architecture, 1791–1861: Problems in Development* (Washington, D.C., 1971); Lee, *Architects to the Nation*; and James M. Goode, *Capital Losses: A Cultural History of Washington's Destroyed Buildings*, rev. ed. (Washington, D.C., 2003). Concerning the engineers, see Albert E. Cowdrey, *A City for the Nation: The Army Engineers and the Building of Washington, D.C., 1790–1967* (Washington, D.C., 1979); and William C. Dickinson, et al., eds., *Montgomery C. Meigs and the Building of the Nation's Capital* (Athens, Ohio, 2001). Concerning builders of the period, see Melissa McLoud, "Craftsmen and Entrepreneurs: Builders in Late Nineteenth-Century Washington, D.C." (Ph.D. diss., George Washington University, 1988).

5. Clay Lancaster, "Gideon Shyrock and John McMurtry, Architect and Builder of Kentucky," *Art Quarterly* 6 (1943): 257–75; Eric Johannsen, "Charles W. Heard, Victorian Architect," *Ohio History* 77 (Autumn 1968): 131–42, 174–75; *John Van Osdel: A Quarter Century of Chicago Architecture* (Chicago, 1898); John Albury Bryan, ed., *Missouri's Contribution to American Architecture* (St. Louis, 1928), 11–14, 33, 35–36, 38, 40, 42, 45–46; George Ehrlich and Peggy E. Schrock, "The Asa B. Cross Lumber Company 1858–1871," *Missouri Historical Review* 60 (October 1985): 14–32.

6. Scott, "Directory," affords crucial documentation. A few architects of some prominence began to practice in the city in the mid to late 1860s, including Henry R. Searle (1864), Paul Pelz (1867), and Norris Starkweather (1868). Many more came during the years that followed, including Harvey L. Page (1871); John Fraser, Thomas Plowman, and John L. Smithmeyer (1872); Richard Ezdorf (1873); Clement August Didden, Paul Lauritzen, and William Poindexter (1874); and Joseph Hornblower (1877). See also William Bushong, et al., *A Centennial History of the Washington Chapter, American Institute of Architects, 1887–1897* (Washington, D.C., 1987).

7. The most detailed account of Schulze is Adolf Cluss, "Paul Schulze," handwritten manuscript, [1897], record group 801, series 3, box 12, folder 5a, American Institute of Architects Archives, Washington, D.C., written to colleagues shortly after Schulze's death. Cluss discussed his former partner's personality on pages 8–10. Published sources include Adolf K. Placzek, ed., *Macmillan Encyclopedia of Architects*, 4 vols. (New York, 1982), 4: 6–7; Bainbridge Bunting and Margaret Henderson Floyd, *Harvard, An Architectural History* (Cambridge, Mass., 1985), 46, 48–49; Kathleen Curran, *The Romanesque Revival: Religion, Politics, and Transnational Exchange* (University Park, Pa., 2003), 236; and his obituary, *American Architect and Building News* (hereafter, *American Architect*) 55 (February 6, 1897): 42. Cluss's competition entry for the Library of Congress has yet to be found.

8. Bushong, *Centennial History*, 1; "A Convention of Architects," *Washington Post*, 16 November 1881, 2; "Officers Elected," *Washington Post*, 7 October 1888, 6. Cluss is first listed as a Fellow of the AIA in *Proceedings*, 1868, 56. He delivered a paper, "Theory, Function and Incidental Uses of Chimneys [sic]," *Proceedings*, 1870, 35–40. Thereafter, he is not again listed as a member until 1874. Throughout this period Smithmeyer and Pelz were associate members, Cluss was the only fellow from Washington save Henry R. Searle, whose membership lapsed in 1875. For a full listing by year, see "Professional Members, Fellows and Associates of the American Institute of Architects, from Its Formation," *Proceedings*, 1902, 155–71 (through 1886).

9. Alan Lessoff, *The Nation and Its City: Politics, "Corruption," and Progress in Washington, D.C., 1861–1902* (Baltimore, 1994), chap. 1.

10. Goode, *Capital Losses*, 427. See also *Annual Report of the Trustees of the Public Schools of the City of Washington* (hereafter, *Annual Report*), 1864, 16–18; and J. Ormond Wilson, "Eighty Years of Public Schools of Washington—1805 to 1885," *Records* 1 (1896): 138–43.

11. Lessoff, *The Nation and Its City*, chaps. 2, 3; Frederick Gutheim and National Capital Planning Commission, *Worthy of the Nation: The History of Planning in the Nation's Capital* (Washington, D.C., 1977), 84–88; William M. Maury, *Alexander "Boss" Shepherd and the Board of Public Works* (Washington, D.C., 1975).

12. Lessoff, *The Nation and Its City*, 48–49, 80–81, 86–87; Alison K. Hoagland, "Nineteenth-Century Building Regulations in Washington, D.C.," *Records* 52 (1989): 60–61.

13. Quoted in Hoagland, "Building Regulations," 71.

14. Gutheim, *Worthy of the Nation*, 80–81; Lessoff, *The Nation and Its City*, 84–85.

15. Lessoff, *The Nation and Its City*, 67, 82; Daniel Bluestone, *Constructing Chicago* (New Haven, 1991), chaps. 1, 2; Bainbridge Bunting, *Houses of Boston's Back Bay: An Architectural History, 1840–1917* (Cambridge, Mass., 1967), chaps. 2, 3, 8; *Back Bay Boston: The City as a Work of Art* (Boston, 1969).

16. Goode, *Capital Losses*, 96–97, 183–85. Cluss never occupied his unit in the row. He probably acquired the parcel for investment purposes as part of a business arrangement with Shepherd and Kilbourn.

17. Ibid., 188, 182. For another example, see page 187.

18. McLoud, "Craftsmen and Entrepreneurs," 248, 253.

19. Harold N. Cooledge Jr., *Samuel Sloan, Architect of Philadelphia, 1815–1884* (Philadelphia, 1986), 28–34, 45–50. Sloan's work received extensive publicity through a detailed treatise by Henry Barnard, *School Architecture, or Contributions to the Improvement of School Houses in the United States*, first published in 1842 and issued in at least five updated editions through 1855. Considerable refinements had occurred by the time Barnard compiled his *Report to the Commissioner of Education on School Architecture* (Washington, D.C., 1870).

20. *Annual Report*, 1866–67, 33; Adolf Cluss, "The School Building," *Order of Exercises at the Dedication of the Franklin School Building...* (Washington, D.C., 1869), 28–32 (quote on page 28). See also *Annual Report*, 1866–70, 116–18; *Annual Report*, 1871–72, 123; and John W. Reps, *Washington on View: The Nation's Capital since 1790* (Chapel Hill, N.C., 1991), 150.

21. For descriptions, see *Annual Report*, 1870–71, 95–96 and plates (Seaton School); *Annual Report*, 1871–72, 109–14 and plates (Jefferson School) and 133–34 and plates (Cranch School); and *Annual Report*, 1874–75, 236–37 and plates (Curtis School).

22. *Annual Report of the Superintendent of Colored Schools of Washington and Georgetown*, 1871–72, 78–92 and plates.

23. Helen Tangires, "Contested Space: The Life and Death of Center Market," *Washington History* 7 (Spring–Summer 1995): 46–67, 95–97; Helen Tangires, *Public Markets and Civic Culture in Nineteenth-Century America* (Baltimore, 2003), 173–80; Goode, *Capital Losses*, 302–3.

24. "The First French Flats," *Washington Post*, 24 April 1880, 2; "The Building Boom," *Washington Post*, 16 April 1881, 1; "The Portland, Washington, D.C.," *American Architect* 15 (April 12, 1884): 174–75 and plate. For a recent assessment, see James M. Goode, *Best Addresses: A Century of Washington's Distinguished Apartment Houses* (Washington, D.C., 1988), 8–10; and Goode, *Capital Losses*, 2003, 212–13.

25. For comparison, see Elizabeth Collins Cromley, *Alone Together: A History of New York's Early Apartments* (Ithaca, 1990); Robert A. M. Stern, et al., *New York 1880: Architecture and Urbanism in the Gilded Age* (New York, 1999), 531–68; and Douglass Shand Tucci, *Built in Boston: City and Suburb* (1978; rev. ed., Amherst, Mass., 1999), 101–6.

26. Important examples of Hunt in this regard include the Studio Building (1857), Stuyvesant Apartments (1869–70), Presbyterian Hospital (1869–72), Lenox Library (1870–77), and Tribune Building (1873–75), all in New York. Most of the scholarly attention given to Hunt has focused on a stylistic rather than functional context. However much valuable material pertaining to these works as building types is found in Sarah Bradford Landau and Carl W. Condit, *Rise of the New York Skyscraper 1865–1913* (New Haven, 1996), 83–90; and Stern, et al., *New York*, 196–201, 256–60, 403–6, 533–38.

27. Concerning Mullett, see Lee, *Architects to the Nation*, chap. 4. Cluss's dislike of Mullett's work is indicated by his comments about the federal building in New York in Cluss, "Paul Schulze," 3.

28. Contemporary accounts of the building include "The New National Museum," *Washington Post*, 26 July 1879, 1; "The Brick Work Completed," *Washington Post*, 14 November 1879, 4; "Our National Museum," *Washington Post*, 27 December 1879, 2; and "The New Building for the National Museum...," *American Architect* 8 (October 23, 1880): 199–200 and plate. See also *Annual Report of the Board of Regents of the Smithsonian Institution..., Report of the U. S. National Museum* (Washington, D.C., 1905), 238–59. As consulting engineer, Montgomery Meigs had a role in the design's development as well, see Cynthia Field, "A Rich Repast of Classicism: Meigs and Classical Sources," in Dickinson, et al., eds., *Montgomery C. Meigs*, 75–79.

29. Concerning Memorial Hall, see John Maass, *The Glorious Enterprise: The Centennial Exhibition of 1876 and H. J. Schwarzmann, Architect-in-Chief* (Watkins Glen, N.Y., 1973); and Ingrid A. Steffensen-Bruce, *Marble Palaces, Temples of Art: Art Museums, Architecture, and American Culture, 1890–1930* (Lewisburg, Pa., 1998), 51–56. Concerning the museum context, see Gwendolyn Wright, ed., *The Formation of National Collections of Art and Archaeology*, National Gallery of Art, Studies in the History of Art, vol. 47 (Washington, D.C., 1996); and Carla Yanni, *Natures' Museums: Victorian Science and the Architecture of Display* (Baltimore, 1999).

30. Francis R. Kowsky, *Country, Park & City: The Architecture and Life of Calvert Vaux* (New York, 1998), 231–37; William Alex, *Calvert Vaux, Architect & Planner* (New York, 1994), 202–5; Stern et al., New York, 182–86; M. Christine Boyer, *Manhattan Manners: Architecture and Style 1850–1900* (New York, 1985), 62–64; Dell Upton, "Inventing the Metropolis: Civilization and Urbanity in Antebellum New York," in Catherine Hoover Voorsanger, et al., *Art and the Empire City: New York, 1825–61* (New York, 2000), 40–42; Maass, *Glorious Enterprise*.

31. Along with Meigs and Architect of the Capitol Edward Clark, Cluss was on the commission that investigated the causes of the 1877 fire. The following year, his firm won the competition. In 1883 work began on remodeling sections unaffected by the fire in order to render their upper portions more fireproof. For background, see Douglas E. Evelyn, "A Public Office for a New Democracy: The Patent Office Building in the Nineteenth Century" (Ph.D. diss., George Washington University, 1997), 449–66. See also Elizabeth B. Del Donna, "Patent Office Building Competition, Washington, D.C., 1878," *Journal of the Society of Architectural Historians* 23 (March 1964): 44–48. Contemporary sources include "Official Report of the Patent Office Competition," *American Architect* 4 (August 31, 1878): 75–77; "Interior of the Model-Room of the Patent Office, Washington, D.C.," *American Architect* 7 (March 20, 1880): 119–20 and plate; and *American Architect* 15 (May 3, 1884): plate.

32. Daniel Bluestone, "Civic and Aesthetic Reserve: Ammi Burnham Young's 1850s Federal Customhouse Designs," *Winterthur Portfolio* 25 (Summer–Autumn 1990): 131–56; and Lee, *Architects to the Nation*, chap. 3.

33. Roula Mouroudellis Geraniotis, "German Architectural Theory and Practice in Chicago, 1850–1900," *Winterthur Portfolio* 21 (Winter 1986): 305–6.

34. Concerning Furness, see Michael J. Lewis, *Frank Furness: Architecture and the Violent Mind* (New York, 2001) and George Thomas et al., *Frank Furness: The Complete Works* (New York, 1991).

35. Concerning his work for the Smithsonian, see Kenneth Hafertepe, *America's Castle: The Evolution of the Smithsonian Building and Its Institution, 1840–1878* (Washington, D.C., 1984), 138–40; and Cynthia Field, et al., *The Castle: An Illustrated History of the Smithsonian Building* (Washington, D.C., 1993), 38–39, 58, 79, 82, 108–9, 124, 148. Concerning the Medical Museum see "The United States Army Medical Museum and Library. . .," *American Architect* 19 (January 16, 1886): 31 and plate; and Goode, *Capital Losses*, 366–67.

36. Jon A. Peterson, *The Birth of City Planning in the United States, 1840–1917* (Baltimore, 2003), chaps. 4, 6; Thomas Hines, "The Imperial Mall: The City Beautiful Movement and the Washington Plan of 1901–1902," Jon A. Peterson, "The Mall, the McMillan Plan, and the Origins of American City Planning," and David C. Streatfield, "The Olmsteds and the Landscape of the Mall," in Richard Longstreth, ed., *The Mall in Washington, 1791–1991*, National Gallery of Art, Studies in the History of Art, vol. 30, reprint ed. (Washington, 2002), 78–99, 100–115, 116–41, respectively; Richard Longstreth, "The Unusual Transformation of Downtown Washington in the Early Twentieth Century," *Washington History* 13 (Fall–Winter 2001–2): 50–51.

37. *American Architect* 88 (August 5, 1905): 41.

Adolf Cluss and Washington's Public Works

ALAN LESSOFF

For most of his American career, Adolf Cluss avoided political controversy. A notable exception occurred in May 1874, when Cluss provided dramatic testimony to a special investigating committee of the United States Congress. The senators and representatives on the committee were examining improprieties in the Comprehensive Plan of Improvements, an ambitious program to upgrade Washington's public works and appearance. At the time, Cluss served as the District of Columbia's chief municipal engineer and as a member of the Board of Public Works, a five-person commission created by Congress in 1871 to oversee the capital city's streets, water and sewage, municipal buildings, and building inspection. He had direct responsibility for paving and sewerage contracts that became the focus of a huge scandal concerning financial manipulation to hide cost overruns and political favoritism in public-works contracts. The immigrant engineer made front-page news across the United States by admitting that he had certified dozens of vouchers for street and sewer contracts that he knew were based on incomplete or false measurements. This left local taxpayers and the federal government responsible for the cost of unauthorized projects and overcharges by contractors with connections to the Republican Party.

According to press accounts, harsh cross-examination during the hearings unnerved Cluss; however, he regained his

self-control and explained that he had inherited a convoluted, deceptive contracting system when he took over the District of Columbia's engineering department in late 1872. Friends had advised him to tolerate the "gross outrages" rather than jeopardize the much-needed infrastructure program. Now, the time had arrived to "vindicate public honesty." Ultimate responsibility for the scandal, Cluss insisted, belonged to his sometime business partner and current boss, Alexander R. Shepherd. As vice-president and de facto head of the Board of Public Works from its creation in 1871, Shepherd had devised and implemented the Comprehensive Plan of Improvements. Even after Shepherd's appointment in September 1873 as governor of the District of Columbia under the territorial system then administering the capital, he remained involved with street and sewer issues. To Cluss's dismay, Shepherd regularly bypassed his chief engineer and made unilateral decisions. Cluss testified that Shepherd personally directed Cluss's assistant engineers to prepare the "irregular" vouchers now under congressional scrutiny.[1]

Shepherd's allies denounced Cluss's "base treachery and perfidity." At Shepherd's request, President Ulysses S. Grant fired Cluss as Washington's chief engineer, thereby ending Cluss's venture into municipal engineering. The city's German newspaper, the *Washingtoner Journal*, lamented

Detail, Street pavings built by the Board of Public Works as of November 1873. See page 127.

Cluss's "entanglement" in the scandal and worried that involvement of such a prominent German-born professional would reflect badly on the local German community.[2] Other witnesses, however, corroborated Cluss's account, and Shepherd outlasted Cluss by only a few weeks. In June, Congress abolished the territorial government and the Board of Public Works, created an appointed federal commission to govern the city, and assigned management of Washington's public works to the U.S. Army Corps of Engineers. Initially conceived as a temporary expedient to oversee the bankrupt District of Columbia through its fiscal crisis, an appointed board of commissioners would rule the capital until the 1960s.

With his personal finances shattered along with his political future, Shepherd spent much of his remaining life managing silver mines in Mexico. Shepherd's supporters proclaimed that Cluss's testimony amounted to professional "suicide."[3] Yet Cluss's career suffered no apparent damage from his having allowed Shepherd to treat him "as a straw man" and from having signed vouchers he had known to be "wrong and fraudulent."[4] Although he never again held a position in Washington's municipal public works, he continued to design schools for the District of Columbia and to secure commissions from the United States government. Indeed, Cluss's candid testimony enhanced his reputation among Republican Party factions opposed to the Grant administration's alleged corruption.

Although Cluss's reputation for probity may have been strengthened by his role in disclosing the 1874 scandal, his reputation as a civil engineer suffered damage in subsequent years. The sewer system he had helped to implement became an example of what to avoid in sewer-system design. The Army Corps of Engineers repaved virtually every street supposedly improved by Cluss. Cluss's inclination towards experimentation with new methods and technologies, found in both his civil engineering and his architecture, seemed to the next generation of civil engineers to be the epitome of a misguided, trial-and-error approach. Neither Cluss's lack of specialized training nor Shepherd's lack of scruples, however, were fully to blame for the backed-up sewers and crumbling pavements that Washington hurried to replace in the late 1870s. In a period of unprecedented urbanization, civil engi-

neers throughout Europe and the United States faced the challenge of devising public works and services of unprecedented scope and complexity. From Berlin to Chicago, the first generation of modern municipal engineers, like Cluss, undertook experiments and experienced wrenching failures.

Visions of a Worthy Capital

During the Civil War, when Cluss was launching his architecture and engineering partnership with fellow immigrant Joseph W. von Kammerhueber, Washington became an inviting field for architects, engineers, developers, and contractors. As the United States capital and the headquarters of the Union war effort against the rebellious Confederate states, Washington attracted unprecedented attention. The District of Columbia's population doubled from 75,000 in 1860 to an estimated 155,000 in 1864. During the war, hundreds of thousands of northerners passed through the city on war-related business. Although Washington's appearance and public services were respectable for a town of its size, Unionists measured the city not against other midsized cities, but against their vision of a "New Washington," a capital "worthy of the nation," as contemporary phrases described it. The capital's disappointing condition seemed a metaphor for the country's unfulfilled ambitions. Northern newcomers blamed Washington's shortcomings on the supposedly languid, Southern character of this slave-owning city, whose prewar elite had close ties to the landed families of Virginia and Maryland.

During the war, army wagons ground to rubble the cobblestones of Pennsylvania Avenue, one of the few thoroughfares with a pretense of paving. Commercial buildings and hotels dismissed by Mark Twain as "mean, and cheap, and dingy" lined the avenue intended as a national boulevard.[5] To the south, on the site of the present Federal Triangle, stood a red-light district and slum known as Murder Bay, because of the brawls that spilled from its bars and brothels and occasionally ended with a death. To the north of Pennsylvania Avenue, Washington's dirt roads petered out within seven blocks. Congress refused to fund and the city could not afford to pave the majestic system of radiating avenues envisioned by the city's designer, Pierre Charles L'Enfant, in 1791. Thus Massachusetts, New York, and New Jersey avenues remained "a great Sahara of dirt" during dry weather and "seas or canals of mud" after rain or snow.[6]

Despite the war, the federal government pushed ahead with the $3.3 million Washington Aqueduct, which upon its December 1863 opening piped twenty-five million gallons of water per day from Great Falls, twelve miles up the Potomac River. Designed by Army Corps engineer Montgomery Meigs, later Cluss's collaborator on the National Museum, the Washington Aqueduct provided a water supply worthy of the city's status. Yet, like most American and European cities, Washington failed to implement adequate drainage for its new water supply. The sinks and toilets of federal and private buildings flowed along with street runoff directly into the Washington Canal, which ran along the line of the current Constitution Avenue. Intended by city promoters in the 1790s as a thoroughfare for commerce, the canal had decayed by the 1860s into a "fetid bayou" bearing "dead cats and all kinds of putridity and reeking with pestilential odors."[7]

Lined by lumber and coal yards as well as Murder Bay and the ramshackle Center Market from the 1820s, the canal separated the Mall from the city's main commercial and residential districts. The Mall itself was landscaped in fragments and marred by railroad tracks. At the Mall's west end, bordering the Potomac River marshes that would be reclaimed in the 1880s, stood the half-finished Washington Monument, abandoned in its scaffolding since 1854 for want of funds. Mark Twain imagined George Washington's ghost alighting on the scaffolding of his "memorial Chimney," surveying what had come so far of his and L'Enfant's vision for the American Rome, and thanking the nation for its "unappeasable gratitude."[8]

The gap between the city's pretenses and its reality humiliated young entrepreneurs such as Alexander Shepherd, who came from the section of southwest Washington nicknamed "the Island," because the canal separated it from the rest of the city. With much of Washington's prewar establishment suspected of Confederate sympathies, business and political opportunities opened for ambitious newcomers or pro-Northern natives such as Shepherd. After youthful success as

a building supplier and developer and service in various civic and political offices, Shepherd emerged by the late 1860s as the leading proponent of a concerted effort to "lift the city out of the mud and make it what it should be as the capital of the nation."[9]

In the post–Civil War years, editors and politicians from the Midwest campaigned for abandoning Washington as a failed relic of the prewar Union. They argued for a fresh start in St. Louis or another Mississippi Valley city. Nevertheless, the Civil War spurred the demand for housing and services, gave new visibility to Washington, and sparked an unprecedented level of private investment in the capital city. The war also strengthened political support for national underwriting of efforts to "make a decent city, with decent ornamentation," a capital that evoked pride and not derision.[10] When leaving federal employment for private practice in 1862, Cluss had thus begun a career as architect and engineer in a city poised to embark on a wave of public and private building.

As support grew for a concerted effort to upgrade Washington's services and improve its appearance, the spectacular rebuilding of Paris between 1853 and 1870 under the Second Empire's relentless Prefect of the Seine Georges-Eugène Haussmann stood as the most renowned international model of the massive reconstruction of a capital city. The best-known feature of Haussmann's work—the construction of grand boulevards, lined with trees and flanked by fashionable apartments—came to define nineteenth-century notions of urban elegance from Istanbul to Buenos Aires. Haussmann's Paris set such an example of modern methods and tastes that architects throughout Europe and the Americas, including Cluss, adopted the style known as "Second Empire" for prestigious commissions. Municipal engineers and public works officials took special note of Paris's improvement in the areas of parks, sewers, water mains, public markets, railroad stations, cemeteries, and other projects intended to make life in Paris healthier, pleasanter, and practical. Like many observers with leftist sympathies, Cluss expressed skepticism of "Imperial Haussmann." He followed Victor Hugo, Karl Marx, and other left-wing writers in charging that Haussmann's broad, straight avenues and macadam pavings were a "ruse" to render Paris less susceptible to barricade-building and easier to control during revolutions.[11] Yet by involving himself in the pursuit of a Washington of tree-lined boulevards, pleasant parks and squares, up-to-date markets, schools, other services, and lavish buildings topped by mansard roofs, Cluss was working towards a Washington that would stand as a "worthy" capital according to the Paris standard.

Cluss was correct in seeking political lessons in Haussmann's work, but the relevant lessons to his situation in Washington were to be found not in Haussmann's alleged antipathy to barricades but in the prefect's deceitful bookkeeping and corrupt dealings with contractors and financiers. These issues, which precipitated Haussmann's downfall in 1870, also provoked Cluss to testify against Shepherd in 1874. Like Shepherd a few years later, Haussmann resorted not only to influence peddling to bolster a rickety political coalition, but also to creative financing when costs far exceeded original estimates and anticipated sources of revenue did not appear. One quality that Cluss shared with later engineers who criticized his work was the notion that public works could stand apart from politics and serve the public good in a neutral fashion. In his relations with Shepherd, Cluss confronted the hard lesson that the ability of an engineer to implement the most necessary improvements hinges on the vicissitudes of politics, especially when the cost of projects appears open-ended and their success uncertain.

Sewage by Trial and Error

Like many of his contemporaries, Cluss described himself as an architect and a civil engineer, believing that the roles overlapped. This belief in the architect-engineer as a generalist contrasted with the viewpoint of subsequent generations that architecture and civil engineering formed separate professions requiring specialized training and a distinct perspective. As Tanya Edwards Beauchamp's chapter in this volume recounts, Cluss won international acclaim for his efforts to deal with both the architectural and the engineering problems posed by school construction, even though his heating and ventilation innovations often proved inadequate.

Impressed by the school design work of Cluss and Kammerhueber, his partner at the time, the Washington City government in December 1864 commissioned the firm to assess a number of schemes then under consideration for diverting sewage from the Washington Canal and rendering it navigable. Cluss and Kammerhueber's report, published in May 1865, explained that no easy method existed for keeping the canal clean and open to traffic. If residents desired a navigable canal through the center of a populous city, they would have to pay not only to dredge and narrow it, but also to construct sewer mains beside the canal to divert street runoff and "the offal of kitchens and . . . filth from water closets" into the Potomac and Anacostia rivers. Cluss and Kammerhueber's report challenged the rationale for maintaining a navigable canal alongside the Mall, and in so doing questioned an article of faith still widespread in Washington that went back to George Washington himself that the city could potentially combine the functions of thriving port and impressive political capital. A "proper system of drainage" was "of more importance," the engineers wrote, than whether or not the canal again became navigable. Washington, "the seat of government of a great and enlightened nation" could not "show any [sewerage] system at all!"[12]

Cluss and Kammerhueber's study helped set in motion a heated debate that would continue until 1871. At that point Shepherd, head of the newly established Board of Public Works, took money that Congress had appropriated to dredge the canal and used it instead to fill the canal and build main sewers along its route, roughly where Cluss's report had recommended. When challenged by political opponents and diehard canal supporters, Shepherd rounded up a contingent of experts, including Professor Joseph Henry of the Smithsonian Institution. During a House of Representatives hearing in the spring of 1872, the experts testified that whatever the legality of Shepherd's action, abolition of the open sewer next to the Mall was essential to the city's beautification and public health. At the same hearing, Cluss spoke in support of the emphasis on sanitation over commerce represented by Shepherd's decision to fill the canal. Cluss added that if given the opportunity, he might "go further than the board of public works" in covering over the

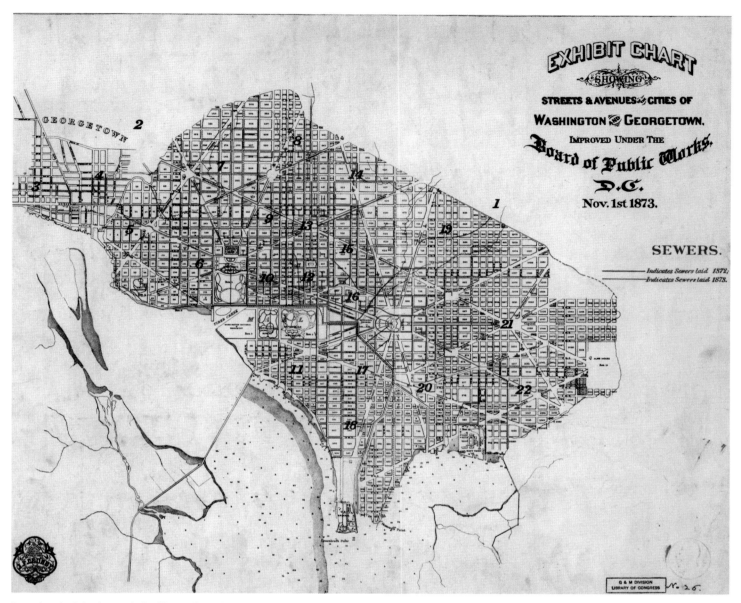

Sewer lines built by the Board of Public Works as of November 1873. The "B Street Intercepting Sewer" runs along the north side of the Mall, on the site of the former canal. From Board of Public Works, Annual Report, 1873. Courtesy Library of Congress, Geography and Maps Division.

city's remaining creeks and channels and replacing them with sewer mains.[13] This he endeavored to accomplish when he joined the board and became the city's chief engineer later that year.

By late 1873, Cluss claimed the sewer system he had helped conceive and now supervised to be "so far advanced that before long the drainage of surface, subsoil, and sewage proper will be within reach of all." Although the Potomac and Anacostia "tidelocked" the main outlets "for a considerable length," Cluss insisted that with minor adjustments, the obvious hazards of sewage stagnating in the mains and backing up during storms could be avoided.[14] This claim proved optimistic. It turned out that the "B Street Intercepting Sewer,"

constructed along the route of the old canal, stagnated daily at high tide, with up to three feet of raw sewage pushed back several thousand feet into central Washington. The B Street main flooded at least five times between 1875 and 1889. This last flood prompted appointment of a commission led by Rudolph Hering, a German-American civil engineer who trained in his family's homeland during the 1860s, about two decades after Cluss, and who had become the country's most respected sewage expert.

Hering's report reviewed a litany of problems that reinforced dismissal of Cluss's sewerage work as ill-conceived to the point of amateurish. Back in 1865, however, Cluss and Kammerhueber's report did endeavor to reflect the state of hydraulic engineering at the time. The report cited examples from Hamburg and "other great and populous cities" to conclude that a "nearly level" main discharging into the tidal Potomac could work so long as precautions were taken to close the outlets at high tides and to flush the mains on a regular basis.[15] Before repeated floods made his program's defects manifest, Cluss asserted "the drainage of tide sewers" to be "part of the knowledge required by engineers," an expression of confidence in wide-ranging knowledge typical of his generation of engineer-architects.[16]

Indeed, whatever their other differences, Cluss shared with Shepherd a confidence in their ability to master the range of public works, planning, and sanitation problems confronting Washington. Such confidence encouraged Cluss and his contemporaries in other European and American cities to tackle urgent infrastructure problems by trial and error. Their successes became received wisdom, while failures such as the B Street sewer set negative precedents.

The Politics of a New Washington

This investigation into Cluss's municipal engineering and urban planning work is not the place to explain the intricacies of Washington's local politics. It is crucial to note, however, that in the decade after the Civil War, the capital city experienced continual political turmoil. Throughout his career as architect and engineer, Cluss exhibited a penchant for experimentation, an engaging quality that also led at times to trouble. Yet even if Cluss had been inclined to approach public works in a strictly systematic manner, Washington's tumultuous political climate would have pushed him towards the inadequate planning and rushed implementation that characterized much of his work with the Board of Public Works.

During the Reconstruction years after the Civil War, much of Washington's turmoil stemmed from the changed status of African Americans after emancipation. Between 1860 and 1870, Washington's black population tripled from 14,317 to 43,422. Most of this increase represented former slaves from Virginia and Maryland, who crowded into slums such as Murder Bay. An influential segment of Washington's

African American community had been free before the war. These people, often educated and politically active, were determined to turn the capital into a model of reformed race relations. The Radical faction of the Republican Party, which sympathized with black ambitions, lobbied Congress and the municipal government to extend the vote to blacks, to desegregate streetcars and public places, and to provide black children with educational opportunities. Cluss's Charles Sumner School counted among the most impressive products of this effort (see Beauchamp, this volume).

Among the District of Columbia's white majority, the prospect of blacks sharing power combined with the influx of northern newcomers into the southern-leaning city to generate bitter factional fighting. Old-line Washingtonians leaned towards the Democratic Party and resistance to black civil rights. As occurred in the national Republican Party, Washington's Republicans split into the Radical faction that supported black aspirations and a moderate faction that was ambivalent about black rights because the issue diverted attention from the party's other priorities: investment in infrastructure and economic development.

In 1868, in a disputed election marred by racial violence, Radical Republican Sayles J. Bowen won the post of Washington City mayor on a promise to work simultaneously for civil rights and public works. Bowen's public works initiatives soon became mired in the city's tense racial politics. Shepherd, who had given grudging support to Bowen in 1868, now emerged as leader of the moderate faction bent on ousting Bowen as mayor and replacing the District of Columbia's existing governmental structure. The plan was to merge the municipal corporations of Washington and Georgetown and unincorporated suburbs known as Washington County into a "Territory of the District of Columbia," ruled by a governor nominated by the United States president, who would also name the upper house of the territorial legislature, along with a Board of Public Works to manage the capital city's infrastructure. Under this plan, the federal district's residents would elect only the lower house of the territorial legislature and a nonvoting delegate to Congress. By placing Washington's public works under the control of officials appointed by the president, this system

In 1873, while chief engineer to the Board of Public Works, Cluss designed this lavish mansion at Connecticut and Massachusetts avenues on Dupont Circle for Nevada senator William Stewart. Nicknamed "Stewart's Castle," this was an especially opulent example of Cluss's fashionable, Second Empire residences. During Cluss's congressional testimony against Shepherd in May 1874, Stewart, a shrewd lawyer as well as a major investor in Washington real estate and a firm ally of Shepherd, helped to unnerve his former architect with harsh cross-examination. Courtesy Historical Society of Washington, D.C.

would divorce the prodevelopment Republicans' priorities of infrastructure and development from the noisy politics of race and civil rights.

While suspicious of the Radicals, Shepherd's prodevelopment Republicans expressed contempt for Washington's Democratic, prewar elite, whom they dismissed as "small-souled," pro-Southern "hunkers" responsible for the city's squalor.[17] The city's so-called old citizens returned this contempt, portraying the Shepherd group as meretricious upstarts. Nevertheless, such old-line Washingtonians as bankers William W. Corcoran and George W. Riggs entered a strategic alliance with the Shepherd Republicans to defeat Bowen in the 1870 municipal elections. Moderate Republican Matthew Emery became Washington's last elected mayor for 104 years. The old-line Washingtonians

then worked with the Shepherd Republicans to persuade Congress to authorize the territorial format in February 1871.

President Grant, Shepherd's friend and a proponent of federal support for upgrading Washington, named Shepherd and several allies to the Board of Public Works. Grant also placed well-disposed Republicans in other key territorial offices. The initial governor, for example, was Shepherd's business partner Henry Cooke, brother of Jay Cooke, the famous Republican banker. President Grant thus handed the prodevelopment group an open opportunity, as Shepherd put it, "to devise and carry out, as rapidly as possible, some system of improvements."[18] Within three weeks of taking office in June 1871, the Board of Public Works published its Comprehensive Plan of Improvements. By the end of the summer contracts had been let for grading and paving and water, gas, and sewage projects throughout the city. Old-line Washingtonians, who had recently cooperated in the movement for the territory, now recoiled from Shepherd's "ill-digested, incoherent, and blundering scheme," which they correctly predicted would cost several times the projected $6.6 million.[19] This turn of events and Grant's exclusion of Democrats with local roots from important District offices pushed Washington's old establishment into relentless opposition. The prominence among Shepherd's enemies of such "rich people content with existing circumstances" in turn helps to explain the imperiousness and ruthlessness with which he pursued his program.[20]

Cluss and the Comprehensive Plan

Although a firm Republican, Cluss took no recorded position on the city's factional disputes. One can only surmise his views from the effort he put into the all-black Sumner School or from his defense of black bricklayers employed to construct the Center Market. Cluss began working for Washington's local government under Mayor Richard Wallach, a vocal opponent of black rights who served from 1861 to 1868. He continued working for the city under Bowen. By 1871, Cluss was easily the leading architect of municipal buildings and a logical choice for building inspector, his first office under the Board of Public Works.

Cluss gained respect from Shepherd and his associates but did not belong to their social or business circle. Cluss did not own stock in any of the contracting or building supply companies identified with the scandal over Shepherd's contracting methods. Cluss did acquire 202 shares, worth $10,100, in the Washington Market Company, which operated the Center Market that he designed.[21] This company's ties to the local and national Republican parties generated much controversy, as Helen Tangires's essay in this volume explains. Furthermore, around the time Cluss joined the territorial government, he entered a direct business arrangement with Shepherd, in which he designed "Shepherd's Row," a trio of ornate townhouses on K Street north of Farragut Square. The two outer houses of the trio belonged to Shepherd and Hallett Kilbourn, a lawyer and real estate broker closely asso-

ciated with Shepherd. Cluss owned the middle house, possibly in exchange for architectural services and probably as an investment, since he never moved there from his house on Second Street, NW. Shortly before his testimony in May 1874, Cluss took steps to sell his interest in Shepherd's Row.[22]

It was Cluss's professional stature as an inventive architect of public buildings and fashionable residences that brought him into association with Shepherd, rather than any social or business connection or political conviction. Cluss heartily supported Shepherd's vision of a New Washington, but he remained an outsider to the circle of Republican developers, contractors, and financiers who dominated Washington during the territorial period.

From spring 1871, when the territorial government went into operation, until October 1872, when Grant appointed Cluss to the Board of Public Works, the architect played a significant role in the improvement program but not an organizing one. Beyond designing Center Market and the city-owned Eastern Market, Cluss oversaw the design or renovation of seven schools. He also supervised construction of the District's new jail, designed by Alfred B. Mullett, the federal Supervising Architect of the Treasury and Cluss's predecessor on the Board of Public Works. As District building inspector, Cluss undertook to transform the capital's "absolutely obsolete, imperfect, and defective" building laws into an effective "system of inspection" for private as well as public buildings.[23]

In December 1872, Cluss's duties expanded to include heading Washington's municipal engineering office. Cluss later told the truth when he asserted that the convoluted practices uncovered by investigators were already in place when he took charge of the engineering department. In devising the content and procedures of the Comprehensive Plan, Shepherd worked with Mullett, who was already a target of controversy for his management of the Supervising Architect's office and for his design of the State, War, and Navy building. Shepherd colluded as well with other favorable federal officials, especially Major Orville Babcock, head of the federal Office of Public Buildings and Grounds (as well as President Grant's personal secretary). Probably the most damaging revelation Cluss made during his testimony

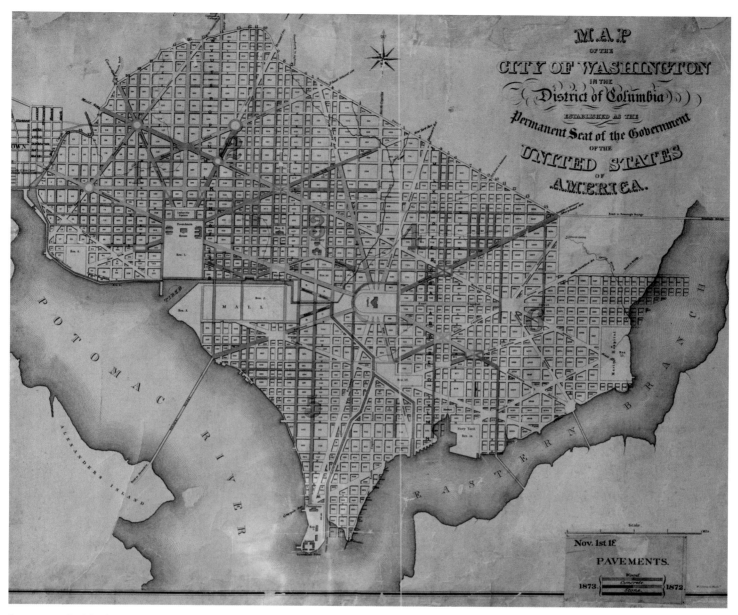

MAP
OF THE
CITY OF WASHINGTON
IN THE
District of Columbia
ESTABLISHED AS THE
Permanent Seat of the Government
OF THE
UNITED STATES
OF
AMERICA.

Nov. 1st 18
PAVEMENTS.
1873. 1872.

Street pavings built by the Board of Public Works as of November 1873. All the wood and much of the concrete paving needed replacement in the years after the territorial government's abolishment in 1874. Courtesy Library of Congress, Geography and Maps Division.

concerned arrangements between Shepherd and Babcock, which enabled the District to shift the costs of unauthorized street work to the federal government.

While Cluss may have found Shepherd's methods arrogant and irresponsible, he raised few objections to the Comprehensive Plan itself, probably because Shepherd was using high-handed methods to push through a variety of projects that had been under discussion for years. Major features of the Shepherd program included the narrowing and "parking" of Washington's broad, muddy streets and avenues, the grading and paving of about 150 miles of thoroughfares, the creation of small parks and circles in the irregular trian-

gles at the intersections of L'Enfant's avenues and streets, and the filling of the Washington Canal as a step towards a city-wide sewerage system. Every one of these projects had appeared between 1865 and 1871 in reports by the Army Corps of Engineers and other federal agencies and in city documents such as Cluss and Kammerhueber's canal report. Even while denouncing Shepherd's tactics, Cluss never indicated substantive disagreement with his program because the Comprehensive Plan conformed to standard, contemporary notions in place throughout Europe and the Americas of how to render a capital city more functional, amenable, and healthful.

Beyond overseeing a sewage plan that he had earlier helped originate, Cluss, once he was appointed city engineer, enthusiastically pursued the widespread "parking" of streets—that is, the narrowing of roadways and the planting of trees and grass alongside or down the middle of the road. The parking program, Cluss wrote, "materially reduced the cost of improved roadways," while giving Washington "a leading feature of rare beauty," reminiscent of the boulevards of Paris or Berlin. The parking plan, Cluss argued, made "the imperial widths of avenues and streets" into "superlative attractions" rather than a source of "rebuke and reproach."[24]

While later engineers found much to praise and little to criticize in this parking program, they came to deplore the Board of Public Works' street paving technologies as much as the dysfunctional sewage system described above. In his 1873 annual report for the Board of Public Works, Cluss warned that dozens of miles of wooden pavements laid since 1871 showed signs of rotting, but he remained hopeful that an effective method for preserving wood pavements would emerge, since the experimental surface was easy to clean and comfortable for horses. Several years later, as the Army Corps of Engineers rushed to replace the Board of Public Works' wood streets worth $5 million, nearly all "in an advanced state of decay," Cluss apologetically confessed in a magazine article that municipal engineers such as himself had "rather hastily" adopted them. In 1873, Cluss also "confidently expected" that the concrete and coal tar pavements adopted by the board because they were cheaper than natural asphalt would prove durable. This was another miscalculation that would cost millions to rectify.[25]

Cluss and Shepherd lived to see the Comprehensive Plan acquire an ambiguous reputation. Washingtonians, even many who had opposed the Shepherd government at the time, came to appreciate the territorial period as the time when Washington overcame its "arrested development" and transformed from "a struggling, straggling village into a modern city."[26] As the passions of these years faded, more observers were willing to accept Shepherd's defense of his imperious and underhanded actions. Washington needed a

shove to overcome indolence and decrepitude, he argued. The old establishment's resistance in combination with Congress's sidestepping of financial responsibility for the capital's infrastructure costs justified heavy-handed, even extralegal expedients. By temperament an outsider to Shepherd's boisterous, promotion-minded circles, Cluss found it painful to participate in the creation of a "worthy" New Washington through less than upright means. As an engineer and architect proud of his professional stature, it also galled him to witness much of his work come to represent a cautionary tale for next-generation municipal engineers and city planners.

Back in 1852, as Sabina W. Dugan recounts in her essay in this volume, Cluss helped arrange publication of a legendary work of political criticism, Karl Marx's *The Eighteenth Brumaire of Louis Bonaparte*. "Men make their own history," runs a famous dictum at the start of Marx's book, "but they do not make it just as they please; they do not make it under circumstances chosen by themselves."[27] Two decades later, Cluss found himself in a situation to which Marx's maxim could apply. By 1872, Cluss had worked his way into the envious position of chief engineer for the capital city of his adopted country, at a time when an ambitious movement gained momentum for upgrading Washington's public works and embellishing its public places. Yet the tense political circumstances surrounding Shepherd's territorial government accentuated the drawbacks of Cluss's trial-and-error approach to civil engineering, as he had no time to reconsider false starts and redo mistakes. Cluss worked for an unstable regime determined to seize a fleeting opportunity and to build quickly on a grand scale, which magnified errors that Cluss could reconsider only when it was too late. His best-remembered contribution to Washington's Comprehensive Plan was his dramatic exposure of its unsavory dimensions. In this episode of his career, Cluss undertook to mold Washington's appearance and services. He ended in a witness chair in a congressional hearing room, a nervous, even embarrassed symbol of public honesty.

NOTES

1. *Affairs in the District of Columbia*, 43d Cong., 1st sess., June 16, 1874, S. Rept. 453, Testimony, 2080–81, 2174–75, 2225.

2. *Evening Star* (Washington), 23 May 1874. *Washingtoner Journal*, 25 May 1874.

3. *Evening Star* (Washington), 26 May 1874.

4. *Washingtoner Journal*, 25 May 1874.

5. Mark Twain and Charles Dudley Warner, *The Gilded Age* (1873; repr., New York, 1994), 177.

6. *National Intelligencer*, 5 November 1862. Noah Brooks, *Mr. Lincoln's Washington: Selections from the Writings of Noah Brooks, Civil War Correspondent*, ed. P. J. Staudenraus (South Brunswick, 1967), 116–17.

7. William A. Croffut, "Lincoln's Washington: Recollections of a Journalist Who Knew Everybody," *Atlantic Monthly* 145 (January 1930): 55.

8. Twain and Warner, *The Gilded Age*, 177.

9. *Evening Star* (Washington), 6 April 1871.

10. *Congressional Globe*, 41st Cong, 3d sess., January 24, 1871, 687.

11. Washington Board of Public Works, *Annual Report*, 1873, Chief Engineer's Report, 11.

12. *Report and Documents on the Present State, and the Improvement of the Washington City Canal* (Washington, D.C., 1865), 10, 31–32.

13. *Affairs in the District of Columbia*, 42d Cong., 2d sess., May 13, 1872, H. Rept. 72, 636.

14. Board of Public Works, *Annual Report*, 1873, Engineer's Report, 18.

15. *Present State, and the Improvement of the Washington City Canal*, 24, 32–33.

16. *Affairs in the District of Columbia*, 42d Cong., 2nd sess., H. Rept. 72, 636.

17. *Evening Star* (Washington), 6 April 1871.

18. *Affairs in the District of Columbia*, 42d Cong., 2nd sess., H. Rept. 72, 736.

19. *Daily Patriot* (Washington), 25 September 1871.

20. *Evening Star* (Washington), 30 June 1871.

21. District of Columbia House of Delegates, "Report . . . Relating to the Washington Market Company," April 12, 1871, copy in District of Columbia Committee papers, File 45A–F 8.2, Records of the House of Representatives, Record Group 233, National Archives.

22. Based on transactions involving Cluss during 1874 found by Joseph Browne in the records of the District of Columbia Recorder of Deeds.

23. Washington Board of Public Works, *Annual Report*, 1872, 91, 94.

24. Washington Board of Public Works, *Annual Report*, 1873, Chief Engineer's Report, 13.

25. Board of Public Works, *Annual Report*, 1873, Chief Engineer's Report, 11; Adolf Cluss, "Modern Street Pavings," *Popular Science Monthly* 37 (May 1875): 84–85.

26. Charles Moore, *Washington: Past and Present* (New York, 1929), 48.

27. Karl Marx, *The Eighteenth Brumaire of Louis Bonaparte* (1852, repr. New York, 1963), 15.

SUGGESTED READING

Abbott, Carl. *Political Terrain: Washington, D.C., from Tidewater Town to Global Metropolis*. Chapel Hill: University of North Carolina Press, 1999.

Gillette, Howard. *Between Beauty and Justice: Race, Planning, and the Failure of Urban Policy in Washington, D.C.* Baltimore: Johns Hopkins University Press, 1995.

Hall, Thomas. *Planning Europe's Capital Cities: Aspects of Nineteenth-Century Urban Development*. London: Spon, 1997.

Jacob, Kathryn Allamong. *Capital Elites: High Society in Washington, D.C., after the Civil War*. Washington: Smithsonian Institution Press, 1995.

Jordan, David P. *Transforming Paris: The Life and Labors of Baron Haussmann*. New York: Free Press, 1995.

Ladd, Brian. *Urban Planning and Civic Order in Germany, 1860–1914*. Cambridge: Harvard University Press, 1990.

Lessoff, Alan. *The Nation and Its City: Politics, "Corruption," and Progress in Washington, D.C., 1861–1902*. Baltimore: Johns Hopkins University Press, 1994.

Melosi, Martin. *The Sanitary City: Urban Infrastructure in America from Colonial Times to the Present*. Baltimore: Johns Hopkins University Press, 2000.

Peterson, Jon A. *The Birth of City Planning in the United States, 1840–1917*. Baltimore: Johns Hopkins University Press, 2003.

Teaford, Jon C. *The Unheralded Triumph: City Government in America, 1870–1900*. Baltimore: Johns Hopkins University Press, 1984.

Fig. 1. Cluss and Schulze, National Museum building, ca. 1885–90. Smithsonian Institution.

Cluss's Masterwork: The National Museum Building

CYNTHIA R. FIELD

The National Museum building of the Smithsonian Institution, now known as the Arts and Industries building, was created between 1879 and 1881 by Adolf Cluss and his partner Paul Schulze (fig. 1). With this one very prominent commission, Cluss created his masterwork, the one that incorporated all of his training and thinking about architectural and design ideas. This building was as unique in appearance as it was in function, because it was the first National Museum building ever designed in the United States. With no established model, Cluss was able to imagine how such a museum would look. He capably considered the ideal relationship of objects and the ideal flow of visitors and of light. For this museum he practiced a modern approach to design, wherein the expression of structure and adaptability to function were embodied in the measure of aesthetic success. All of his decisions reflected European intellectual currents and the thinking of progressive writers on the history of architecture and the decorative arts.

This structure was designed to hold the Smithsonian's National Museum collection that was overflowing its quarters in the original Smithsonian building, now known as "the Castle." The space problem had become especially dire after 1876, when the Smithsonian acquired a large quantity of artifacts from the Philadelphia Centennial Exposition. The architects' goal was to provide maximum floor space for exhibitions, and so they created a one-story plan with open arches instead of walls so that visitors could find all exhibitions easily. According to the Smithsonian secretary at the time, Joseph Henry, the new museum marked the separation of the institution's museum function from its research and publication mission.

The Plan

The Smithsonian first turned to Montgomery Meigs (1816–1892), trained as a civil engineer at West Point, to draw up plans for a new museum in 1875 (fig. 2). Meigs had achieved considerable prominence in Washington for building the Washington water supply system, the extension of the U.S. Capitol with its massive iron dome, and the General Post Office building, and for serving in both war and peace times as Quartermaster General of the Army for over twenty years. In 1878, Meigs's plan was the basis for an architectural competition won by the firm of Cluss and Schulze. Cluss added the axial halls that subdivided Meigs's large concentric spaces and reduced the central rotunda (fig. 3).[1]

The large number of similarities between the two plans suggests a common source: the model plan for a museum published by J.N.L. Durand in the book *Précis des leçons d'architecture données à l'École Polytechnique* (1802–1805) (fig. 4). Durand's museum plan was known to architecture and civil-engineering students throughout the nineteenth century.

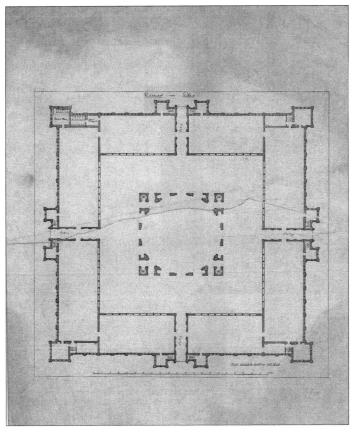

Both Meigs and Cluss, who were engineers and architects, would have learned design as Durand demonstrated in his published works. Durand taught architecture to engineers at the École Polytechnique from 1796 to 1833. His lessons, published in the *Précis*, had the scientific virtues of regularity, almost mechanical progression of spaces, structural integrity independent of decoration or style, and simple numerical measurement and relation of parts.[2] All of the characteristics can be found in the National Museum design.

As a result of the wide knowledge of this text, Durand's museum design was often used for museums in nineteenth-century Europe, whereas the model for the South Kensington

Fig. 2. Montgomery Meigs, Plan for the National Museum, 1876 or 1877. Smithsonian Institution Archives, Record Unit 92, Prints and Drawings, Series 1, #113.

Fig. 3. Cluss and Schulze, Plan of National Museum, ca. 1878. Smithsonian Institution Archives, Record Unit 92, Prints and Drawings, October 1879.

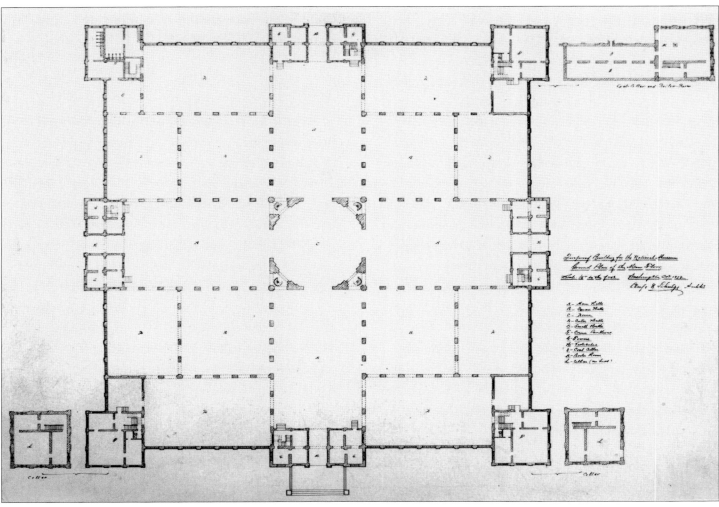

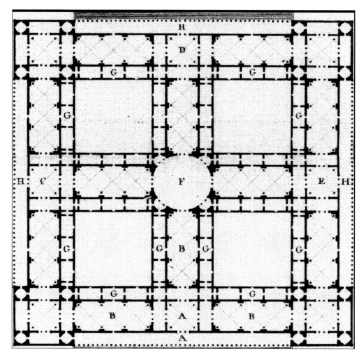

Fig. 4. J. N. L. Durand, ideal museum plan from the *Précis des leçons d'architecture*, (1802–5).

museum, London, was more common in the United States at this time.[3] A Spanish architect used it for a National Library and Museums building in Madrid in 1865. Two famous German museums, the Glyptothek (1816) in Munich by Leo von Klenze and the Altes Museum in Berlin by Karl Friedrich Schinkel (1823) were adaptations. Meigs remained close to the Durand model by adopting the equilateral floor plan with a high dome over the center. Cluss added exhibition space by covering the courts. Cluss's insight into the origins of Meigs's plan allowed him to draw on the same principles for his winning design in the competition.

Meigs and Cluss worked closely on the new museum building. Cluss was the architect supervising all aspects of the project, but also shared his responsibility with Meigs who represented the interests of the Smithsonian.[4] While not paid for his work as Honorary Engineer on the museum building, Meigs was later rewarded by appointment to the Smithsonian's prestigious Board of Regents. The two men, Meigs and Cluss, so alike in temperament and interests, had both the opportunity and the inclination to maintain strong professional ties.[5]

Durand asserted that a building should have fitness to its purpose and economy in its design. In this spirit, the National Museum featured seventeen exhibition halls with

80,300 square feet of floor space. Galleries located at the ends of three of the four axial halls provided "an unobstructed view of the ensemble" as well as small exhibition space for the discrete temporary show.[6] Since a primary goal of the museum was to provide maximum floor space for exhibitions, a largely one-story plan resulted with peripheral portions allowing multiple stories for office spaces. These 135 rooms caused little interruption of the public space.

What was unprecedented about the Meigs-Cluss plan was its use of pierced walls through which light from above filtered into every public space. Meigs had specifically recommended the building's open-wall plan to save space and construction costs.[7] As a result of this design visitor flow was unstructured, guided by simple line of sight through the open arches (fig. 5). It seems to have been Cluss who introduced the idea of skylights with vertical windows (fig. 6). An undated note in Cluss's handwriting described the building from Vienna's 1873 World's Fair with special attention to its rotunda. He suggested that the light gained from the glass panels in the dome was excellent for viewing the art. It is likely that he was considering such an arrangement of windows and skylights for the National Museum building when he wrote this note.[8] His skylight stratagem avoided the direct sunlight and allowed it to enter at an angle from every direction throughout the day. By using window assemblies alone without the addition of fixed glass panels in the roofs, he provided both circulation of air and abundance of light at the skylight level. Cluss also selected the fire-resistant materials. Although the building's open structure would have done little to contain a fire, the building was always known as "the fireproof building," because all the architectural materials (bricks, wrought iron, tile, and slate) were fire resistant. From 1865, when the original Smithsonian building burned, through 1887, Cluss was the Smithsonian's architect of choice for all projects having to do with fireproof construction.

As mentioned earlier, the new museum would house the preexisting collection plus all those objects acquired from the Centennial Exposition, which filled sixty boxcars.[9] As so many of the objects had not yet been exhibited at the Smithsonian, the system for their presentation was being developed at the same time that the walls were going up.

Fig. 5. Cluss and Schulze, National Museum, west hall interior between 1881–90, showing open walls and painted decoration. Smithsonian Institution.

Cluss had developed a close relationship with then Assistant Secretary Spenser Baird, for whom he executed private commissions, such as houses for both Baird and his sister. Surely the two men discussed such matters as how to present the collection in the new museum.

Within each gallery a system of organization had to be devised. It could well have been in Cluss's mind that his square plan with galleries flowing together fit the museum concept described by Gottfried Semper in his *Plan for an Ideal Museum* (1852). Semper wrote that public collections are "a potent means of assisting national education." A diagram illustrated his point, showing how a collection should be arranged for clear and logical presentation. His square format permitted the curators to organize exhibitions in four categories, which might overlap where the quadrants ran together.

Semper based his concept on the idea that ". . . a good classification based on compatibility will make it possible for researchers to observe the objects in their ever-changing relationships and dissimilarities."[10] At the time that this new building opened, George Brown Goode, assistant director in charge of the National Museum, espoused exactly the same museum objective, where the arrangement and classification by curators would encourage visitors to study the objects as well as to simply examine them.[11] Cluss's use of Semper's exhibition ideas clearly contributed to the notion that the National Museum was to be a source of education, for its final configuration was intended to further the public's understanding of the relationships between objects and cultures.

The Interior Decoration

The National Museum's interior, which was plastered in sand finish and lightly colored, was deliberately plain, in order to "heighten rather than interfere with the objects on

134

Fig. 6. Cluss and Schulze, National Museum, upright skylight and other windows. Photograph by C. Field, 2004.

exhibition."[12] However, for the decorative detail, Cluss and Schulze planned a didactic message. Geometrized flowers and stalks were based on the design vocabulary of late nineteenth-century English design reformers Charles Eastlake, Owen Jones, and Christopher Dresser. Their flattening of naturalistic branches into repeated textilelike patterns recalls the principles of Jones and Dresser that flowers should never appear in natural form as ornament, but only as flattened and abstract representations that do not contravene the architectural unity of a wall. To communicate the fundamentals of good design, these reformers published guides showing the authentic decorative styles of all known cultures. Thus the new museum's progressive architects consciously chose decorative details from design reform sources; the large Moorish patterns on the walls of each hall seem closest to the style of August Racinet, a French follower of Jones, while the urns and spiky stalks recall Dresser (see fig. 5).[13]

The decorative designs clearly followed one of the three-color combinations recommended by Johann Wolfgang von Goethe (1749–1832). Goethe's *Theory of Colours (Zur Farbenlehre)* was published in Germany in 1810. The book was most popular in the ensuing years with those of a philosophical and artistic bent rather than a scientific one. Goethe declared that the use of any of three specific color combinations created a harmonious juxtaposition of colors that had a gladdening effect.[14] The predominant yellow and lilac combination of the National Museum's decorative detail was one of these schemes. Goethe's theory of color was so well known in Cluss's youth that it was translated into English by Charles Eastlake.[15]

The museum's colorful floors were suited to function. The four main halls, those entered directly from exterior doors, were paved with black, white, and red marble squares that resisted wear. Slate borders of blackish gray served to access the ditches for air-system pipes. A strongly reticulated, radiating pattern of terra cotta and beige encaustic tile—a type of colored tile whose process guaranteed that the colorful patterns would not be ground off by wear—announced the break from the rectilinear halls to the circular center hall. In the spaces known as courts and ranges, wooden floors were used until replaced in 1900. The walls were colored and scored to resemble stone blocks (see fig. 5).

Exterior Articulation

The National Museum's use of a deeply colored, pressed red brick might well have been intended to distinguish it from public buildings of an earlier period. Brick probably represented that which was new, modern, and not tied to other cultures, classes, or styles. For Cluss the use of brick in building the National Museum had several meanings: he could deliver an economical, fireproof structure; use of brick ensured an equal material to the good building stone that was rare in the Washington region; and he could use a variety of brick to achieve rich color effects. A deeply colored sandstone was commonly used in cities north of Washington. The capital area's similar Seneca sandstone was exhausted early, but brick flourished as an industry, delivering a strong color effect. In France, Germany, and England building associated with contemporary functions employed brick for color effects. In Europe, brick had become modernism's expression of cleanliness, structural strength, and planar smoothness. For this museum building, Cluss used bricks glazed in buff, black, and blue as well as red. In the mid-nineteenth century,

Fig. 7. Caspar Buberl, Columbia Protecting Science and Industry, National Museum, ca. 1880. Smithsonian Institution.

architectural polychromy became an area of academic debate related to the historical development of architecture itself. Cluss showed his knowledge of this debate through his confident use of decorative brick. By contrast, a less structurally restrained use of color, to be found in such contemporary museums as the Boston Museum of Fine Arts and the Metropolitan Museum of Art, was another instance of their dependence on the English example at the South Kensington museum. With his masterwork, the National Museum, he signaled a greater academic knowledge of theory than was general in the United States.

Sculpture

Above the museum's entrances, Cluss apparently planned to have monumental sculptural groups and four inscription plates. The architect intended these decorative details to mark the four naves or two-story halls; the external architecture would clearly express the prominence that the four naves or halls occupied in the internal arrangement's hierarchy of space.[16] In this intent, Cluss again showed his adherence to the modernist theory of expressing function through his design.

For the entrance sculpture, Cluss and Schulze chose the sculptor Caspar Buberl of New York, who had not had any previous commissions in Washington. Schulze and Buberl were not only members of the same New York art club, The Palette, but also had served together on its governing council only five years before the National Museum commission.[17]

By late 1879, the first sculptural group was in place over the building's north entrance. Cluss referred to it as "Columbia as Protectress of Science and Industry" (fig. 7).[18] The figure of "Columbia," the female figure representing the nation, stood above two seated figures. The figure of "Science" was identified by a book and an owl, symbols of Athena, goddess of wisdom, for the figure was seeking knowledge, *scientia* in Latin. The other figure, "Industry," held building tools: a surveyor's instrument and a stonemason's mallet. The composition recalls a similar grouping occupying a prominent place above the entrance to the Hall of Machines built for the 1867 World's Exposition in Paris. This symbolic grouping, *La France couronnant Art et Science* (France crowning Art and Science) depicted a female figure representing the nation with representational figures of art and science. Cluss would certainly have seen the Hall of Machines, a famous example of industrial design to this day, as it continued to be an exhibition hall until the end of the

nineteenth century. In the absence of any discussion in the notes of the Building Committee meetings or any exchange in letters, we must assign the choice of subjects as well as the choice of sculptor to the architects. Buberl was commissioned to provide a second group, apparently unexecuted, depicting Peace and the Fine Arts, possibly also under the protection of Columbia.[19]

Correspondence in the Smithsonian archive does show that Cluss took the initiative of suggesting the inscription to be placed above the Mall-side doors of the building. He suggested "Dedicated to Science, Art and Industry, A.D. 1879."[20] Secretary Baird rejected this suggestion, preferring the simple "National Museum." Did Baird realize that Cluss's inscription echoed the title of Gottfried Semper's famous article on the inter-relations between art and industry, *Wissenschaft, Industrie und Kunst?*[21] Unmistakably Cluss understood the new museum as containing the elements Semper identified as embodying a national consciousness about the culture of man. Had he been able to choose the inscription, he would have expressed on the building the ideas in Semper's essay, which called for the study of natural science, art, and industry as a single entity. As it turned out, Cluss had to be content with expressing the same idea in his sculptural groups representing science and industry and the fine arts.

The building's exterior was enlivened by sculpted roundels in a low relief (fig. 8) and elaborate, wrought-iron

Fig. 9. Cluss and Schulze, National Museum, illustration of curtain wall section with buttresses. Photograph by C. Field, 2004.

gates. The patterns of both ornamental features include variants of the interior's geometrized plants. The strong resemblance of two designs executed by craftsmen of very different building trades suggests that Cluss himself created them. (Schulze's known buildings are completely without ornament.) The design approach suggests an abstract, pattern-forming logic imposed on natural elements. These plant details are a modern feature, reflecting a clear acceptance of the contemporary movement in the decorative arts that has been previously discussed; yet they coexist with the classically robed figures crowning the pediment, which belong to a historical tradition of sculptural symbolism.

Function and Form

Cluss and Schulze carefully chose the stylistic articulation of the new National Museum. They were sensitive to the neo-Romanesque style of the original Smithsonian building and so used a round-arched window motif. While this window could be considered a modernized Romanesque element, it was also a rigorously unadorned wall of light-transmitting glass. These walls of round-arched windows provided, as the architects wrote, "a well calculated and pleasing admission of light."[22] In function and material these window-walls presage the glass curtain walls of twentieth-century buildings. Semper has been celebrated as a theorist who directed architects to "let materials speak for themselves and appear, undisguised . . . each according to the structural laws that apply to it."[23] The visible face or cladding of a structure should express the way it works as an entire construct. As a nineteenth-century man, Semper would have the architect express the physical forces of stress and resistance in the structure, not actually reveal the structure itself as would his twentieth-century successors. The National Museum's exterior buttresses are the easily readable expression of the structure bearing the forces exerted by the roof trusses (fig. 9).

Semper famously interpreted the earliest architectural history as a development from which man hung woven textiles to create walls. Thus was born the concept of the "curtain wall," an architectural component that was not supporting any load. In the National Museum, bricks in contrasting colors are used in textilelike patterns in the areas of wall in between the weight-bearing structural piers (fig. 9). When we see them, we know that we are looking at a curtain wall, the very term conveying the sense of a light fabric with no weight-bearing strength. The expressive, colored-brick patterns appear only between these buttresses, never across them. Cluss used glazed, colored bricks that both highlight the appearance of primitive weaving and recall the general debate about the use of polychromy that was so prominent in the theoretical debate of the mid-nineteenth century. While familiar to the European architect, these debates were little recognized by the American audience, making the National Museum a remarkable building in the American context.

Theory and Practice

The National Museum building shows Cluss interpreting ideas of Gottfried Semper, arguably the leading architectural theorist of the mid-nineteenth century.[24] Semper's influence appears in practice in the clear expression of structure emphasized by the use of polychromy to articulate curtain-wall construction, but also in theory relating to his more abstract thinking about the ideal museum. Like Semper, Cluss was an ardent supporter of both social and aesthetic reform; both participated in the revolutionary activities of 1848; both were influenced by Durand, an architectural teacher of France's revolutionary generation. Cluss fit into the category of nineteenth-century revolutionary architects who "saw architecture as a response to a need." These architects increasingly sought to base their designs on actual structure and on the response to actual use, rather than on tradition.

On one level, the National Museum represents the theoretical ideas Cluss wrestled with throughout his career. His spirit of inquiry was broad in so many fields of learning that it is consistent to find that his work reflects the influence of the great design theorists of his age—Durand, Semper, Hübsch, Jones, Dresser, Racinet, and Goethe. Both his expressive choices and his written articles reveal that he was in agreement with the leading design reformers of his day. He used their plates as guides and cited their work in his texts. He was keeping current on buildings in England, Germany, and France throughout the 1860s, when his career in Washington was beginning in earnest, and in the 1870s when it was flourishing.

In 1902, Cluss gave the American Institute of Architects (AIA) the serials he still had of contemporary architecture in France, Germany, and England, covering the period of his active career. Unfortunately no record has been found of the specific journals he donated. Cluss's references to contemporaneous French architecture and urban systems suggest that he probably received the *Revue générale de l'architecture et des travaux publiques*, France's leading architectural magazine in the second half of the nineteenth century. The stated aim of this publication "to serve as a bond between men of special aptitudes of all countries, in constituting among them an intellectual association for the profit of science, humanity,

and themselves" befits Cluss and his record. For fifty years (1840–1890), this magazine's editor, César Daly, himself trained in a polytechnic school, took the approach that in linking architects and engineers the publication would "show the intimate correlation which exists between science and art."[25] This stated goal pervaded Cluss's National Museum, from exhibit spaces that flowed together like branches of the same river to the sculpture above the door.

In his book *Social Radicalism and the Arts* (1970), Donald Drew Egbert calls this linkage of architects and engineers for the improvement of man a typically Fourierist statement. The Fourierists, a utopian socialist group that flourished in nineteenth-century France and established colonies in the United States, drew its principal leadership and membership from the École Polytechnique. Their debate, in turn, inspired the young German social philosophers including Karl Marx, who were living in Paris in the early 1840s. The thirst for social progress was as strong among those French students trained to build civic-improvement projects as it was for the young Adolf Cluss in the heady years of the 1840s. Years later when Cluss combined the ideas of French liberals and German progressives in the National Museum building, he was also translating his early socialism into mature architectural accomplishment.

In the centennial year of 1876, the honor of delivering a speech on the history of Washington architecture and architects for the AIA's Tenth Annual convention went to Adolf Cluss. His idea of "architectural language" emerged in the last third of this paper. In the tradition of Heinrich Hübsch and ultimately Gottfried Semper, Cluss insisted that architecture using historical design elements had to demonstrate a correct understanding of the meaning of structures within their ancient cultures. Moreover, a truly modern building for a modern function could not look like a traditional building. Cluss declared his unwavering belief in that tenet of modern architecture, which stated that a building must be expressive of the functions, technology, and philosophy of its own age. He declared in this paper that "Architecture is defined as the material expression of the wants, faculties and sentiments of its age."[26] This sentence is verbatim from the text of *The Grammar of Ornament* (1856) by Owen Jones, whom Cluss mentioned by name elsewhere in this address. Jones believed that his century should produce a style of its own that would be expressive of its construction and contemporary materials. In attempting to carry through this ideology in his own work, Jones used brick polychromy. Cluss, in his larger public buildings such as the National Museum, demonstrated another of Owen Jones's principles when he used decoration to articulate construction. The idea of an architecture that fit its own time lay at the base of Cluss's preference for the modern style of his own period.

The National Museum was unique because it demonstrated theoretical and functional thinking that was a product of its forward-looking era. Out of Cluss's liberal political philosophy emerged a design that utilized the architectural theories of the reformers in order to enrich the notion of "education and science," which the National Museum represented. Cluss became a conduit for ideas from Europe, first politically but gradually in the fields of architecture, engineering, and city planning. Through his continued links with Europe by means of his avid scholarship, he became an agent of change in the United States, whose legacy is most truly represented in his masterwork, the Smithsonian's National Museum. 🏵

NOTES

1. This drawing, S01/1113, is related to the letter from Montgomery Meigs to Spenser Baird, 7 March 1879, describing the changes between the Meigs plan of 1876 and the Cluss plan of 1879 and acknowledging the fact that Cluss and Meigs were exchanging drawings based on the earlier Meigs sketch and plan. Smithsonian Institution Archives, RU 71. There are many documents on which I have constructed the history of this design. In the *Annual Report of the Board of Regents of the Smithsonian Institution Showing the Operation, Expenditure, and Condition of the Institution for the Year 1876* (Washington, D.C., 1877), in the "Report of the Secretary" (page 13) declares that "General M. C. Meigs . . . has gratuitously furnished a plan for a new building for the Museum" (page 47). "The idea of this was suggested by General Meigs as the result of his special inquiries into public buildings and museums abroad, and the details have been worked out by Mr. Cluss." Again in the *Annual Report of the Board of Regents of the Smithsonian Institution Showing the Operation, Expenditure, and Condition of the Institution for the Year 1878* (Washington, D.C., 1879), 42, "A plan was prepared on the basis of suggestions from General Meigs, and approved by the Committees on Public Buildings and Grounds of both the House and Senate." For Meigs see Russell F. Weigley, *Quartermaster General of the Union Army; A Biography of M. C. Meigs* (New York, 1959); David Miller, *Second Only to Grant : Quartermaster General Montgomery C. Meigs* (Shippensburg, Pa., 2000); and William C. Dickinson, Dean A. Herrin, and Donald R. Kennon, eds., *Montgomery C. Meigs and the Building of the Nation's Capital* (Athens, Ohio, 2001).

2. Renato De Fusco, "Afterwords: Didactic Semiotics," in Sergio Villari, *J.N.L. Durand (1760–1834)* (New York, 1990), 71.

3. See Jay Cantor, "Temples of the Arts: Museum Architecture in Nineteenth-Century America," *Metropolitan Museum of Art Bulletin*, N.S. 28 (April 1970): 331–54; Margaret Henderson Floyd, "A Terra-Cotta Cornerstone for Copley Square: Museum of Fine Arts, Boston, 1870–1876, by Sturgis and Brigham," *Journal of the Society of Architectural Historians* 32 (May 1973): 83–103. Floyd showed that the South Kensington museum was named as the model for the Museum of Fine Arts in correspondence between the client and the architect in 1870.

4. For instance, the minutes of the Building Commission for April 24, 1879 show that thirteen bids were received. On their meeting of April 25 the commissioners, along with Cluss and Meigs, selected the lowest bidder, Rothwell and Floyd. Smithsonian Institution Archives, RU 71.

5. There is reason to believe that Meigs and Cluss had become acquainted during the war years, when both were part of the war effort. Both Meigs and Cluss served on the three-person commission established to determine the cause of the 1877 fire in the Patent Office. Their relationship must have been already established for them to have worked together so well between 1878 and 1881 on the National Museum building. In 1885, when he designed and built the Pension building, Meigs used the same upright window transoms Cluss had created for the museum skylights. Like Cluss, Meigs used a concrete slab laid directly on the earth for most of his floor surface.

6. Adolf Cluss and Paul Schulze, "The Report of the Architects," in *Annual Report of the Board of Regents of the Smithsonian Institution Showing the Operation, Expenditure, and Condition of the Institution for the Year 1879* (Washington, D.C., 1880), 130–31. "The Report of the Architects," dated January 1, 1880 appears on pages 130–40.

7. Meigs to Baird, 9 December 1875, Smithsonian Institution Archives, RU 201.

8. Adolf Cluss, note, Smithsonian Institution Archives, RU 71. This note was found in Box 10 in the file: Cluss. The question should be posed as to whether Cluss himself attended the exhibition at Vienna. Although there was no passport issued to him for such a trip, his existing passport was probably still good. He was part of the Washington section of the education exhibition at the fair, which won a prize. The personal satisfaction Cluss might have experienced to have this European recognition of his work can be readily imagined. During his youth, the Austrians occupied Mainz where he was in active rebellion; now the Austrians were honoring him, through his adopted city, Washington.

9. *Annual Report of the Board of Regents of the Smithsonian Institution Showing the Operation, Expenditure, and Condition of the Institution for the Year 1877*, 41.

10. I am grateful to Rudolph Hirsh, a volunteer in Architectural History and Historic Preservation at the Smithsonian Institution, who prepared the English translation of "Plan für ein Ideales Museum" (1852), published in Gottfried Semper, *Wissenschaft, Industrie und Kunst und Andere Schriften über Architektur, Kunstwerk und Kunstunterricht*, ed. Hans M. Wingler (Mainz, 1966), 77–80. The translation can be found in the Cluss project files along with a xerox copy of the original.

11. George Brown Goode, "Organization and Scope of the National Museum," in *Proceedings of the United States National Museum*, vol. 3, 1881, Appendix 5.

12. Cluss and Schulze, "Report of the Architects," 132.

13. August Racinet, *L'Ornement Polychrome* (1871–73). In both the brilliantly colored lithographic plates and in the subject matter, Racinet proved himself an admirer of Jones, the leader of the design reform movement in England, by devoting his chapter on Moorish ornament to that found in the Alhambra in close imitation of Jones's *Plans, Elevations and Details of the Alhambra* (1835–45). In his choice of Racinet as source over the more famous Jones, Cluss revealed that, although he quoted from Jones in the Washington article for the AIA, he was equally familiar with and already using contemporary French sources.

14. Johann Wolfgang von Goethe, *Zur Farbenlehre* (1810), published in English as Charles Lock Eastlake, *Goethe's Theory of Colours* (London, 1840), reissued with an introduction by Deane B. Judd (Cambridge, Mass., 1970), section 808, 318.

15. Deane B. Judd, introduction to Eastlake's *Goethe's Theory of Colours*, x.

16. *Annual Report . . . 1879*, 131.

17. "Membership of the Art Association Palette, July 1, 1872," quoted in Esther Mirpaas, "Caspar Buberl, Renaissance Revival Sculptor, 1834–1899," an undated paper in the records of the Office of Architectural History and Historic Preservation, Smithsonian Institution.

18. *Annual Report . . . 1879*, 131.

19. "The New Building for the National Museum, Washington, D.C.," Smithsonian Institution Archives, RU 71, 4.

20. Adolf Cluss to Baird, 4 August 1879, Smithsonian Institution Archives, RU 7002.

21. Gottfried Semper, *Wissenschaft, Industrie und Kunst*, Braunschweig; Friedrich Vieweg und Sohn, 1852.

22. *Annual Report . . . for 1879*, 130–31. The building would provide a large and well-lit exhibition space, but would not include adequate collections storage and study space. As early as the *Annual Report . . . for the Year 1888*, 15–16, the staff reported overcrowded conditions for collections and curatorial work.

23. Hanno-Walter Kruft, *A History of Architectural Theory: From Vitruvius to the Present*, trans. Ronald Taylor, Elsie Callander and Anthony Wood (New York, 1994), 311.

24. The source for all interpretations and quotes in this paragraph is Kruft, *Architectural Theory*, 310–11.

25. Both quotes are from Daly's first editorial in the *Revue générale de l'architecture et des traveaux publiques*, in Donald Drew Egbert, *Social Radicalism and the Arts* (New York, 1970), 141.

26. *Proceedings of the Tenth Annual Convention of the American Institute of Architects*, Committee on Publications of the American Institute of Architects, 1877, 44.

Schools for All: Adolf Cluss and Education

TANYA EDWARDS BEAUCHAMP

"Schools for all; good enough for the richest, cheap enough for the poorest."[1] This was the rallying cry for Washington City as a modern, urban public school system was established during the tumultuous years of Civil War and Reconstruction. The schools of the capital city would serve as a model for the reunited nation. Universal education would safeguard the freedoms established by the Founding Fathers, erase social distinctions, create equal opportunity for all to better themselves, and raise moral standards. These ideas were the outgrowth of the educational reform movement that had flourished in America and abroad in the 1830s to 1850s. New England, under the leadership of Horace Mann, Henry Barnard, and others, had led the way, looking to Europe and especially to Germany for ideas. German American architect and engineer Adolf Cluss, long an advocate of universal education and knowledgeable in the design of school buildings here and abroad, would be selected to design and supervise construction of eight prototypical public schools for Washington.

Although free public schools for white males had been organized in Washington in 1805, they were poorly funded and taught, and located in inadequate, often makeshift quarters. Known as "pauper schools," they were shunned by families of means, who relied on private schools, as did the large, free black population. A few private schools taught girls.

Slaves were denied education. In 1845, the mayor and city council began the slow process of public school reform by adopting the New England plan for universal education supported by real estate taxes.[2] The city was divided into four school districts with a centralized Board of Trustees composed of representatives from each district. The board classified schools as primary and district, adopted a uniform code of rules for their conduct, and, in 1856, appointed a teacher of vocal music to serve all schools. The Columbian Teachers' Association (1855–1860), composed of both public and private school teachers as well as interested citizens, met on a regular basis to discuss the practical issues of public education. The group held public lectures featuring prominent educators from abroad. The association did much to improve the schools and publicize educational issues.[3] In 1858, the city amended its charter, finally authorizing support of the schools through real estate taxes. It unsuccessfully renewed earlier appeals to the federal government for financial aid equal to that provided the states.

As the Civil War began in the spring of 1861, city officials pursued their educational goals with new vigor to meet the challenges imposed by a burgeoning wartime population, shortages of both labor and building materials, and the threat that the rebellion posed to the future of the city and the nation. Construction of state-of-the-art school buildings, like the uninterrupted construction of the United States Capitol dome by the federal government, symbolized their faith that the Union would prevail. On April 16, 1862, the United States Congress acted to free slaves in the nation's capital. On January 1, 1863, President Abraham Lincoln issued the Emancipation Proclamation abolishing slavery in the rebellious Southern states. Freedmen fled to the city from the South, seeking the protection of the federal government, and tripling the size of the African American community in Washington. They settled near the forts that ringed the city and within established free black neighborhoods. The city did not at first accept responsibility for the education of these illiterate, indigent newcomers, considering them the responsibility of the federal government. Congress established a separate school system for African Americans under control of a Board of Trustees for the Colored Schools of Washington and Georgetown.

In 1862, a portion of the property tax was set aside for the purchase of sites for new schools and for their construction. At the same time, the Board of Trustees clarified the earlier classification of school grades as either primary or district by establishing primary, secondary, intermediate, and grammar grades—each with a duration of two years. They carefully chose courses of study, methods of teaching, student desks, blackboards, books, and other teaching tools. The board planned to erect a large schoolhouse in a central position in each of the four school districts to accommodate the upper grades. Smaller schoolhouses for primary grades would be conveniently located in neighborhoods.[4] Girls would be educated equally for the first time, but would be taught separately from boys. African Americans would be educated in a segregated school system. On October 18, 1862, the mayor and city council appointed a joint committee of elected officials and school trustees with full authority to purchase a site and build the first, large multiclass schoolhouse. The committee chose an entire square in Capitol Hill's populous third district, today's historic district, and solicited a request for proposals for the design of the building from the city's architects. They selected the newly formed architectural and engineering firm of Cluss & Kammerhueber, which had made a study of the best school architecture here and abroad.

As a young man in Germany, Adolf Cluss, in common with American reformers, had been inspired by the humani-tarian teaching methods of Johann Heinrich Pestalozzi, who had advocated universal education, professional training for all teachers, establishment of teachers' associations, and separation of the church from the schools. In 1862, married to the daughter of a teacher and father of a growing family, Cluss accepted the challenge of designing prototypical schools for his adopted American city. Although he had listed his occupation as architect at the time of his emigration in 1848, his employment, except for a brief period in the Office of the Supervising Architect of the U.S. Treasury Department, had been primarily as an engineer, first in the U.S. Coast Survey and then at the Navy Yard. Now, in 1862, he formed a partnership with Joseph W. von Kammerhueber, a fellow worker at the Navy Yard, and embarked upon a remarkable career as an architect and engineer in private practice.

School architecture had long been a concern of educational reformers in New England. The earliest literature on the subject appeared in 1829. In 1838, Horace Mann and Henry Barnard both prepared detailed illustrated reports on the subject which were subsequently published and widely circulated. Barnard republished his essay in 1848 under the title *School Architecture*, including the most useful plans by Mann and others. He offered extensive, specific recommendations on the location, siting, interior layout, lighting, heating, ventilation, furniture, books, apparatus, teacher accommodations, playgrounds, privies, and even dedicatory celebrations for schools. Briefly touching on external appearance, Barnard recommended "a design in good taste and fit proportion, in place of the wretched perversions of architecture, which almost universally characterize the district schoolhouses of New England."[5]

In October 1849, the National Convention of the Friends of Public Education, with Horace Mann as president, appointed a committee to prepare a report on school architecture, which was then presented at the following year's convention by committee member Joseph Henry, secretary of the newly established Smithsonian Institution. The report favorably critiqued Barnard's *School Architecture* and served as the introduction in subsequent editions of this work. Barnard had taken little systematic interest in the external design of schools, and his publication included designs in the Greek

Revival, Italian villa, Gothic, and other currently popular styles of architecture. Addressing the convention, Henry criticized adoption of historical styles unsuitable for school design. He advocated a modern architecture in which form would follow function, incorporating the new materials and methods of construction made possible through industrialization. In this architecture of "perfect adaptation, the outside is an exposition of the in, and the in is an arrangement expressly intended to subserve a definite end. No part of a good architectural structure should be made for mere ornament but should always spring from some useful object."[6] A member of the Columbian Teachers' Association, Henry became one of Cluss's earliest and most important clients, selecting him to reconstruct the Smithsonian building after a disastrous fire on January 24, 1865. His influence is apparent in Cluss's designs of "perfect adaptation" for public schools in Washington.

The program given to Cluss & Kammerhueber for the design of Washington's first modern urban school building required that it 1) be located in the center of the square with fully developed facades on three fronts, 2) accommodate six hundred pupils of both sexes in ten rooms with a large hall for general purposes, and 3) entirely separate the girls from the boys.[7] The architects demonstrated their familiarity with the latest thought in modern schoolhouse architecture. They followed the general principles laid out in Barnard's *School Architecture*, developed their design from the inside out as recommended by Henry, and creatively met the program requirements. They took advantage of the large, open site by designing an approximately square building with entrances at the midpoint of all four sides and a cruciform interior stair hall and utility core. There were separate entrances, classrooms, and basement playrooms for boys and girls. All shared a large, third-story auditorium. Reached by spacious stair halls, the auditorium was a public amenity for neighborhood cultural and educational events. The architects located eight of the ten classrooms on two floors at the corners of the building in structurally independent bays. They placed the remaining two classrooms on the second floor over the front and rear entrances and the janitor's rooms in the basement. The latrines were approached through covered walkways at the rear of the building. Heating and ventilating flues were exuberantly expressed on the exterior of the building as major design features. Architect James Renwick had introduced this handling of a difficult modern problem in his design for the Free Academy in New York City,[8] but, unlike Cluss, had subordinated it to historical style.

Construction began in May 1863, and, surmounting the extreme difficulties imposed by an ongoing state of war, was completed in June 1864 (see page 78). Named for Mayor Richard Wallach, the building was dedicated on July 4, 1864. Attendees at the dedication crowded into the spacious hall and filled the new building's corridors and grounds. The impressive and colorful dedicatory ceremonies were inspired by those recommended in Barnard's *School Architecture*. The Lincoln Hospital band marched in procession to the new building, playing patriotic songs and making its way through the crowds to the third floor auditorium. Grammar school pupils sang a hymn written for the occasion by nationally prominent educator Zalmon Richards, who had been president of the Columbian Teachers' Association and who would be appointed as the first superintendent of Washington's public schools in 1869. Dedicatory speeches reflected upon the long struggle for educational reform in Washington and elsewhere, the skill with which Cluss and Kammerhueber had designed the building, and the success with which a new era of schoolhouse architecture had been launched.[9]

Planning for the Benjamin Franklin School, named for the patriot who had been an early advocate of universal education, began while work on the Wallach School was underway (fig. 1). A high, prominent site was purchased in the First School District at 13th and K streets, NW. This was a prestigious new neighborhood near the White House whose politically powerful residents included Secretary of War Edwin M. Stanton, Ohio senator John Sherman, future president James Garfield, and Commodore A. S. Wadsworth. Franklin was to be the flagship building of the new school system. Its planners hoped that Congress would see the building from the U.S. Capitol, understand the significance of public schools in the city and the nation, and lend its support. A commission of educators from Boston toured American cities in 1866, inspecting schoolhouses. They

Fig. 1. Benjamin Franklin School (built 1869), 1876. Photograph by Alexander Gardner. Charles Sumner School Museum and Archives.

Fig. 2. Plan of Franklin School. Charles Sumner School Museum and Archives.

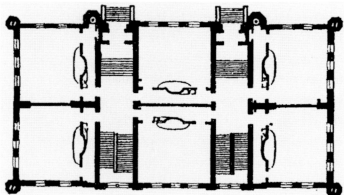

reported that "Wallach school was in external architecture the most attractive school visited, while the Franklin school (not then finished), in its size, plans, etc., promises to be unsurpassed in the country."[10]

Franklin School's site was steep and more constricted and urban than Wallach's location (fig. 2). The footprint of the three-story, brick-masonry building occupied the entire site with the exception of a small, rear utility yard, where the water closets and janitor's yard were originally located. The building's design was based on a system of three structurally independent and fireproof classroom bays linked internally by two separate stair and corridor units running front to rear.

The north bay was assigned to girls and the south to boys, with separate entrances for each. All classrooms were entered indirectly through cloakrooms. In the central bay the cloakrooms provided a longitudinal corridor with doors that could be locked to allow the classrooms on either side to be used exclusively by either girls or boys as the need arose. A library

Fig. 3. Elementary school class at Franklin School, ca. 1895. Photograph by Frances Benjamin Johnston. Library of Congress, LC-USZ62-76888.

and an administrative office for the superintendent and Board of Trustees were located over the entrances on the second floor. Grammar school rooms, a lofty and spacious auditorium, and a recitation room were located on the third floor. Janitor's rooms and boys' and girls' playrooms were located in the basement.

The classrooms provided a unique learning environment in an aesthetically pleasing setting. The spacious proportions of the rooms, careful choice of congenial colors, views through a progression of doors and transoms and over Franklin Park, beautifully grained finishes, and simple elegance of design in moldings, doors, and windows all contributed to this effect. Rich interior detail included the marble floors and ornate, cast-iron stair railings of the entrance halls and the dry-frescoed walls, paneled ceiling, and richly designed music-gallery of the auditorium. The educators hoped to instill an

understanding and appreciation of beauty by exposing all students to such a setting in their daily workplace and creating a sense that this beauty was for all and not just for the privileged classes (fig. 3).

For Cluss the isolation of classrooms was the answer to certain design problems. Sound transmission between the classrooms and the halls was minimized. Students were provided with a learning environment in which outside distractions were virtually eliminated. The teacher's desk was placed on a platform at the entrance end of the classroom, allowing clear sight lines between students and teacher. A semicircular niche at the rear of the platform reinforced the dignity and authority of the teacher, while creating an interesting design feature. Acoustics were also improved by this arrangement, with the niche acting as a sounding board. In the later schools, the corners of the rooms were also curved to

Fig. 4. A class in an African American school, ca. 1895. Photograph by Frances Benjamin Johnston. Library of Congress.

enhance acoustics. The rectangular classrooms were spacious and carefully proportioned, with high ceilings and extraordinarily large areas of glass. They were designed to allow sixty students to sit facing the teacher with maximum light entering from the side and rear. This was a revolution to students and teachers who previously had been holding classes in dark church basements and stables. Picture moldings and blackboards were present on all walls. Use of an oil-finished wainscot ensured ease of care for the classroom walls. Window sills were integrated with the chair rail at the top of the wainscot. Sand-finished plaster—painted in pastel shades of orange, pink, blue, and violet—was confined to the walls above the blackboards, out of the children's reach, where it could be easily maintained by periodic repainting. Providing entrance of the students through cloakrooms ensured that clutter and damp clothing would remain outside the classroom, preserving its orderliness.

Disdaining the excesses of the baroque, Cluss described his school design style as Modern Renaissance and linked it aesthetically with the brick architecture of the cinquecento in Lombardy.[11] In his work, Renaissance purity of line and proportion and structural integrity were combined with the most modern technology to create a new architecture for a new era. Using traditional brick masonry construction methods with two-foot-thick walls and supporting arches, Cluss planned structurally independent, vertical classroom units that would provide the basis for optimal classroom design. These units were joined by broad, fireproof stair halls, using segmental brick arches sprung from rolled-iron beams and prefabricated cast-iron staircases. Pressed brick, laid up with a fine mortar joint over the structural brick, provided uniform, richly colored facade surfaces. Contrasting stone detail was supplemented with manufactured cast-iron elements, with sand added to the paint to simulate stone. Decorative detail was restrained and purposeful. In his Franklin School, for example, the modern heating and ventilating system is expressed on the exterior through the prominent, symmetrically grouped octagonal central bell towers and corner towers,

Fig. 5. Normal school class at Franklin School, ca. 1895. Professional training of teachers began in 1873, here in the third-floor recitation room. Practice teaching was done within the school. The superintendent and Board of Trustees were also located at Franklin, where they could directly observe and participate in the evolving educational program. Photograph by Frances Benjamin Johnston. Library of Congress, LC-USZ62-30193.

becoming a defining design feature of the building. As Cluss once commented, "Architecture itself constitutes the decoration of architecture."[12] Each architectural element grows from and complements the whole. The central section of the building, with its steep mansard roof covered in polychrome slate shingles and distinctive cast-iron cresting, rises high above the end-pavilions, dominating the composition. A colossal bust of Benjamin Franklin, above a pedimented clockface, crowns the facade. The upper portions of the building are discreetly gilded so that they will catch the light and bring attention to the building from afar.

At its completion in 1869, Franklin School was immediately successful, creating an entirely new perception of public schools and their significance. Critics suggested that the building was too fine for a public schoolhouse and would be better suited as offices for the State Department. Presenting the keys of Franklin to the mayor at the dedication ceremonies, Alderman W. H. Chase commented, "I hope the time

may never come when we would make less beautiful and attractive the places where our children are to receive an education, where lasting impressions are to be made upon the young mind, than we would the offices of State. It has been well said by an eminent thinker, 'Show me the churches and school houses of a nation, and I will tell you what is its civilization and enlightenment.'"[13]

Demand for attendance at Franklin exceeded the available space from the very beginning (fig. 5). Pupils came to the school from all social classes and from all neighborhoods of the city, fulfilling one of the principal objectives of its planners. The prominent location and distinguished architecture of the building made it a landmark in the vernacular sense, a tourist attraction for visitors to the nation's capital. J. Ormond Wilson, superintendent of the Washington public schools from 1870 to 1885, later recounted: "General Francis A. Walker said that whenever he passed that noble American public school-house he turned to look and felt like lifting his

Fig. 6. Washington public school exhibit at the Centennial Exposition in Philadelphia; Franklin School model by Adolf Cluss at center, 1876. Stereographic view by Centennial Photographic Co., Philadelphia. Library of Congress, LC-USZ62-96853.

hat in token of respect."[14] Wilson went on to recall that in 1871, Sir Stafford Henry Northcote, member of the American and British Joint High Commission who lived near Franklin School, wrote to Wilson as he was about to leave the city that "he had so highly enjoyed the singing of the children in that school, as their sweet young voices had reached him through the open windows, that he desired to visit the school, hear them sing again before his departure, and personally thank them for the greatest pleasure he had experienced during his stay in Washington."[15] Music was emphasized in the school curriculum from the beginning. Public concerts were regularly held at Franklin, raising more than $50,000 and paying for all the musical instruments used in all the schools, including pianos. These funds also covered the purchase of costly reference books and all the expenses of school-related American and European exhibits.

In 1873, a model of Franklin School, together with drawings and photographs of other school buildings, was sent to the World Exposition in Vienna as part of an American educational exhibit. The exhibit also included samples of student work. The model, which was built to scale in one-story sec-

tions, cost $1,000 to construct, and elicited considerable interest (fig. 6). It was disassembled and carefully examined. Educators from all over Europe made drawings of the exterior. A Medal for Progress in education and school architecture was awarded and accepted by Superintendent Wilson. This international recognition of the work of the Board of Trustees was richly deserved. At last the public schools of Washington were perceived as a model for the nation and as an equal of European schools. Similar prizewinning exhibitions were made at the international expositions in Philadelphia in 1876, in Paris in 1878, and in New Orleans in 1884.

Adolf Cluss went on to design and build six more prototypical school buildings for Washington, including the William Seaton School on I Street between 2d and 3d streets, NW (1871); the William Cranch School, 12th and G streets, SE (1871); the Charles Sumner School, 17th and M streets, NW (1872); the Thomas Jefferson School, 524 Virginia Avenue, SW (1872); the William Curtis School, Wisconsin Avenue and O Street, NW (1875); and the Joseph Henry School, 7th and P streets, NW (Cluss & Schulze, 1880). Each of these schools had its own purpose and character, but each shared Cluss's innovative design features for multiclass urban public schools. Again, this was a new building type for a new and developing institution. All were designed with aesthetic considerations foremost in order to inspire students, dignify the educational profession, elevate the free public schools to a position of prominence and respect in the community, and provide a model of universal education to the nation.

Named for the abolitionist senator from Massachusetts, the Charles Sumner School was the flagship school of the segregated, African American school system. It was located on the site of an earlier freedmen's barracks school in an established, traditionally free black neighborhood where education had long been a primary concern. In 1851, Miss Myrtilla Miner, an idealistic white teacher, had established one of the nation's first high schools for black women nearby. Miner had abolitionist support for this school, intended as a national model for the education of African American teachers. Another school was located in a Quaker meeting house at 17th and N streets, and in 1862, an evening school was opened by the abolitionist American Tract Society in the basement of the Union Bethel Church on M Street between 15th and 16th streets. Funding for the construction of public schools for blacks was not available until the 1866 to 1867 school year when two substantial schools were built. The Thaddeus Stevens School, at 21st and L streets, NW (1868), was the first school for black children considered equal to those designed for white children.

At the dedication of Sumner School, William H. A. Wormley, chairman of the building committee, expressed his hopes for the elevation of his race and the acceptance by all of the scriptural teaching, "Of one blood we were all made." Still hoping for an integrated school system, he declared that he had done his best to erect "a house that none need be ashamed to enter, and from which none shall be turned away while there is room to accommodate; be he white or black, high or low, rich or poor, if they seek for education they shall be welcome."[16] The builder, Robert I. Fleming, paid tribute to "the colored mechanics, who have been denied the rights of mechanics," and declared that "this edifice, which has been mainly constructed by their handiwork, will ever stand as a monument to their genius."[17] Smaller than Franklin, the school gained presence through its corner location and its monumental campanile entrance. The tower housed the administrative offices of the African American school system. In 1872, the first public high school for African American students was moved to Sumner.

Seaton School was erected in 1871 near Judiciary Square in the populous second school district. Intended as a prototypical neighborhood school, the ten-classroom building design is simplified while incorporating the essential programmatic features earlier introduced by Cluss. A single-sex school for boys, the interior arrangements are less elaborate than those in the earlier schools. One of Cluss's sons attended this school. The Cranch School was located in the third school district and completed in 1872 (fig. 7). It was designed as a model primary school that could be built in every city neighborhood, allowing children to walk to school. No auditorium was provided.

The Jefferson School (1872), south of the National Mall in the fourth school district, accommodated twelve hundred students in twenty classrooms (fig. 8). Before construction of the school, students—who came from the immediate neighborhood—were housed in inadequate temporary structures on the site. The design of the Jefferson School addressed the need for a large neighborhood school. With two end pavilions sited perpendicular to a long central section, it foreshadowed the schools designed by the municipal architect's office after World War I, when large population increases required more schools. Cluss commented that Jefferson was unique in many ways, benefiting from refinements of earlier school plans. The design of the auditorium was similar to that of the nearby Smithsonian Institution building. The room was fan-shaped with a gallery. The seating was built so that each row was higher than the row in front, allowing unobstructed sight lines. Walls were built with an insulating air space between the plastered interior surface and the brick outside walls to improve the acoustics and heating and to reduce condensation, which had been found on the walls of earlier schools, where the plaster had been applied directly to masonry.[18] The Jefferson School burned in 1882. The boilers were suspected at first, since the fire spread through the hot

Fig. 7. William Cranch School (built 1872; returned to commissioners 1949, razed), 1876. Photograph by Alexander Gardner. Charles Sumner School Museum and Archives.

air ducts to the insulating space of the exterior walls and into the attic of the mansard roof, eventually engulfing the entire building. The investigation, however, found that the fire had begun in the janitor's rooms, either by arson or spontaneous combustion of cleaning materials.

The Curtis School was erected in 1875 in Georgetown. The riverfront tobacco port, founded in 1751, had been assimilated into the District of Columbia in 1871. The neighborhood had hoped for a high school and community center and so housed the privately funded Peabody Library and Linthicum Institute within the Curtis School. It was not until 1890 that the college preparatory Western High School would be located here, on the top floor of Cluss's 1875 building. As at Sumner, a central entrance tower with clock and bell asserted the building's presence near the center of Georgetown on commercial Wisconsin Avenue at O Street, NW.

The Henry School was designed as a prototypical grammar school for students in grades seven to eight, and a model of it was exhibited at the Paris Exposition in 1878. In the commissioner of education's report to Congress, the school was described as having "some original features but which represents very well the best grammar school-houses found in American cities."[19] Here the success of the exhibit was such that the French government requested it be placed permanently in the Palais Bourbon's pedagogical museum.

Heating and ventilating these large multiclass school buildings was of paramount importance, but the technology for successfully accomplishing this was untried. Earlier one- and two-room schools had been heated with woodstoves and ventilated by opening and closing windows. Cluss designed a system using safe, low-pressure steam heating and down-draft ventilation. Two boilers, normally located in the vaults beneath the entrance stairs, were used either alternately or

Fig. 8. Thomas Jefferson School (built 1872; razed 1960). Alexander Gardner, photographer, 1876. Charles Sumner School Museum and Archives.

together as conditions dictated. They heated vertical tube coil radiators contained within fireproof brick chambers located centrally in the basement and connected by vertical shafts with cold outside air. The warmed air was conveyed to, and the vitiated air expelled from, each classroom through a system of arched brick ducts and flues. Operation, which required a resident janitor, combined maximum safety with the most efficient heating then available.

This innovative system was introduced by Cluss in the Wallach School and developed and refined in his subsequent school buildings as he learned from experience. Problems were cited at Wallach from the beginning. The Board of Trustees reported in 1867 that even the introduction of additional boilers had failed to adequately heat the schoolrooms. The open exposure of the site and large areas of glass, reported as 170 square feet per room, were blamed.[20] The ventilation of the building was also insufficient, and in 1878

the committee on buildings and repairs requested funding for improvements, commenting that "the building was erected when the subject of ventilation was but little understood, and though flues were constructed for the purpose, they are small, and quite inadequate."[21]

In 1878, the Board of Trustees reported on their progress in establishing a free public school system in Washington. Standards for all aspects of the system, including school buildings, were detailed. Cluss's improved heating and ventilating system for a school he was currently designing— probably Henry—was attached to the report. The description of an alternative system developed in Cleveland, Ohio, using radiators placed directly in the classrooms, under windows instead of in a central air chamber in the basement, was also attached. The report concluded that ventilation in the Cluss buildings was insufficient and recommended that the Cleveland method be used to correct the problems at Wallach.[22]

Eventually the Cleveland method was adopted in all of Washington's public schools.

The prototypical schools designed by Adolf Cluss continued to provide a baseline for the design of Washington public schools well into the twentieth century. After the District lost home rule to the federal government in 1874, the urgent need for new schoolhouses was balanced against congressional budgetary constraint and oversight. Funding requests often asserted that new buildings would be plain and efficient, specifically promising that they would not be of the architecturally grand Franklin type. A typical compromise eliminated auditoriums and utilized stair halls for assemblies, with students seated on the steps.

Cluss had designed these schools at a time of rapid technological change. The need to develop sophisticated heating, ventilating, and fireproofing systems for the new multiclass, urban school buildings had been identified as a primary concern in Barnard's *School Architecture* in 1848. Engineering technology progressed rapidly during the period in which these schools were designed. Similarly, outdoor latrines had been provided at Wallach School, but within five or six years, interior water closets and washrooms were included in the new schools. Gas lights, battery-powered bells and clocks, and speaking tubes which provided early public address systems were new inventions implemented in these state-of-the-art buildings. In 1879, Alexander Graham Bell first tested the photophone, an invention for the transmission of sound by light waves, from Franklin School (see page 82). The night the Jefferson School burned, there had been a demonstration of Edison's phonograph in the auditorium. Schools for a system of universal education were being invented in America by educators like Barnard, Mann, Richards, and Wilson. Cluss had been an advocate of universal education as a young man in Germany and clearly envisioned the new building type that his clients needed. Franklin became a laboratory for exploration of educational ideas. All of the programs of the school system were first introduced there. Cluss and all those involved in establishing a public school system in the nation's capital were recognized here and abroad as pioneers.

Today, only the Franklin and Sumner schools remain standing. The Sumner School, listed in the National Register of Historic Places, was restored and rehabilitated in 1984 to 1986 as the Charles Sumner Museum and Archives—part of an innovative, award-winning public/private partnership project. A vital, community-based institution, it hosts a full and varied schedule of lectures, concerts, meetings, exhibitions, and other cultural events. The exterior of the Franklin School, a National Historic Landmark, was restored in 1990 to 1991 but the interior remains in deteriorated condition. Vacant and endangered, it is being used temporarily as a homeless shelter, although planning is underway to transform it into a hotel.

NOTES

1. J. Ormond Wilson, "Eighty Years of the Public Schools of Washington: 1805 to 1885," *Records of the Columbia Historical Society* 1 (1897): 18.

2. Ibid., 13.

3. Ibid., 16.

4. Ibid., 20–21.

5. Henry Barnard, *School Architecture or, Contributions to the Improvement of School-Houses in the United States* (New York, 1854), 47–48.

6. Joseph Henry, "Thoughts on Architecture," *A Scientist in American Life: Essays and Lectures of Joseph Henry,* ed. Arthur P. Molella et al. (Washington, D.C., 1980), 32–34.

7. Adolf Cluss, "Description, Plan, Cost, &c., of the Wallach School Building," *Twentieth Annual Report of the Board of Trustees of the Public Schools of the City of Washington* (Washington, D. C., 1865), 50–51.

8. Barnard, *School Architecture,* 234–42.

9. "Dedication of the Wallach School Building," *Twentieth Annual Report of the Board of Trustees of the Public Schools of the City of Washington* (Washington, D. C., 1865), 52–62.

10. Wilson, "Eighty Years," 23.

11. Adolf Cluss, *Order of Exercises at the Dedication of the Franklin School Building, Corner of Thirteenth and K Streets, Washington, D. C., October 2, 1869* (Washington, D.C., 1869), 28–29.

12. Cluss, *Order of Exercises,* 29.

13. Ibid., 17.

14. Wilson, "Eighty Years," 26.

15. Ibid., 28.

16. William H. A. Wormley, *Annual Report of the Superintendent of Colored Schools of Washington and Georgetown, 1871–72* (Washington, D.C., 1873), 85.

17. Robert I. Fleming, *Annual Report,* 84.

18. Adolf Cluss, *Twenty-Fifth Report of the Board of Trustees of the Public Schools of the City of Washington, 1871–72* (Washington City, 1872), 109–14.

19. *Report of the Commissioner of Education for the Year 1878* (Washington, D.C., 1880), CLXXXI.

20. *Twenty-Second Annual Report of the Board of Trustees of the Public Schools of the City of Washington,* (Washington D.C., 1867), 80.

21. *Minutes of the Board of Trustees of the Public Schools of the City of Washington, 1878,* (Washington, D.C., 1879), 135.

22. *Report of the Board of Trustees of the Public Schools of the City of Washington,* (Washington D.C., 1879), 16–21.

Adolf Cluss and Public Market Reform

HELEN TANGIRES

THE ARCHITECTURAL CAREER of Adolf Cluss coincided with unprecedented reform of the public market system in Europe and the United States. This ancient form of urban food retailing, whereby local government administers public space for the sale of fresh food, demanded new architectural strategies, as cities looked for ways to improve public order, hygiene, and urbanity while providing affordable food for wage earners and their families. In the process, cities removed marketing from their principal streets and thoroughfares, standardized market houses, extended them into growing neighborhoods, and developed distinct building types for the wholesale and retail trade. New market houses, usually major public works projects, were critical to the city-building process as architects and engineers experimented with ways to incorporate them into a growing and changing urban infra-structure.[1]

This essay explores the three market houses designed by Adolf Cluss during pivotal years for urban food marketing: Center Market (1871–1878), the Alexandria City Hall and Market House (1871–1873), and Eastern Market (1873). Different in size, scope, and function, these markets reflect the specific standards and requirements of their clients—the Washington Market Company, the City of Alexandria, Virginia, and the Board of Public Works of the District of Columbia, respectively. Yet they also demonstrate Cluss's

awareness of the range of market reforms openly debated by government officials, architects, and civil engineers nation-wide and abroad.

Market Reform in Europe

During the second half of the nineteenth century, the European nations were particularly active in market reform because conflicts over the food supply threatened the public order. The high cost of living was a source of widespread dis-content and a central theme of strikes and worker protests. Each country therefore developed its own strategy for main-taining physical and financial control of the food supply—an important element in the city-building process.[2]

In France, Louis Napoleon supported earlier demands to renovate the central market district, Les Halles, shortly after becoming president in 1848. In 1851, he approved the plans of Victor Baltard, architect of the state, and Felix-Emmanuel Callet. Baltard had visited the public markets of England, Belgium, and the Netherlands before submitting his design. The new market comprised twenty acres, with nearly half covered by ten iron and glass pavilions. By 1870, Les Halles was the heart of a highly centralized, wholesale food market-ing and distribution system that supplied over sixty retail markets around Paris.[3]

The largest number of market halls built in Britain in any single decade of the nineteenth century occurred in the

1870s, when sixty-six new markets were constructed. This British market-hall boom, which also corresponds to a national building boom, was in response to rapid urban growth, improved methods of public funding, cheaper and more plentiful food, increased powers of local government, and new theories concerning the moral and physical arrangement of public space.[4]

Officials in Berlin openly debated reforms and launched major market projects shortly after the city became capital of the German Empire in 1871. Members of the market commission visited the great markets of other European capitals in order to develop the best plan. Hoping to make Berlin a world-class city, the German Assembly approved the commission's plan to close seventeen open-air street markets and to replace them with thirteen enclosed retail markets and a new central wholesale market in Alexanderplatz. Built between 1886 and 1891, the new market houses were intended to alleviate traffic, improve sanitation, and facilitate a more diverse and reliable food supply.[5]

The Dissemination of Ideas

Nineteenth-century architecture and engineering journals contributed to the dissemination of these market projects. Readers of *Allgemeine Bauzeitung* or *Zeitschrift für Bauwesen* would have been able to review the latest designs for markets not only in Berlin, Frankfurt, Leipzig, Munich, and Vienna, but also those in Brussels, London, Lyon, and Paris. Likewise, market plans, elevations, and construction techniques were available to a French-speaking audience in such journals as the *Gazette des architecture et du bâtiments, La construction moderne,* and *Revue générale de l'architecture. Builder* and *Building News* disseminated most of the designs available to the English-speaking world.[6]

European civil engineers and municipal authorities studied the public market's administrative demands, complex social and economic networks, and reciprocal relationship to the urban infrastructure. In 1865, James Newlands, engineer for the borough of Liverpool, published the comparative study, *A Short Description of the Markets and Market Systems of Paris: with Notes on the Markets of London,* for the Markets

Committee of Liverpool.[7] Likewise, Alexandre Friedmann, civil engineer for the City of Vienna, promoted large central market halls modeled after the recently demolished pavilions of the 1873 exposition. He published his plans in *Nouvelles Dispositions pour la construction de halles, marchés et entrepôts* in 1877. These amateur economic geographers promoted a system of government-controlled retail markets supplied by a central wholesale market. The union of wholesalers under careful municipal administration and regulation, they argued, would stabilize food prices and supply throughout the city.[8]

Promoting a market typology were public officials such as Theodor Risch, member of the Berlin city council. His extensive handbook, *Bericht über Markthallen in Deutschland, Belgien, Frankreich, England und Italien,* published in 1867, provided architects, civil engineers, and municipal authorities with descriptions of the present market systems in twenty-five European cities. The choice of style was also a matter of interest. The chapter entitled "In What Style Should Markets Be Built?" was Risch's effort to bring public markets into the decades-old architectural debate in Germany.[9]

To what extent Cluss was familiar with the European literature on markets is only speculative, but it is certain that the literature was available in Washington. Cluss frequented the Library of Congress, where he would have had access to specialized architecture and engineering journals, or to books such as Risch's *Bericht über Markthallen.* He also may have read James Newlands' *A Short Description of the Markets and Market Systems of Paris* and Newlands's other writings on municipal streets, sewers and water systems, which were available at the Library of the Surgeon General's Office in Washington—the predecessor to the Army Medical Museum and Library designed by Cluss in 1886.[10] Cluss also maintained his own library of German language publications well after emigration to the United States and asked the Smithsonian to obtain the 1865 edition of *Erbham's Zeitung für Bauwesen* in 1880.[11]

Market Reform in the United States

It is also possible that Cluss absorbed some of the latest ideas about market design from Horace Capron, the United States

Commissioner of Agriculture from 1867 to 1871. Capron was the first commissioner to deal with issues of food marketing and distribution in American cities. He published the results of his nationwide survey on the state of public markets in his 1870 annual report. In it, he noted and admired the Philadelphia market houses, where the Pennsylvania farmer met the consumer face to face. He also observed that food shoppers and dealers came in different classes, particularly in large cities. Realizing the potential of modern markets, he recommended that cities develop systems that satisfied a diversity of buyers and sellers. He also recommended improved marketing facilities, extended market days and hours, and fewer ordinances that discouraged farmers from selling direct.[12]

Capron would have been able to observe the principal marketplace in Washington firsthand from his headquarters—the new Agriculture Department Building designed by Cluss and Joseph W. von Kammerhueber in 1867 to 1868.[13] Looking northeast across the Mall, Capron would have seen a hodge-podge of low-frame market sheds that extended from Seventh to Ninth streets, with open space for farmers between Tenth and Twelfth streets—a sight that was soon to change. Just as Capron promoted elegant market houses, separate accommodations for the different classes of buyers and sellers, and the benefits of direct marketing between farmer and consumer, Adolf Cluss was busy incorporating similar principles into his designs for the new Center Market.

Center Market: Showpiece for the National Capital

Following the trend in other cities, federal officials concluded that the time had come for the national capital to have a modern market house—one that would place Washington among the ranks of the great European capitals. According to Congress, however, a new market on Pennsylvania Avenue, the ceremonial link between the Capitol and White House, was beyond the means, vision, and capability of the District government.[14]

In 1869, the federal government entrusted its dream of a world-class market to the Washington Market Company, which proposed to erect "instead of the loathsome pile of rubbish . . . a stately and elegant structure [with] magnificent entrances and porches to the edifices. . . . Nothing will be seen of the Market and its operations, by passers along Pennsylvania Avenue, and no evidence of the existence of such a place will be observed, except the flood of people, entering and retiring from the capacious space within."[15]

When the Washington Market Company looked for an architect, Cluss was in the right place at the right time. He had a well-established practice in Washington, where he had earned a reputation for his innovative public school buildings. As a fellow of the American Institute of Architects in New York, he was among peers involved in some of the country's most significant architectural commissions. He was also active on the south side of the Mall, across from Center Market, where he was primary architect of the Smithsonian Institution and architect of the recently completed Agriculture Department building.[16]

The company hired Cluss to prepare plans during the summer and fall of 1869, while Congress debated the terms of the company's charter.[17] Center Market's reconstruction became a reality when Congress authorized an act to incorporate the Washington Market Company on May 20, 1870. The company was empowered to construct and manage a new market house to replace the old, city-run market within two years or less. The act also authorized the company to issue capital stock in the amount of one million dollars and gave the company title to the market space for ninety-nine years, after which the property and buildings would revert to the United States, unless Congress chose to extend the agreement.[18] Cluss was in powerful company. Among the twenty-six incorporators were some of the city's most influential leaders, including Alexander Shepherd, leading figure in the District's territorial government from 1871 to 1874 and key player in the building of the "New Washington."[19]

The incorporation act detailed elaborate specifications for the market buildings and made reference to elevation drawings and floor plans on file in the State Department. It also specified that all work be done under the direction of, and according to, the designs of the company architect. None of the original drawings for Center Market are known to have survived, but its architecture can be reconstructed from the

Fig. 1. Interior view of one of the market wings, Center Market, Washington, D.C., 1923. National Archives (RG 83-G).

published building specifications, subsequent testimony from Cluss, and photographs of the market as it was completed.

Specifications in the company charter called for four buildings arranged in a square around an open court: 1) the main building facing Pennsylvania Avenue, 2) a market wing along Seventh Street, 3) a market wing along Ninth Street, and 4) a market wing along B Street. The precise function of the main building was vague, but the building specifications describe what would have been an elaborate multistory hotel, complete with servants' quarters, lobbies, parlors, elevators, suites and single rooms, bathtubs, speaking tubes, electric bells, and clocks.

The market wings were completed and open to the public on July 1, 1872. With the main building still noticeably absent, a series of congressional investigations and litigation with stallholders ensued.[20] For the purposes of this essay, Cluss's testimony and affidavits on behalf of the company, in the public record, provide a rare glimpse of his grasp of public market design and engineering.[21]

Continuity and Innovation at Center Market

Cluss used the same architectural vocabulary on the market exterior that he employed in the Agriculture Department Building, namely, the combination of a French mansard roof with features that were characteristic of the German Renaissance Revival, such as generous use of the *Rundbogenstil*, or round arch style (see page 163). The Agriculture Department building also served as a model for parts of the market's interior—at least in theory. Although the second floor offices of the Seventh Street wing were never built, the charter of the Washington Market Company specified that the offices should "be equal in substance and style to that of the office rooms in the new building lately erected for the department of agriculture."[22]

Contrary to specifications in the charter, Cluss omitted a second floor over the Seventh Street wing and introduced large, ventilating skylights based on the latest principles of sanitation and public market design (fig. 1). Cluss was inspired by high-storied markets after visiting New York and Philadelphia in 1871 with N. G. Ordway, stockholder and member of the Market Company's building committee. Ordway reported that he and Cluss found "nearly all the modern markets in those cities with walls high enough for two stories."[23] Cluss built the exterior walls of the market wings in compliance with the original plan, but in such a way that a second floor could be inserted later. Inside, the exposed high ceilings featured skylights with elaborate ventilators that could be pivoted and adjusted by machinery.[24]

Following company orders, Cluss also designed the Ninth Street wing without a grand hall above, as required by the charter. Justin Morrill, chairman of the Senate Committee on Public Buildings and Grounds, defended the omission, arguing that "it is true the public may miss a grand hall for national occasions, and for large mechanical, horticultural, and agricultural exhibitions, but the ventilation of the market, a great desideratum, is obviously most successfully obtained without the addition and interference of the second or the upper stories."[25]

Heavy use of pressed brick was another characteristic feature of Cluss's work, and one that he employed to good effect

Fig. 2. B Street (Constitution Avenue) facade, Center Market, Washington, D.C., 1920. National Archives (RG 83-G).

throughout Center Market (fig. 2). According to Isaac P. Childs, the city's largest brick manufacturer, the brick order was so large—1.2 million common and one million pressed brick—that he had to deliver in installments. Childs boasted, incidentally, that the bricks were far superior to those used in the Agriculture Department building, and that Daniel Green, an African American contractor, did an exceptional job on the market's brickwork. Green employed a majority of men of his own race, many of whom were unaccustomed to laying the pressed brick required for the decorative exterior walls of Center Market. Green finally found experienced white men to do the work but had to pay them extra wages, compensation for risking future rejection for employment on the grounds of having worked "on the same scaffold as colored men."[26]

Unlike older market houses, the new Center Market had few alleys and driveways, because Cluss considered them dangerous to the market-going public, and he did not want to expose himself and the offices of the company to manslaughter charges. He wanted to encourage shoppers to stroll in and around the market without the nuisance of traffic. Cluss was also proud of the large icehouses located in the courtyard, which he considered "indispensable appendages of a modern market in a southern climate." By placing the icehouses outside, Cluss avoided the usual problems that they caused indoors, where they tended to block air circulation and the view of the market floor. Interior icehouses, Cluss noted, were also reputed to provide hiding places for rats and vermin.[27]

The Washington Market Company, plagued by accusations that it did not comply with its original charter, could

Fig. 3. Stall No. 226, John Ockershausen's condiment stand, 1917. National Archives (RG 83-G).

still boast that it had "erected at great expense, the largest, best ventilated, and most imposing Market structure in this country, if not in the world."[28] According to Cluss, Center Market was indeed the largest market in the country, with 57,500 square feet of floor space, compared to 52,000 at New York's Washington Market, 32,400 at the Philadelphia Farmer's Market, and 27,500 at Boston's Faneuil Hall Market.

Center Market contained 666 stalls, which varied in size and character according to the needs of the different trades (fig. 3). Cluss arrived at this number based on the market's occupancy rate over the past several years and after making a minute survey of the grounds before construction. He argued that the final number of stalls would insure a healthy competition among the market men without ruining their interests by over-competition. The "tasty modern market stalls," as

they were described in the charter, had uniform overhead signs that identified the stall number and vendor. Butcher stalls were forty-eight square feet, compared to thirty-six square feet for butter stalls; and the most moderate stalls were for bacon dealers and hucksters. Outside of the market, the "country people," as they were often called, furnished their own benches under the eaves and awnings, where they occupied their spaces for a nominal fee (fig. 4). According to Cluss, modest facilities for this type of vendor were important because they drew the "great mass of purchasers" to the market.[29]

Center Market reached out to a female, upper-class clientele by installing an elegant ladies lounge, equipped with stylish wicker furniture and a telephone (fig. 5). This feature set a new standard—or at least an expectation—for other markets in the city. Center Market, in short, provided an

Fig. 4. Hucksters, Center Market, Washington, D.C., ca. 1900. Washingtoniana Division, D.C. Public Library.

Fig. 5. Ladies Lounge, Center Market, Washington, D.C., 1917. National Archives (RG 83-G).

Fig. 6. Wholesale stores, Center Market, Washington, D.C., ca. 1885. Library of Congress, Prints and Photographs Division, LC-USZ62-26704.

Fig. 7. "Buildings for Market-House, Court-House, Offices, etc., Alexandria, Va., as submitted by Adolph Cluss, Architect," ca. 1871. Alexandria Library, Special Collections.

enclosed, hygienic, controlled environment for the retailer and bourgeois shopper, while at the same time it offered modest outdoor facilities for vendors and consumers of low-cost, seasonal goods.[30]

The controversy over the main building was settled in 1878, when the company constructed a handsome row of wholesale stores instead of a hotel on the north front between the Seventh and Ninth street wings (fig. 6).[31] N. G. Ordway testified that the company chose not to build a hotel for the front building on Pennsylvania Avenue because it would be "a disastrous failure," being so close to a market.[32]

Describing the ornate fixtures in the front row of wholesale stores, Cluss remarked that they were designed without regard to expense for a certain class of market men from the old market. The Washington Market Company also lured

two important tenants to the wholesale section of Center Market: Armour and Swift. Both companies were among the nation's largest wholesale dealers in Chicago dressed beef. Armour occupied Store No. 2 for the storage of canned goods, corned beef, pork, and pickled meats in barrels. Store No. 3 contained the company offices, salesroom, and weighing room. In Store No. 4 was a large icebox for fresh meat. Lard, oils, and margarine were stored on the upper floors. Swift, located in Store Nos. 13 and 14, housed a pressed corned beef tank with a capacity of forty barrels at one time. The company also handled fresh meat at its weighing station, where reportedly one man could weigh a side of beef, swing it onto a moving track, and hang it in the refrigerator in fifteen seconds.[33]

Center Market proved to be a highly contentious project

for Cluss, but he always remained loyal to the company and committed to the success of the market. He informed himself by visiting the principal markets in other cities, he responded to company departures from the original plans without compromising quality and safety in construction, and he defended his design strategies when questioned. Cluss also argued that any changes from the original plan were made with the best interests of the city in mind. Ultimately, he thought his greatest accomplishment at Center Market was the replacement of combustible sheds with a series of massive, substantial buildings. In addition to solid construction and fireproofing, he carefully considered the classification of space by goods, separate facilities for the wholesale and retail trade, parking for farmers' wagons, the availability of meeting space, restrooms, offices, ventilation, state-of-the-art refrigeration, and cold-storage facilities. In short, Cluss's Center Market, despite the controversies, epitomized the mammoth central market of the late nineteenth century.

The Alexandria City Hall and Market House

At the same time that Cluss proved capable of designing a mammoth central market, he was involved in other projects of a different type and scale. In 1871, after a fire on May 19 destroyed the city hall in Alexandria, Virginia, the city council received proposals and accepted Cluss's plan for a city hall and market house on June 28.[34]

The new building, designed primarily in the Second Empire style, was U-shaped around a central courtyard. The west wing, on Royal Street, contained the city council chambers and offices on the upper level, with market stalls on the ground floor. The other wings contained an engine house, police headquarters, courthouse, Masonic Temple, rental space, and other city offices. The ground floor beneath the courthouse section may have been used for additional market stalls, and there were also market sheds in the courtyard of the complex.

Cluss basically worked with a traditional market type—one that combined governmental functions on the upper floors with an open market arcade on the ground floor (fig. 7). This market type was common in small cities and towns

that did not justify a freestanding, fully enclosed market house. The combination of a market with a town hall or courthouse was common practice in the United States as well as in England and on the Continent. In Heilbronn, where Cluss spent his childhood, the *Fleischhaus*, built from 1598 to 1600, had served as meat market and courthouse through the period of the imperial city.[35]

According to the *Alexandria Gazette*, Cluss visited the site regularly to review the plans with the builders, to inspect construction, and to monitor progress. About a year into construction, the market commissioners visited Center Market with Cluss to see if the style of stalls, pavement, and internal arrangements could be applied to the Alexandria market. Benjamin F. Price was the contractor and builder for most of the details for the market section of the Alexandria City Hall, including the central clock tower, entrance doors, and butcher and huckster stalls. Cluss's contribution to the market's interior was primarily the layout and arrangement of stalls, aisles, and doorways. Each stall was provided with a locked closet beneath the counter, but the marble tables, other furniture and fixtures, and ornamentation were the responsibility of the dealer.[36]

Eastern Market

Eastern Market, Cluss's third and final market house, typified the neighborhood retail market of the late nineteenth century (fig. 8). Cluss worked on the project in his capacity as the city's engineer and member of the Board of Public Works in the early 1870s. Constructed in 1872 to 1873, Eastern Market still stands on Seventh Street between C Street and North Carolina Avenue, SE, in the heart of Capitol Hill.

Void of the architectural elaboration and scale required at Center Market, Eastern Market was noted for its economy of construction, unostentatious design, and standardized architectural vocabulary. The original brick building was approximately 180 feet long (20 bays) and 50 feet wide (5 bays) and covered an area of around 10,000 square feet (about one-sixth the size of Center Market). Cluss made generous use once again of the round arch style, which features promi-

Fig. 8. Eastern Market, east front, 1972. Library of Congress, Prints and Photographs Division, HABS DC, WASH, 415-1.

nently in the alternating windows and doorways. Three projecting entrance bays are capped by massive brackets carrying a deep, overhanging cornice. A detached open shed for farmers runs the length of the Seventh Street facade. Inside, Eastern Market features an open, three-story plan with iron-bar trusses supporting an exposed ceiling.[37]

The District of Columbia seems to have followed the European practice of developing a model municipal retail market, whose architectural vocabulary could be repeated throughout the city, as in Paris and Berlin. Eastern Market bears a strong resemblance in style and scale to Western Market, once located on Twenty-first and K streets, NW, another municipal market built by the District around 1876. Western Market, at least judging from its exterior, was also a simple rectangular brick building, with high, arched windows and multiple entrances on all sides.[38]

Eastern Market's ornamental red-brick character blended well over the years with the surrounding Capitol Hill neighborhood, and the market became a proven success. The city expanded it after Cluss's time, more than doubling its length with an addition to the north, designed by Snowden Ashford in 1908. Eastern Market continues to serve the neighborhood not only as a market but also as a community center.[39]

In conclusion, Cluss demonstrated a keen awareness of the various market typologies that were at his disposal. At Center Market, he created a showpiece for the nation's capital, while simultaneously satisfying the practical need of the wholesale and retail trade. Backed by private capital, the Center Market commission allowed him to employ the latest technology in fireproof construction, cold storage, refrigeration, electrical lighting, and ventilation. By contrast, the Alexandria City Hall and Market House required a more traditional design approach. As the seat of local government, this project demanded a multipurpose structure that combined city hall, courthouse, police department, fire station, and public market into a single facility. Eastern Market demanded yet another market type, namely a municipal market designed exclusively for the retail trade in a neighborhood.

Among Cluss's three markets, only Center Market did not survive, having been demolished in 1931 to provide a site for the National Archives. Center Market, however, was dispensable not because its Victorian brick character was out of fashion, but because large central markets were considered unnecessary by the 1920s, with the proliferation of chain grocery stores and later supermarkets. Nonetheless, Cluss's market houses stand as testimony to the value of markets in the late nineteenth century, when cities still considered buildings for the sale of fresh food to be important civic landmarks and basic public amenities. ✽

NOTES

1. Helen Tangires, *Public Markets and Civic Culture in Nineteenth-Century America* (Baltimore, 2003), 172.

2. Charles Tilly, "Food Supply and the Public Order in Modern Europe," in *The Formation of National States in Western Europe*, ed. Charles Tilly (Princeton, 1975), 380–455.

3. Frances H. Steiner, *French Iron Architecture*, Studies in the Fine Arts: Architecture 3 (Ann Arbor, 1984), 46–53; Arthur Drexler, ed., *The Architecture of the Ecole des Beaux-Arts* (New York, 1977), 422.

4. James Schmiechen and Kenneth Carls, *The British Market Hall: A Social and Architectural History* (New Haven, 1999), 146–53.

5. Andrew Lohmeier, "*Bürgerliche Gesellschaft* and Consumer Interests: The Berlin Public Market Hall Reform, 1867–1891," *Business History Review* 73 (Spring 1999): 91–113.

6. An excellent bibliography of nineteenth-century market projects in Europe can be found in Georg Osthoff and Eduard Schmitt, "Markthallen und Marktplätze," in *Handbuch der Architektur*, ed. Josef Durm (Darmstadt, 1888–1923), vol. 4, 3:2, 200–204.

7. James Newlands, *A Short Description of the Markets and Market Systems of Paris: With Notes on the Markets of London* (Liverpool, 1865).

8. Alexandre Friedmann, *Nouvelles Dispositions pour la construction de halles, marchés et entrepôts* (Paris, 1877).

9. Theodor Risch, *Bericht über Markthallen in Deutschland, Belgien, Frankreich, England und Italien* (Berlin, 1867); Wolfgang Herrmann, ed. *In What Style Should We Build? The German Debate on Architectural Style* (Santa Monica, Calif., 1992).

10. The Army Medical Museum and Library is now the National Library of Medicine, National Institutes of Health, in Bethesda, Maryland.

11. I wish to thank Sabina Dugan, Architectural History and Historic Preservation, Smithsonian Institution (AHHP), for providing information on the Cluss library.

12. U.S. Department of Agriculture, Commissioner of Agriculture [Horace Capron], "The Market Systems of the Country, Their Usages and Abuses," in *Report of the Commissioner of Agriculture in the Year 1870* (Washington, D.C., 1871), 241–54.

13. The agriculture building was demolished in 1930. Pamela Scott and Antoinette J. Lee, *Buildings of the District of Columbia* (New York, 1993), 73.

14. This author published a detailed account of Center Market's reconstruction in "Contested Space: The Life and Death of Center Market," *Washington History* 7 (Spring/Summer 1995): 46–67. See also Tangires, *Public Markets*, 174–80.

15. The Washington Market Company, *Copy of Statement Made to the Senate Committee on Public Buildings and Grounds*, ca. 1869, in Records of the House of Representatives, RG 233, National Archives.

16. Cynthia R. Field, Richard E. Stamm, and Heather P. Ewing, *The Castle: An Illustrated History of the Smithsonian Building* (Washington, D.C., 1993), 78–79.

17. U.S. Senate Committee on the District of Columbia, *Papers Relating to the Washington Market Company*, 60th Cong., 1st sess., 1908, S. Doc. 495, 46–47.

18. An *Act to Incorporate the Washington Market Company*, Statutes at Large, 41st Cong., 2d sess., May 20, 1870, chap. 107–9: 124–33.

19. Cluss owned $10,100 of the $500,000 shares in the Washington Market Company, perhaps in lieu of payment for architectural services. District of Columbia House of Delegates, "Report . . . Relating to the Washington Market Company," April 12, 1871, copy in District of Columbia Committee papers, File 45A–F 8.2, Records of the House of Representatives, Record Group 233, National Archives.

20. Alan Lessoff, *The Nation and Its City: Politics, "Corruption," and Progress in Washington, D.C., 1861–1902* (Baltimore, 1994), 50–51.

21. Unless otherwise stated, Cluss's personal accounts of Center Market are from 1878 testimonies reproduced in *Papers Relating to the Washington Market Company*, 31–33, 49–51.

22. *Act to Incorporate the Washington Market Company*, 131.

23. "The Market Investigation. Corrected Testimony of N. G. Ordway before Madison Davis, Esq., Sub-Committee on Laws and Judiciary of the House of Delegates, August 10, 1871," newspaper clipping in Justin S. Morrill Papers, microfilm, Library of Congress.

24. *Report of the Committee on Laws and Judiciary*, 76.

25. U.S. Senate Committee on Public Buildings and Grounds, *Report of Justin Morrill on the Washington Market Company*, 43d Cong., 1st sess., June 13, 1874, S. Rept. 449.

26. *Report of the Committee on Laws and Judiciary*, 1871, 41, 61–62.

27. U.S. Senate Committee on the District of Columbia, *Papers Relating to the Washington Market Company*, 50.

28. Letter from P(?). S. Smith, Clerk, to A. S. Williams, Chairman, House Committee on the District of Columbia, November 1, 1877, RG 233, National Archives.

29. U.S. Senate Committee on the District of Columbia, *Papers Relating to the Washington Market Company*, 33, 49–50, 70.

30. For more on the interior space of the late nineteenth-century market hall as a sanctuary to bourgeois femininity, see Lohmeier, "*Bürgerliche Gesellschaft* and Consumer Interests," 108–9; and Schmiechen and Carls, *The British Market Hall*, 165–66.

31. Benjamin D. Whitney, *Answer of the Washington Market Company to the Interrogatories of the House Committees*, January 21, 1878, RG 233, National Archives.

32. *Report of Justin Morrill*, 2, 8, 30, 32.

33. "Armour & Co." and "G. F. Swift & Co.," *Washington Post*, 1 March 1885.

34. *Alexandria Gazette*, 26 May 1871; 28 June 1871.

35. This building is now Heilbronn's Museum of Natural History.

36. "Alexandria Market House & City Hall (Masonic Hall), 301 King Street, Alexandria, (Independent City) County, VA," typescript, 1981, in Library of Congress, Prints & Photographs Division, Historic American Buildings Survey, HABS VA, 7-ALEX, 171.

37. "Eastern Market, Seventh Street Southeast, Washington, District of Columbia," typescript, 1983, in Library of Congress, Prints & Photographs Division, HABS DC, WASH, 415.

38. Western Market was demolished in 1967.

39. Scott and Lee, *Buildings of the District of Columbia*, 260–61.

EPILOGUE: The Lost Buildings of Adolf Cluss

CHRISTOF MAUCH

I F ADOLF CLUSS were to stroll through Washington, D.C., today, he would not recognize the city where he spent the largest portion of his life. The American capital, which had a provincial air in the mid-1800s (Washington was in many ways more backward than Cluss's hometown of Heilbronn), has since become a cosmopolitan metropolis, the hub of an expansive economic region with more than five million inhabitants. Furthermore, Cluss would not recognize "his Washington" because most of the buildings that he had planned and realized as master builder, engineer, and architect disappeared over the course of the twentieth century. The few which still stand have taken on new functions—his Masonic Temple, for example, is now an office building—in a fully transformed urban landscape.

By the same token, the world of Adolf Cluss is equally foreign to twenty-first-century observers. The transformation of buildings—and, even more so, their demolition—both marks and reflects changes in society. The physical is intrinsically bound up with the social. Cluss's Shepherd's Row, for example, an ensemble of elegant three-story homes on Washington's K Street, was a center for the sumptuous banquets of the upper echelons of society for fifty years. In the 1870s, President Ulysses S. Grant paid visits to Governor Alexander Shepherd there and, in subsequent decades, Chinese and Russian diplomats held receptions on the premises. A high point in the social life of Shepherd's Row was

the 1917 wedding of Prince Boncampagni of Rome to the daughter of an American ambassador, at which thousands of butterflies were released in the ballroom. A few years later, the blue and scarlet-red brocaded satin hangings in the posh residences gave way to a plainer interior decor. The drawing rooms became offices and, after the Second World War, the Cluss buildings on K Street—which once embodied the pomp and social vitality of the Gilded Age—were torn down to clear space for a high-rise office complex. A similar fate befell the first luxury apartment building in the District of Columbia, Portland Flats, which Cluss built in the late 1870s in a Renaissance Revival style. The Thomas Circle building, with a corner tower and exotic design allusions that prompted contemporaries to compare it to an ocean liner, had to make way for a nondescript building after eighty years.

With every demolished building, a bit of the memory of Cluss vanished. Memory is intimately bound up with material realities, with buildings and artifacts. For that reason, we construct monuments as memories etched in stone. But a collective loss of memory admittedly does not stand in the way of a reconstruction of history. Each building by Cluss that was demolished had its own story. There were specific reasons for each choice the urban planners made. Often, the fate of a given structure was known years before it was taken down. Yet beyond the individual reasons for which his buildings were destroyed, and apart from the rather lax standards for historic preservation that prevailed in the United States well into the post–World War II era, the great speed with which Washington transformed itself from a provincial late-nineteenth-century city into a metropolis with national allure also played a role. Washington wanted to become "worthy of the nation." Decisive for Washington's new image was the fact that, since the late nineteenth century, the city attracted more than congressmen: financially powerful industrialists and investors from the Midwest also moved to the city and wanted to express the sort of national pride which reached a highpoint during the Spanish-American War of 1898.

Ironically, as a participant in the expansion of Washington, Adolf Cluss himself contributed to the acceleration of the urban development to which his own buildings eventually fell victim. Cluss arrived in Washington at a time when the city experienced an intellectual awakening. Like no other architect, Cluss helped to change the image of the city, even during the Civil War, when construction in the District of Columbia was largely stagnant. He designed the Foundry Methodist Church, which was the only large church built during the war, and he was commissioned with planning the first public school system, which was one of the few large-scale public projects that could be realized despite the war. (The Wallach School was dedicated in the last year of the war.) For contemporaries, the name Cluss signified innovation and reform; notably, he was awarded a medal of progress in school architecture. Admittedly, Cluss primarily focused on single buildings, in contrast to Washington's twentieth-century urban planners. The structures he designed often set the tone for the direction in which a neighborhood would develop. They set trends. His buildings often towered over others in the area, until similarly-sized ones were built. This led to increased land prices, speculation, and new, town-planning initiatives. Such developments were, to be sure, often coincidental and affected specific areas of the city or individual streets, rather than the city as a whole.

City planning in the modern sense, with a focus on the entire physical and functional structure of a city, first developed in America during the Progressive Era. Cluss perceived and noted the beginnings of the city planning movement but did not take an active role. In Washington, it was precisely the application of modern principles of urban planning in the downtown area that resulted in the functional transformation or demolition of his buildings. Added to this was the idea of the McMillan Commission, which dictated new priorities for the implementation of L'Enfant's formal plans for the National Mall. One consequence was the tearing down in 1930 of Cluss's Agriculture Department building on the Mall (with its formal gardens and neoclassical pavilions). In 1931, his Center Market followed into oblivion; the National Archives building was erected on the site.

Cluss had the good fortune to arrive in Washington when he did. He was drawn there because of his political interests, but it was architecture and engineering that proved to be the real challenge for him. In contrast to the majority of German American architects who (aside from church architecture, a field in which they played a leading role) by and large dedicated themselves to smaller projects, Adolf Cluss had substantial public funds at his disposal in Washington. Interestingly, Cluss found himself in the company of politicians, planners, and architects who were open to new things and had vision. This could hardly be said of Washington after the First World War.

By the same token, Washington was fortunate that the German American Cluss came to the capital city. The cultural transfer of ideas and technology through Cluss's architecture was inspiring and, to a certain extent, style-forming. The improvement of the streets, the innovative extension of the sewer system, the construction of modern apartment buildings, the farsighted design of new school buildings—all of these consolidated and boosted Washington's reputation at a time when the possible transfer of the capital to St. Louis was still being seriously mentioned. The planting of 75,000 trees in downtown Washington had a lasting effect and shapes the image of the city to this day. Even if most of Cluss's buildings have vanished from the twenty-first-century cityscape, they have had an enormous influence on the transformation of Washington from the seat of the government and a "federal village" (Kenneth Bowling) to a prestigious "global metropolis" (Carl Abbott). However, although Cluss has left his mark in these influential but subtle ways, the most visible traces of his legacy—his buildings—have, for the most part, vanished.

1825
born July 14 in Heilbronn, Württemberg (now Germany), fourth child of Heinrich Abraham Cluss and Anna Christine Neuz

1827
May 3, mother died; October 30, father married his wife's first cousin, Jakobine Roth

1831–44
attended public schools in Heilbronn, probably including the *Realklasse* of the Karlsgymnasium, a kind of technical high school

1844–46
received government permission to travel as a journeyman carpenter; educated in the "architectural arts and sciences," possibly at a polytechnical university

1846–47
employed with the Hessische Ludwigs Railroad between Mainz and Worms; August 1846, first German *Turnfest* in Heilbronn to which Cluss invited twenty-eight of his fellow *Turner* from Mainz; 1847, became member of the Communist League in Brussels

1848
March, elected secretary of the newly formed *Mainz Arbeiterbildungsverein*; April to July, wrote articles for Mainz newspaper *Der Demokrat*; June 14 to 17, attended the Democratic Congress in Frankfurt; September 15, arrived in New York from Le Havre, France, on board the ship *Zurich*

1849
March, arrived in Washington to witness the inauguration of President Zachary Taylor

1849–50
employed as draftsman for the United States Coast Survey

1850–55
employed as draftsman for the Ordnance Laboratory at the Washington Navy Yard

1851–55
corresponded with Karl Marx

1852
helped found and was elected secretary of the local *Turnverein*; published articles for the following newspapers: *Die Revolution* in New York, *Baltimore Wecker* in Baltimore, *Hochwächter* in Cincinnati, and *Philadelphier Demokrat* in Philadelphia

1852–53
wrote articles for the following newspapers: *New-Yorker Criminal Zeitung* in New York, *Neu England Zeitung* in Boston, and *The People's Paper* in London

1852–54
wrote articles for *Die Turn-Zeitung* in New York

1853
with Sam Briggs organized the Workingman's National Association and published the *Workingman's National Advocate*; wrote articles for the following newspapers:

Washington Union in Washington and *Der Demokrat* in
New York

1853–54
wrote articles for and financially backed *Die Reform* in
New York

1855
June 5, became U.S. citizen

1855–58
employed as draftsman at the Treasury Department, Bureau
of Construction

1857
father Heinrich Cluss died, leaving each of his seven children
a substantial inheritance

1858
traveled to Württemberg, France, and England

1859
February 10, at Zion Church, Baltimore, married Rosa
Schmidt, daughter of Jacob and Elizabeth Schmidt, both
natives of the Palatinate (ruled by Bavaria, now Germany);
honeymooned in Europe

1859–63
employed at the Ordnance Laboratory, Washington
Navy Yard

1860–94
lived at 130 Second Street West (later renumbered
413 Second Street, NW)

1860
January 2, daughter Lillian born

1861
September 6, daughter Anita born

1862–68
private architectural and engineering practice and
partnership with Joseph W. von Kammerhueber

1862–88
designed sixty-seven new or renovated buildings with
partner or in solo practice while engaging in numerous
building supervision and civil engineering projects

1863
January 29, son Adolph born; September 17, wrote article
for *Scientific American* on new Tumbrill railroad cars for
transporting ammunition and shells

1864
initiated as Mason, LaFayette Lodge No. 19

1864–65
appointed by Mayor Wallach to study city canal and sewage
problems; report submitted and published as *Present State and
the Improvement of the Washington City Canal* with recommendation for building a sewer system

1865
August 14, son Carl born

1865–88
employed as architect for the Smithsonian Institution

1867–1905
member of the national American Institute of Architects
(AIA)

1868
office located at the corner of Seventh and F streets, NW;
November 18, presented paper to the AIA on history and
uses of chimneys

1869
March, AIA published Cluss's report, *The Office of the
Supervising Architect: What It Was, What It Is, and What It
Ought to Be*

1870
appointed Chief of Bureau of Buildings for the City of
Washington; December 2, daughter Flora born

1870s
employed Otto Wolfsteiner for eleven years as draftsman

1870–72
office located at 529 Seventh Street, NW

1871
elected president of the German Republican Party in
Washington

1871–74
Inspector of Buildings by appointment of the Board of
Public Works

1872
office relocated to Fifteenth and G streets, NW; wrote *Report
of Inspector of Public Buildings* for Board of Public Works

1872–74
City Engineer and member of the Board of Public Works by
appointment of President Ulysses S. Grant

1873
design awarded medal at the World's Exposition in Vienna, Austria, for "progress in school architecture"; wrote *Report of Chief Engineer* for Board of Public Works; November 4, son Robert born

1874
May 20 to 22, provided damaging testimony against the Board of Public Works; May 25, removed from Board of Public Works by President Grant; November 5, withdrew Masonic membership

1875
published article on street pavements in the *Popular Science Monthly* and another on the underground telegraph system in the *New York Daily Tribune*; wrote paper on the functions and properties of building materials for AIA Convention; September 30, son Richard born

1875–83
employed T. F. Schneider as apprentice

1876
design awarded gold medal at the International Exhibition in Philadelphia, Pennsylvania, for "progress in school architecture"; October, lectured on the history of Washington architecture at the AIA convention in Philadelphia, Pennsylvania; October 24, son Robert died, age two, from pneumonia

1877–78
partnership with Frederick Daniel

1878
office at Fifteenth and Pennsylvania Avenue, NW; design awarded gold medal at the World Exposition in Paris, France, for his Force School plan (later used to design Henry School)

1879–89
partnership with Paul Schulze

1880
published article on governmental water use in the *Washington Post*

1881
chaired Hall and Promenade Reception Committee for Inaugural Ball; April 29, daughter Lillian secretly married Israel Kimbell

1881–1905
daughter Anita performed professionally as harpist; toured in United States and Europe; taught at Fairmont Seminary in Washington

1883–85
son Adolph employed as clerk for the reconstruction of the Patent Office

1884
completed engineering report on the Winder Building at request of Treasury Department; son Carl employed as a pharmacy clerk

1886
June, daughter Lillian's marriage annulled; September 6, son Adolph died, age twenty-three, from typhoid fever in Indianapolis; December 15, daughter Lillian married William H. Daw, pharmacist

1887
spring, traveled to Mexico City; helped found Washington chapter of AIA

1888
elected second president of the Washington AIA; lectured on the history of mortars and concrete at the annual AIA Convention in Buffalo, New York

1889–94
employed as inspector of U.S. public buildings

1890
served on the national Board of Directors for the AIA

1893
April 3, son Richard died, age seventeen, of tuberculosis

1894
April 10, wife Rosa died, of pneumonia and bronchitis; October 12, son Carl died, age twenty-nine, of typhoid fever

1895
moved to 2301 H Street, NW, home of Lillian and William Daw; summer and fall, traveled to Europe

1895–97

worked for Office of Public Buildings and Grounds, U.S. Army Corps of Engineers, supervising construction of the Annex to the Government Printing Office and work at the White House

1898

wrote paper on acoustics for the annual AIA convention in Washington; visited family in Heilbronn for three months

1900

designed at no cost a summer house in Bethesda, Maryland, for Washington Hospital for Foundlings

1901

January 19, daughter Flora married Henry S. Lathrop, a marine engineer; they moved to Yokohama, Japan

1905

July 24, Adolf Cluss died, age eighty, of heat prostration; July 27 interred at Oak Hill Cemetery, Washington, D.C.

Buildings Still Extant

Calvary Baptist Church
777 Eighth Street, NW
1864–65, rebuilt 1869

Masonic Temple
910 F Street, NW
1868–70

Franklin School
Thirteenth and K streets, NW
1869

Sumner School
Seventeenth and M streets, NW
1871–72

Alexandria City Hall, Market House, and Masonic Temple
Alexandria, Virginia
1871–73

Eastern Market
Seventh and C streets, SE
1872–73

National Museum (now Arts and Industries building)
the Mall
1879–81

Churches

Foundry Methodist Church
Fourteenth and G streets, NW
1864–66, demolished 1902

Calvary Baptist Church
777 Eighth Street, NW
1864–65, rebuilt 1869

St. Stephen's Catholic Church
Pennsylvania Avenue and Twenty-fifth Street, NW
1866, demolished 1961

The Tabernacle Congregational Church
Ninth and C streets, SW
1881–82, demolished

The Universalist Church of Our Father
Thirteenth and L streets, NW
1882, demolished

Branch of St. Matthew's School and Chapel
Fifteenth and V streets, NW
1886, demolished 1950

Commercial and Office Buildings

Thomas Brown office
1413 F Street, NW
1878, demolished

John M. Young stores and residences
429 C Street, NW
1885, demolished

Lansburgh Department Store
420–426 Seventh Street, NW
1882, subsumed by later building

John L. Vogt store
429 Seventh Street, NW
1884, demolished

Corcoran office building, addition
Fifteenth and F streets, NW
1885, subsumed by later building

John Young store and residence
Seventh Street, NW, between P and Q streets
ca. 1880–86, demolished

Government Buildings

Agriculture Department with conservatories
the Mall
1867–68, demolished 1930

Patent Office, reconstruction
between F and G streets and Seventh and Ninth streets, NW
1877–78

U.S. Fish Commission
1443 Massachusetts Avenue, NW
1881, demolished

Hospitals

Garfield Hospital, new wing
Tenth Street between Boundary and Sherman avenues, NW
1886, demolished 1960

Washington Hospital for Foundlings
Bethesda, Maryland
1899, demolished

Hotels and Boarding Houses

Seaton House, extension
622 Louisiana Avenue, NW
1867, demolished

John A. Gray's Hotel
920 Fifteenth Street, NW
1868, demolished

Welcker's Hotel, six-story extension
723 Fifteenth Street, NW
1884, demolished

Markets

Center Market
B Street (now Constitution Avenue) between
Seventh and Ninth streets, NW
1871–72, demolished 1931

**Alexandria City Hall, Market House, and
Masonic Temple**
Alexandria, Virginia
1871–73

Eastern Market
Seventh and C streets, SE
1872–73

Military Commissions

New Ordnance Foundry
Washington Navy Yard (west of main courtyard)
1860–62, demolished

Powder Magazines for Navy
Washington Navy Yard
1864, demolished

Powder Magazines for U.S. Arsenal
Fort Lesley J. McNair
Four and One-half and P streets, SW
1864, demolished

**Officers Barracks, remodeling of east and west wings of
the penitentiary for officers quarters**
Fort Lesley J. McNair
Four and One-half and P streets, SW
(north of Arsenal grounds)
1869, one wing demolished 1903

Museums

Smithsonian Institution building, reconstruction
the Mall
1867, 1883–84, 1887–88

National Museum (now Arts and Industries building)
the Mall
1879–81

Army Medical Museum and Library
the Mall
1886, demolished 1969

Schools

Wallach School
Seventh and D streets, SE
1864, demolished 1950

Franklin School
Thirteenth and K streets, NW
1869

O Street School, built second story
O Street between Fourth and Fifth streets, NW
1871, demolished 1951

Lincoln School
Second and C streets, SE
1871, demolished

Seaton School
I Street between Second and Third streets, NW
1871, demolished 1969

Sumner School
Seventeenth and M streets, NW
1871–72

Cranch School
Twelfth and G streets, SE
1872, demolished

Jefferson School
Sixth Street and Virginia Avenue, SW
1872–73, demolished

Curtis School
O Street between Thirty-second and Thirty-third streets, NW
1875, demolished 1951

Henry School (based on the Force School plan)
P Street between Sixth and Seventh streets, NW
1880, demolished

PRIVATE SCHOOLS, COLLEGES, AND UNIVERSITIES

Bennet School, next to St. Dominic's Church
Sixth and E streets, SW
1866, demolished

Academy of the Visitation
Connecticut Avenue between L and DeSales streets, NW
1877, demolished 1923

St. Matthew's Institute (Christian Brothers property, later called St. John's College)
Thomas Circle, Vermont Avenue between
M and N streets, NW
1880, tower addition 1889, demolished 1940s

Design Submissions

District of Columbia Jail, 1866

War Department building, 1866–67

Library of Congress, won third prize, 1873

Library of Congress, second design submission, 1878

Dickinson College building, Carlisle, Pennsylvania, 1880

Catholic University, Divinity Hall, won first prize, 1887

National Monument in Commemoration of the Independence of Mexico, won first prize, Mexico City, 1887

Criminal Court and Municipal Building, New York City, 1888

Soldier's and Sailor's Monument, Indianapolis, Indiana, 1888

St. John the Divine Cathedral, New York City, 1888–89

Grant Memorial, won first prize, New York City, 1889

Partnerships

1863–68 Adolf Cluss & Joseph W. von Kammerhueber
1877–78 Adolf Cluss & Frederick Daniel
1879–89 Adolf Cluss & Paul Schulze

Tanya Edwards Beauchamp is an architectural historian and preservation consultant whose research and writing about Cluss includes her 1972 master's thesis at the University of Virginia, "Adolph Cluss and the Building of the National Museum." She published the first scholarly article on Cluss, "Adolph Cluss: An Architect in Washington during the Civil War and Reconstruction," in the *Records of the Columbia Historical Society of Washington, D.C*, 1971–72. With architect Marc Fetterman, she has taken part in numerous projects for the restoration and preservation of Franklin and Sumner schools. She has lectured often about Cluss and his architecture.

Joseph L. Browne, director and researcher for the Adolf Cluss Project, holds a Ph.D. in American Studies and Education from the University of Maryland. Author of a Maryland regional history and articles on Maryland's post–Civil War, African American schools, he has written teaching guides for educational materials produced by Maryland Public Television, the World Bank, Carnegie Corporation, and the Capital Children's Museum. Browne taught history for thirty years in schools in the United States, Germany, England, and Italy.

Kathleen Neils Conzen is professor of American history at the University of Chicago, where she has taught since 1976. Her research has focused on migration and immigration in American history, particularly on the German immigration experience. She is the author of *Immigrant Milwaukee, 1836–1860* (1976), in addition to numerous articles and chapters. Among her recent publications is *Germans in Minnesota* (2003).

Sabina W. Dugan, an architectural history specialist at the Smithsonian Institution, studied art history as an undergraduate before receiving a master's degree in historic preservation. In addition to her preservation work, she has spent six years applying her German fluency to studying Adolf Cluss's affiliation with Karl Marx and Cluss's activities in Germany and the United States. Her paper on the Cluss-Marx correspondence, given in May 2000 at the Brandenburgische Akademie der Wissenschaften in Berlin, was published in 2002.

Cynthia R. Field, chair of the Architectural History and Historic Preservation department at the Smithsonian Institution, is an expert on the Smithsonian buildings and on Washington planning and has been conducting research on Adolf Cluss and the National Museum for three decades. With a Ph.D. from Columbia University, she has published extensively on public buildings and urban planning, 1865–1915. She is coauthor of *The Castle: An Illustrated History of the Smithsonian Building* (1993).

Sabine Freitag, who received her Ph.D. from the University of Frankfurt, has focused her research on the 1848 Revolution and the emigration of political refugees from that revolution to England and the United States. She is author of *Friedrich Hecker: Biographie eines Republikaners* (1998), coeditor of a multivolume series, *British Envoys to Germany, 1815–1866* (2000, 2002), and editor of *Exiles from European Revolutions: Refugees in Mid-Victorian England* (2003). Currently a researcher at the University of Cologne's History Department, she is working on a history of criminal law, culture, and policy in England, 1850–1930.

William Gilcher directs projects with and about electronic media in North America for the Goethe-Institut/German Cultural Center in Washington, D.C. His doctorate is in French and American film history, and he specializes in cross-cultural projects between the United States and Europe. He wrote, photographed, and directed the virtual tour Web site, *Everywhere You Look: German-American Sites in Washington, D.C.*, a precursor of the Adolf Cluss Project.

Harriet Lesser, exhibition coordinator and curator for the Adolf Cluss Project, has graduate training in fine art and arts administration from New York's Bank Street College and Parsons School of Design. She was previously curator of exhibits at the Charles Sumner Museum and Archives. She has taught at the Corcoran School of Art, the Fillmore Arts Center, and the University of Maryland. A professional artist for more than twenty years, she has exhibited in the Washington area and internationally.

Alan Lessoff is professor of history at Illinois State University in Normal, Illinois, and editor of the *Journal of the Gilded Age and Progressive Era*. A specialist in United States and comparative urban history, he has written articles and chapters on nineteenth-century Washington, along with the book, *The Nation and Its City: Politics, "Corruption," and Progress in Washington, D.C., 1861–1902* (1994). With a Ph.D. from Johns Hopkins University, he has been a Fulbright professor at the University of Kassel, Germany.

Richard Longstreth is professor of American civilization and director of the Graduate Program in Historic Preservation at George Washington University. A past president of the Society of Architectural Historians, he has written extensively on Washington and on many topics related to architecture, landscape, urbanism, and preservation in the United States during the nineteenth and twentieth centuries. Currently he is writing "The Department Store Transformed, 1920–1960," to be published by Johns Hopkins University Press.

Christof Mauch is director of the German Historical Institute in Washington, D.C., and professor of modern history at the Anglo-American Institute of Cologne University. In recent years, he has written *Shadow War against Hitler: America's Covert Wartime Operations during World War II* (2003), and edited *German-Jewish Identities in America* (with Joseph Salmons, 2003), *Nature in German History* (2004), and *Berlin-Washington, 1800–2000: Capital Cities, Cultural Representations, and National Identities* (with Andreas Daum, 2005).

Christhard Schrenk has been director of the Stadtarchiv Heilbronn since 1992. He studied mathematics and history at the University of Konstanz and holds a doctorate in economic history. He has published many articles, monographs, and illustrated volumes, given numerous lectures, and organized exhibitions on local and regional history. Since 1993, he has also held a faculty appointment at the Heilbronn Polytechnic University.

Helen Tangires is administrator of the Center for Advanced Study in the Visual Arts at the National Gallery of Art in Washington, D.C. She holds a Ph.D. in American Studies from George Washington University. A frequent contributor to books and journals on urban foodways, she is author of *Public Markets and Civic Culture in Nineteenth-Century America* (2003). Currently, she is writing an illustrated book on public markets around the world, which draws on the visual resources of the Library of Congress.

Peter Wanner, a native of Heilbronn, is head of the Department of City History and alternate director of the Stadtarchiv Heilbronn. After studying history, political science, and German literature at the University of Heidelberg, he worked as a freelance historian, wrote several local history books, and directed the regional museum in Hardheim before taking his current position in 1999. He is responsible for the Adolf Cluss Project in Heilbronn.

Place names are in Washington, D.C., unless otherwise indicated.